CHALLENGE OF CHANGE

THE WIZDOM OF OZ

OZ MUTZ

CREATION
HOUSE

CHALLENGE OF CHANGE by Oz Mutz
Published by Creation House
A Charisma Media Company
600 Rinehart Road
Lake Mary, Florida 32746
www.charismamedia.com

Unless otherwise noted, all Scripture quotations are from the Holman Christian Standard Bible® Copyright © 1999, 2000, 2002, 2003, 2009 by Holman Bible Publishers. Used with permission by Holman Bible Publishers, Nashville, Tennessee. All rights reserved.

Scripture quotations marked KJV are taken from the King James Version of the Bible.

Design Director: Justin Evans
Cover design by Justin Evans

Library of Congress Cataloging-in-Publication Data: 2015934807
International Standard Book Number: 978-1-62998-431-5
E-book International Standard Book Number: 978-1-62998-432-2

While the author has made every effort to provide accurate telephone numbers and Internet addresses at the time of publication, neither the publisher nor the author assumes any responsibility for errors or for changes that occur after publication.

First edition

15 16 17 18 19 — 987654321
Printed in Canada

DEDICATION

To

Jean G. Mutz, my wife of sixty-seven years.

Marcy Mutz-Wickenkamp and H. William ("Bill") Mutz, my two children, who have helped me through the Challenge of Change.

My fifteen grandchildren:

Joshua, Laura, Caleb, Cari, Jonathan (deceased), Jacob, Lori, Oscar III, Kelli, Michael, Eric, Mark, Kirsti, Stephen, Emma

My twenty-two great-grandchildren:

Alexandria, Blaine, Connor, Avery, Michaela, James, Calvin, Bradford, Gracie (deceased), Kate, Hudson, Isaac, William, Molly (deceased), Lily, Piper, Rainey, Zeke, Noah, Alonna, Lucy, Brooklyn, Shiloh, Theodore

CONTENTS

PART FIVE:
HOME AGAIN

PREFACE

MANY OF THOSE who assisted me in writing this book will remain nameless and were numerous. They were my teachers across the years. My personal intentions and inexperience as an author dictates that. There are several unwritten chapters that I would like to have shared in substance but must save for a later time.

Those who provided consistent and important assistance to me include:

Dr. Annette Graves, who spent long hours working with me on the manuscript. She often knew what I was going to dictate before I did;

My wife, Jean Mutz, who edited and re-edited the manuscript;

Martha Linder, who provided unique, experienced editing skills to us;

Linda Karnes, our long-time associate who kept the whole process glued together;

Chuck Colson, my dear friend and Christian mentor, who gave me the courage to start this book, and the stamina to finish it. If he were still with us, I could not thank him adequately.

PROLOGUE

THINK MY MOTHER was as stunned as I. Usually the first to respond in an emergency, she seemed to have momentarily forgotten the eight-year-old boy at her side. By the time she had recollected me and done an about-face, marching me firmly and purposefully in the opposite direction, it was too late. My eyes had seen too much. The picture in my mind is as fresh today as it was seventy-eight years ago.

My father commuted to Indianapolis from the little Indiana town of Edinburgh. Sometimes he would take my mother, my sister, and me with him, dropping us off under the clock of L. S. Ayres department store at the corner of Meridian and Washington. While we might browse the luxuries of Ayres's upper stories, any purchases Mother made came from the store's bargain basement. We would lunch in the "bargain" cafeteria as well, and then wait for Dad to pick us up once he had finished work.

Shopping was never something I looked forward to, but no one, not even an unwilling recruit like me, could resist the aura L. S. Ayres created in the 1930s at the heart of downtown Indianapolis. Their ten thousand-pound bronze clock had just been hung at the corner of Washington and Meridian, overlooking the Crossroads of America like a watchman on the city walls. The clock's four enormous faces, each one eight feet in diameter and illuminated from within, maintained their steadfast lookout. They saw what was coming, even if those of us on the ground did not.

Mother and I were on the east side of Meridian Street. Traffic was lazy, and the city was rather quiet for the middle of the morning. I had anticipated more hustle and bustle from downtown Indianapolis on a shopping day, although for me, at eight, any foray into the world outside Edinburgh was an adventure.

A man on a motorcycle had just turned north onto Meridian from East Pearl Street. He was in our line of vision because we had stopped in front of the clock at L. S. Ayres to survey the State Soldiers and Sailors Monument and the Circle Tower. The midmorning light dancing on the tower in Monument Circle is worth a pause on even the busiest day. The motorcyclist must have turned too short coming off of the alley. His front tire hit some loose gravel and slid out from beneath him, spraying fine pebbles and dust at the bystanders on the walk.

Perhaps the impact had rendered him unconscious. He made no movement nor uttered any sound to suggest he was trying to either help himself or secure help from someone else. His body spun with the motorcycle on top of him, which ricocheted from side to side as it ground his flesh into the pavement.

I stood riveted to the sidewalk. I could not pull my eyes from the picture of the man beneath his spinning motorcycle.

It seemed a long time before anyone tried to help him. My mother and the security guard from the front entrance to Ayres sprang into action at the same time. My mother spun me around to face the clock over the crossroads and propelled me back toward the department store, being careful to block my view as I twisted my head around my shoulder, trying to see what would happen next. The morning's quiet had fled. I don't remember the motor of the cycle ever being silenced; I only knew that women were screaming and men were shouting and my mother seemed determined to put as much distance as possible between her son and the corner of Washington and Meridian.

I was left looking at the clock over my shoulder.

In a figurative sense, I am still looking at that clock, and it still sits at a crossroads.

That crossroads is the intersection of generations. What lives and what dies rests in the hands of the generation that is coming, not with the generations of the past. Such decisions need to be informed, intentional, and purposeful. In the story that follows, I have endeavored to communicate my negotiation of that generational crossroads from one Mutz generation to another. I pray that it will directly benefit those coming after me: that it will inform their decisions, strengthen their noblest intentions, and inspire purpose.

Indeed, we look forward to the challenge of change that follows.

TAKE AWAYS

- What lives and what dies rests in the hands of the generation that is coming, not with the generations of the past.
- Operate from the basis of informed decisions, strong and noble intentions, and inspired purposes.
- Good work ethics create the basis for success.

SALVATION FOR ZION

Look to Abraham your father, and to Sarah who gave birth to you
in pain. When I called him, he was only one; I blessed him and
made him many. For the LORD will comfort Zion; He will comfort
all her waste places, and He will make her wilderness like Eden,
and her desert like the garden of the LORD. Joy and gladness will
be found in her, thanksgiving and melodious song.

—ISAIAH 51:2–3

PART ONE:

EDINBURGH

Chapter 1

"LOOK TO THE ROCK FROM WHICH YOU WERE CUT"

O N JULY 4, 1876, a brief historical sketch of Shelby County, Indiana, was deposited with the county clerk to celebrate the great "Centennial of American Liberty." The document's authors pondered the accomplishments of the fifty-four short years since the county's formal settlement in 1822.

"Where now we may see broad fields and wide pastures of open woodland," they wrote, "then stood the great oak, the poplar, the beech, the maple, the walnut, and the ash...so dense that they shut out the sun from May to October." The underbrush, they noted, often presented an impenetrable barrier to the horseman, and the level lands stood in water for more than half the year.[1]

Making this part of Indiana suitable for agriculture was a Herculean task. "Without money, and without the assistance which money brings," wrote an eyewitness, "these men had come here to make war upon nature in her most forbidding forms...But they went to work with a dauntless and unconquerable energy, buoyed by the hope of leaving their children a good inheritance."[2] Within fifty years, one generation, men who had possessed little or nothing of the world's goods owned taxable property amounting to fifteen million dollars. Out of the soil recovered from marshland and almost impregnable forest, the settlers of Indiana had made a very "large and substantial prosperity."[3]

Among the names of men notable for their contributions to this growth, the authors of Shelby County's first history cite "Jacob Mutz, Representative in Indiana Legislature, 1861–1865."[4]

Barnabas C. Hobbs, appointed Earlham College's first president in 1867 and the Superintendent of Public Instruction for the State of Indiana in 1868, characterizes this "first generation" of Hoosiers:

> High toned and patriotic, [with a] great regard for law and order. It was not safe for any man to swear profanely when in the presence of any authority that could impose a fine. Men had to obey for wrath if not for conscience. There was a strong repugnance

1

to immorality generally... They were intensely but sincerely sec-
tarian in their religious view [and] though religious they were men
of honor, and ever held themselves in readiness to vindicate their
honor by hard knocks when they thought it necessary.[5]

Described elsewhere as "social and industrious," the people who developed the agricultural resources of Indiana's wealth possessed a strong
work ethic coupled with a high regard for moral behavior. They realized
the American Dream within one lifetime, but never at the expense of the
American character.

In every sense a faithful representation of the people who elected him,
Jacob Mutz consequently functioned as a "citizen legislator" during his
tenure in the Indiana government and never as a career politician.

In fact, in his *Biographical Sketches of the Members of the Forty-first
General Assembly of the State of Indiana*, James Sutherland describes the
freshman representative from Shelby County as exercising "a degree of
industry not practiced by many farmers in Indiana."[6] Sutherland expands
further:

> He is not of that class who never have time to do anything
> except sit on pine boxes in front of stores in the county seats, plying
> their jaws on tobacco and their jack knives on the boxes to which
> they are anchored. Neither does he belong to that class that always
> get done planting corn, harvesting, or any other piece of work, pre-
> cisely at noon on Friday. There are thousands of them in Indiana;
> and nothing short of an interposition of Providence could induce
> them to perform any labor from that time until Monday morning.
> No, Jacob Mutz is not of this order of agriculturalists; but a thrifty,
> judicious cultivator of the Western staples.[7]

Sutherland goes on to commend Mutz for his first term in the Indiana
Legislature:

> [He] has so performed the duties committed to his care as to receive
> the approbation of his constituents, and the confidence and respect
> of all the members of the House. He has filled several township
> offices in a manner that redounded to the interests of the township,
> and secured him much popularity among his neighbors.[8]

Such was the rock from which the Mutz family is hewn.

Ethical, pragmatic, industrious, just—these are our family core values, our family characteristics. The "good inheritance" Jacob Mutz entrusted into his children's care encompassed more than the prosperous Indiana farmland carved out of swamp and wood; it was more than his neighbors' approbation or the recognition of the quality of his public service as a legislator, member of the Indiana Board of Agriculture, or trustee of Purdue University.

His legacy to us is the lifestyle of the good steward who multiplies the talents his Master has given him intentionally and faithfully and avoids—as the framers of the Shelby County centennial history would phrase it—the temptations of "those pleasures too dearly purchased."

A FAMILY INHERITANCE

Born in Lancaster County, Pennsylvania, in 1825, Jacob Mutz was raised in Montgomery County, Ohio, and settled in Edinburgh, Indiana, with his new wife, Anna Maria Snepp, in 1847. Oscar Ulysses Mutz was the youngest of Jacob and Maria's ten children. His oldest brother, Charles, became a doctor, and two of his four sisters (Catherine and Emma) married doctors. Oscar and his wife, Emma, owned and operated the O. U. Mutz Hardware Store in Edinburgh.

In the first half of the twentieth century, Edinburgh was a small but prosperous town with a population hovering around 2,200. Franklin and Columbus were the nearest population centers of any consequence, and Franklin lay a little under eleven miles to the north, Columbus a little over eleven miles to the south.

In the thirty years between 1900 and 1930, Indianapolis, twenty-two miles north of Franklin, doubled in size to over 350,000 residents and became firmly entrenched as one of the country's major manufacturing centers. While the first generation of its settlers were considered "industrious but unenterprising, content with small gains and pleasures not too dearly purchased, nor shared in with an eye to business" by the writers of the Shelby County centennial history, their children and grandchildren had shifted the scale and scope of local ambitions.

This change is reflected in the Shelby County document itself. The authors—reflecting the vision of a rising generation—conclude their description of the area's development by lamenting the fact that, though ornamented with "crowded, thrifty streets" and "graceful...frame houses that loom up in every direction and indicate the comfortable circumstances and taste of their owners," "...now, as in the past, [the county's] mercantile interests largely outweigh its manufactures."

More pointedly, the writers state:

> However much this fact is to be deplored, it is nevertheless true. It
> is not because there are not manufacturing facilities. Upon every
> land are large forests of timber satisfactory for manufacturing pur-
> poses. Already we have furniture, carriage and wagon shops, but
> not upon the scale that should exist. Abundance of walnut and
> ash for all grades of furniture can easily be obtained and man-
> ufactured here; and with Cincinnati, Louisville, Indianapolis, St.
> Louis, and Chicago as distributing points, will command a ready
> market throughout the West. The same holds true in regard to
> other branches. Competition in railway freights secures cheap
> transportation, and wood and water are in abundance. Even the
> facilities of a HYDRAULIC are within our reach. At a point six
> miles above town a canal can be built at a moderate cost…suffi-
> cient for immense manufacturing purposes.[9]

These sons and daughters of those first settlers who cleared the forests
and drained the swamps and founded towns based on a thriving agriculture were not content to live off their parents' inheritance. They sought,
instead, new opportunities to expand and multiply that inheritance, confident they would pass on a better world to those who came after them.

As part of this "bridge" generation, Oscar Mutz had translated his portion of the agriculturally based wealth of his father, Jacob, into a prosperous
hardware enterprise in downtown Edinburgh. He had married the daughter
of the local baker, a wealthy citizen whose family name—Winterberg—was
attached to many of the small business concerns dotting the municipality
at that time, among them, a grocery, millinery, and shoe store, as well as
the original bakery.

Emma Sanders Winterberg was something of a musician. Her father had
acquired a Steinway grand piano custom-built at the governor of Indiana's
specifications for his nine-year-old daughter. This magnificent instrument
graced the Winterberg home. Its frame was of rich, inlaid woods, and the
piano bench legs were shod in crystal. The piano's large, rectangular shape
would have dominated any but the most generously sized rooms.

On such the wife of Oscar Mutz practiced her art.

Since the task of domesticating the Indiana wilderness was completed by
the previous generation, parents turned their attention to the more pleasant
challenges of educating and preparing children for higher positions in life.
Emma had been educated at the Cincinnati Conservatory of Music in 1885,
and, in due course, enrolled her daughter Evelyn there.

Music was a nonnegotiable in the equipping of a new generation for the task of extending the family's fortunes. Oscar and Emma's youngest son, Harold Winterberg Mutz—my father—played flute and piccolo in the symphony orchestras of both nearby Franklin and Columbus and in the local Edinburgh band. While studying at Coe College in Cedar Rapids, Iowa, Harold managed to combine business with pleasure in his own typically eclectic fashion by assuming the management of Coe's Girls' Glee Club. His business acumen as well as his aesthetic appreciations were exercised in booking the Glee Club programs; arranging travel, lodging, and board; and chaperoning the Club on tour throughout Iowa, Illinois, and Indiana every spring.

"The party started when your dad arrived," my maternal aunt Marguerite confided to me later, "and it didn't start until then."

The Mutz family's commitment to education did not begin or end with just immediate family concerns. O. U. and Emma Mutz not only reared four children of their own—Marie, Evelyn, Frank, and Harold—but continued the care and education of an orphaned child, J. Richard Francis, assuming the responsibilities of provision and oversight from Oscar's father, Jacob.

Francis was sent to Purdue University where he studied pharmacy in Purdue's School of Pharmacy and dabbled in engineering. With the rapid advance of the new automotive industry, his pharmaceutical concern in downtown Indianapolis—Hooks Francis Pharmacy—became the site of intense research on carburetors. In 1908 Francis funded the initial manufacture of a carburetor, invented by Indianapolis fiddle maker and woodworker Burt Pierce at Hooks Drug Company.

So began the Marvel Carburetor Company. By 1912 the company had relocated to Flint, Michigan, where it serviced its largest client, a new automobile manufacturer by the name of General Motors.

Francis maintained his home in Indianapolis after the move to Flint, but the investment made him wealthy beyond local imaginations. He purchased a tract of land in Dade County, Florida. After Francis's death, his widow continued to visit the Mutzes in Edinburgh once a year. As the chauffeur maneuvered her car into our street, it seemed to us children to be half a block long. The tan-colored car inevitably sported a soft top and side mount tires and spares. Francis's wife would arrive in a new one every time she visited.

The vision of those who wrote the county's centennial history in 1876 was coming to pass: mercantile interests were giving way to "manufactures," and the Mutz family was perfectly poised to take advantage of this shift.

AN ERA OF OPPORTUNITY

The success of "Cousin Dick" was not immediately mirrored in the fortunes of the Mutz family itself. O. U. Mutz was a gentle man with a keen appreciation for the joys of domestic life and the pleasures, as well as duties, of civic living. At the turn of the twentieth century, Edinburgh was thriving, his hardware establishment was thriving, and his family was thriving. He was a man at peace with his neighbors and himself, a quality of character that must at least partly explain the singular closeness and lack of conflict in the relationship between his two sons.

Frank Mutz, the elder of O. U. Mutz's two boys and the third of his four children, was born in 1896. His younger brother, Harold Winterberg Mutz, was born October 4, 1902. Although different in temperament—or more likely because of this difference—the two brothers would forge life together, partnering on every level to secure the success of each other's families, finances, and futures. Except for Harold's college years in Iowa, Frank and Harold never lived more than a few minutes' drive from each other. Their sons would be born in the same house. They would take turns managing their father's hardware business. They would build successful careers with the same company during the leanest years of the Great Depression. They would retire together to neighboring farms.

This degree of family harmony is not just the product of random chance. O. U. Mutz sowed good seed into his sons' lives. Although I was not quite five years old when my grandfather died in 1932, his memory is vivid. I was frequently parked at my grandparents' house and just as frequently parked on his shoulders. I can't begin to tell how far I rode on those shoulders.

And when he was gone, I carried his name into the future.

My grandfather Mutz was a marvelous man. He did honor to his middle name, Ulysses, a name undoubtedly reflecting the singular challenges his father had faced as state senator during the Civil War. When my mother was carrying me in her pregnancy, he dogged her footsteps, asking her to name her child after him. "I liked your grandfather so much," my mother later explained (or apologized?) to me, "in a moment of weakness I said yes, and then prayed for a girl!"

In my four short years with him, Oscar Mutz taught me two lessons I remember well: how to shine my shoes and how to wash and stay clean—lessons small boys do not always appreciate but that come in handy later!

I remember only one spanking from my grandfather. My Mutz grandparents lived only two blocks from us. While playing ball with some neighbors, I swung the bat through the window of the house behind and immediately sought shelter with my grandparents. When Grandpa Mutz heard about the broken window, he asked me if I had done it, and I fibbed. I said, "No." He believed me until the neighbor man came and blew my cover.

Grandpa didn't say anything. He pulled me over his knee, and I knew I was in for it. Then he reached up and took the felt hat from his head (Oscar Mutz had a thin spot up there he liked to keep warm) and spanked me with it. It's the only spanking I can remember from him. "Now," he admonished me when he had my full and undivided attention with the spanking, "always tell the truth right away!" The lesson was memorable.

The first corpse I ever saw was that of my grandfather in his casket. He died in 1932. By that time, the Great Depression had hit. He had sold his hardware store shortly after the crash in 1929, and my father had begun commuting to Indianapolis to work, having secured a sales position with the Peerless Foundry, Inc., where his brother Frank had recently been promoted into management.

For many, the onset of the Great Depression was the end of an era of opportunity, an era that had realized the "American Dream" in the histories of many families like the Winterbergs (my grandmother Emma's family) and the Sawins (my mother's family). Dick Francis, an orphan who rode to wealth in a GM car, was raised by Jacob Mutz and educated by his son Oscar. He epitomized the thousands of real-life counterparts to the heroes peopling Horatio Alger novels.

But that party had come to a crashing end.

For the two Mutz brothers—Harold and Frank—opportunity had, however, just knocked.

TAKE AWAYS

o Work with dauntless and unconquerable energy with the hope of leaving a good inheritance.

o Develop a strong work ethic coupled with a high regard for moral behavior. The American Dream can be realized in one's lifetime but never at the expense of the American character.

o Core values such as *ethical, pragmatic, industrious, just* make a strong foundation for a good inheritance.

- The good steward whose lifestyle multiplies the talents his Master has given him intentionally and faithfully and avoids the temptations of "pleasures too dearly purchased" is a good legacy.

- Seek new opportunities to expand and multiply the inheritance, confident of leaving a better world to those who follow.

- Seek peace with yourself and those around you and minimize conflict in relationships. Harmony is not the product of random chance.

- Tell the truth—right away!

Chapter 2

TO EVERYTHING ITS SEASON

L AND WAS WEALTH for the first generations of Indiana settlers. Financial solvency from the acquisition and sound management of their land gave parents the resources to expand the next generation's opportunities through higher education. But it was the ability to acquire—and keep—land that made this possible. If a family could not make their land pay, they lost the benefits of owning it and often forfeited the land itself.

My mother's family history, stretching all the way back to Governor William Bradford of Plymouth Colony, followed the fortunes of those members who could keep their land and make it pay. My mother herself suffered personal injury to her educational opportunities when her father could no longer reap a profit from his land. One can only speculate how those changes in fortune might have affected her life's story in other ways.

I can't remember a time when Mother wasn't sick. She had missed a year of high school battling rheumatic fever and really never recovered from it. She always had some kind of illness. I was only thirty-two when she died at the age of fifty-eight, the still-young mother of two young adult children.

But to think of Laura Sawin as sickly or weak or wanting in any way is never to know her or understand the power of her influence and example in others' lives. My mother's example has guided my response to living with Parkinson's disease, a pacemaker, one lung, a replaced hip, and five levels of reconstruction in the back. I can still hear her saying, "You can do things with handicaps if the handicaps don't rule you."

"So I have a broken leg," she would shrug, "What's wrong with that?"

Her father, Asa Sawin, had known personal tragedy in his own life. He had two siblings: twins, a sister and a brother. The brother, Lon Sawin, an alcoholic, took his own life. Lon's son, my mother's first cousin Brent, also committed suicide. At the time of my mother's birth, my grandfather and grandmother lived in Hope, Indiana, about fifteen miles from Edinburgh. Grandpa owned a hardware store on the town square. He had either inherited the store or been given it by his father. In either event, he eventually traded it and a substantial part of the family farm for a watermelon farm near Rensselaer, Indiana. Watermelon was promoted then as the panacea for faltering Indiana farmers. It was going to take them all to heaven, economically.

It didn't.

Asa lost his farm at Rensselaer. He and Anna moved back to what remained of the original Sawin farm three-and-a-half miles east of Edinburgh with three sons and four daughters. My grandfather owned twenty-one head of dairy cattle, milking fourteen regularly and keeping seven dry and calving. He also raised hogs and grew enough grain and hay to feed all his livestock. His wife, my grandmother Anna, had been more accustomed to affluence. Her brother had inherited the Riggs family's home, a graceful, imposing residence near Nineveh, Indiana—the typical abode of a successful farmer. I remember well going there for family picnics. Strategically located next to a spring that flowed twenty-four hours a day, it was the perfect location for outdoor feasts in those days, conveniently providing land, shelter, and fresh water on one site!

Anna's sister, too, had married into a family who knew how to succeed at farming.

Not that the Sawins had lacked agricultural savvy in the past. Grandma "Great" Caroline Harvey Sawin, Asa Sawin's grandmother, was born on September 13, 1808, in Tompkins County, New York. In 1818 her parents pushed westward, first to Sharon, Ohio, and from there by wagon to the relatively unsettled county of Shelby, Indiana, "arriving April 1, 1821," according to an article published in the *Indianapolis News*, April 25, 1902. "Caroline Harvey," the writer continues, "was united in marriage to James H. Sawin, February 23, 1826. Her husband was born in New York, April 29, 1802. His father was of English parentage and his mother of French ancestry. James H. Sawin, previous to his marriage, had entered land at the government office at Brookville, State of Indiana, settling in German township, Bartholomew County in 1824, and had made such improvements as were common in those days in the wilderness—a round log house with puncheon floor and stick chimney."[1] His deed carried the signature of President Andrew Jackson.

The story describes the challenges our family overcame when first settling Indiana:

> The writer well remembers the cabin, where all the family but two were born. They experienced all the hardships incident to the life of the settlers in that early day. For several years an annual trip was made to Madison, about sixty miles distant, with a two-wheeled

cart, loaded with wheat selling then at fifty cents a bushel, [and] returning with the annual supply of coffee, salt, etc.

Thirteen children resulted from the union, ten reaching manhood and womanhood. Six are still living, three of whom are ordained ministers of the primitive Baptist church. Caroline Harvey Sawin is now in her ninety-third year, and though quite bent with the weight of years, she retains well her mental faculties. She is small of stature, weighing but seventy-three pounds. At no time did her weight exceed ninety pounds. She is the oldest pioneer settler living on the same land where she and her husband first went to housekeeping. It is probably the only farm in the county that has never been transferred from the original government deed and purchase.

Her husband cut wood at twenty cents a cord where Washington Street now runs through the heart of the city of Indianapolis. He died in the seventies. Since then, Mrs. Sawin has superintended her own affairs. The only remaining daughter, with her husband, live at the old homestead, tenderly caring for the aged woman. Five generations now represent the line of descent.[2]

Kate Milner Rabb, the well-known columnist for the *Indianapolis Star* and respected Hoosier historian, reported on a letter by J. G. Sawin, one of Caroline Harvey Sawin's sons, in "Hoosier Listening Post":

About 1823 my father, James Sawin, entered a quarter of timber land east of Edinburgh.

A young man of limited means, James Sawin learned the Bates House wanted substantial cords of wood cut, and walked thirty miles to Indianapolis. He and Colonel Bates looked at timber together.

My father proposed fifty cords of wood at 35 cents per cord. Bates was willing to pay only thirty cents. "That's my price—not one cent less." Realizing James was serious, Bates said, "If you'll cord the wood so close I cannot throw my hat through the open spaces, I'll pay your price." Father closed the deal and completed the job. Bates inspected the work, periodically flinging his slouch hat. It would not go through the spaces. Satisfied, Bates told Sawin he'd earned his money.

Years after the Sawin cabin had given way to a substantial frame house, my parents went to Indianapolis to purchase shrubbery and trees, staying at Little's Hotel. After their return home, my father mentioned the proximity to the spot where he cut the cord wood for Colonel Bates.

The frame house was built in the forties by contractor Sanford Rominger of Hope. All finishing lumber was handmade on the premises. The job was long and tedious, but the house has stood storm and tempest.

The homestead still belongs to the Sawin family, whose ancestors came to America before the middle of the seventeenth century, settling near Boston. Succeeding generations of the family have spread throughout New England into most states since then. Sawin ancestry traces back to Robert Sawin, Bottsford, Suffolk County, England, 1642.[3]

Tintypes of "Granny Great," the matriarch of this long-lived line of Sawins, show a very slight woman, but she must have been very tough and was most certainly brave, living over a hundred years. And the section of land she had made productive was the very farm that sheltered Asa and Anna Sawin when the promise of wealth from watermelons failed them. They were less than a mile from the farm pioneered by Jacob Mutz; only one farm lay between the Sawins' and the Mutzes'.

LIVING WITH THE TIMES

My mother may not have been as tough physically as Grandma Great, but she was every bit as brave. She may have lived only half as long, but her legacy to her children, grandchildren, and great-grandchildren will perhaps be more enduring.

Laura Sawin was the youngest of the four girls when her family moved back to the farm outside Edinburgh. Her three older sisters graduated from high school and were sent to college. Nell, the firstborn, graduated from Indiana University and became the head administrator of the resident centers of the University of Chicago. Edith, the second sister, studied design at the Western School for Girls (now Miami University) in Oxford, Ohio. The third, Mary, taught Domestic Science on the faculty of Coe College and married the music director of Coe. And then there was my mother, who worked in the fields like a man until she contracted rheumatic fever at age sixteen while she was attempting to fill the shoes of the oldest male offspring, Ransom. Nell, the oldest, helped Edith and Mary, sisters two and three. Edith and Mary helped the two boys who followed my mother: Bill and Fred attended Coe. Fred started medical school at the University of Chicago.

Laura completed a twelve-week teacher's course one summer at Franklin College in nearby Franklin, Indiana. At the end of those twelve weeks, she was certified to teach all eight lower grades and was installed as the teacher of a one-room schoolhouse visible from her maternal home. She taught Bill and Fred, her two younger brothers, and promptly flunked Bill in third or fourth grade English. A remarkable teacher with only a modest education of her own, she instilled academic rigor in her students (and in me) and enabled them to achieve what might have been dreams she once had for herself.

If the only thing that suffered as a result of her father's issues had been her educational opportunities, Laura Sawin would probably not have battled bitterness as well as ill health.

Later in life, when as a young father I worked long hours for my dad and Uncle Frank in Indianapolis, my sole companion in the office late at night was a man who worked in the foundry during the day and cleaned the office after hours. We burned the midnight oil together; I could tell when he was in the room without even seeing him. One night he paused long enough in his methodical labors to remark to me, "Mr. Oz, yer son is mo' like yer daddy than you is."

"How's that, Kelly?" I asked over my shoulder.

"He likes people mo' better than you," Kelly replied.

There in the half-dark of my office, his comment stuck. I paused, fixed by the sudden revelation.

He was right. I had a little too much of my mom in me. My mother understood people too well; she was always looking to see what the other angle was.

No one could fault Mother's oldest sister, Aunt Nell, who exercised the privileges of her position at the University of Chicago to advance the family fortunes of her younger sisters Edith and Mary. Nell loaned my father the money to pay my mother's hospital bill at the University of Chicago's Lying-In Hospital in 1933 (Mother had almost died then). When Mother and Dad needed a babysitter to take care of me, Nell would put the nail on somebody and exchange the use of the family car for babysitting duties. If my mother did not benefit as directly from Nell's largesse as her siblings, it was because Nell had selflessly drained her resources to take care of her older brother's children.

Even so, it must have given Laura pause to know that Nell sent Ransom's two oldest children to college—one to Yankton and one to Purdue—while she, Laura, had merited only twelve weeks at Franklin's Teachers College and a career as the schoolmarm of the local one-room schoolhouse.

But then, by that time, Laura must have been accustomed to being overlooked and perhaps taken for granted by the other members of her family. She had been filling Ransom's shoes since he left for college in 1914. Mother was only ten years old at the time; Ransom, Asa and Anna's firstborn son and second only to Nell in the family hierarchy, eventually graduated from Purdue University.

That education translated into rank when he was drafted, and Ransom entered military service in 1918 as an ensign in the navy.

After the war, Ransom went to work for Kingan & Company, an Indianapolis-based meatpacking firm. While working for Kingan, he contracted encephalitis (sleeping sickness). The sickness left him clearly limited in physical strength, but he was less physically than mentally impaired. The only other children left at home were the youngest boys, Fred and Bill, who were hardly ready for any level of real responsibility.

By the age of sixteen, within two years of the war's end, my mother, shouldering the agricultural role of an oldest son, contracted rheumatic fever and lost a year of high school. Although physical illness did nothing to dull my mother's inherent brilliance as it had her older brother, both Laura and Ransom died relatively young: Ransom in 1957 at age fifty-nine, my mother at age fifty-eight in 1963.

Often the events that most greatly affect the course of our lives and the forging of our identity and character are beyond our control and, perhaps more significantly, just beyond the radar of our awareness. I am not sure my mother struggled with resentment, particularly toward her father because of the hard work he extracted from her so much as his apparent lack of attention to or appreciation of the sacrifices she was forced to make to keep the Sawin farm going when there was no one else available to help.

From Grandfather Asa's point of view, he had taken a big hit. Just when he needed him most, the only son old enough to take up the reins of what farm he had left and make it successful had effectively been taken from him.

Ransom himself seemed mercifully unaware of the complications his "condition" engendered for others. His old college roommate from Purdue, Hank Schindler, purchased a farm at Nineveh and placed Ransom there to run it. Ransom had married by then. He had two children older than my sister and me and two children younger than us. We would gather for Sunday dinner at my grandparents Sawin's house, and the men could almost set their watches by Ransom getting up and saying, "We got to leave. It's time to go milk."

Ransom farmed for Hank, who took care of him like a younger brother, until World War II began. Then the farm at Nineveh was taken by eminent domain as part of Camp Atterbury, maintained by the Indiana National Guard as a significant Joint Maneuver Training Center since September 11, 2001.

My mother, meanwhile, put her considerable natural gifts to work, equipping the next generation too. She was never one to waste time feeling sorry for herself or to dwell on might-have-beens. She was, after all, a child of "Hope," and the Sawins were people of strong Baptist character. At least two of Asa's uncles (the offspring of Grandma Great) were Baptist preachers who had "beards that were too long and [who] talked too much," according to my Uncle Fred and Uncle Bill. At least, they pronounced the beards too long, so that made them officially so for me.

Only five feet four inches tall, pleasingly plump, and physically active in spite of the ongoing complications from rheumatic fever, Mother was filled with zip and vinegar. A vivacious brunette with a pretty, expressive face and vivid blue eyes (when she smiled it was always a big smile, and when she scowled, you were in trouble!), she walked fast and loved horseback riding. She was unusual in that regard, as horses were not a passion common to girls then, yet she rode one to and from school almost every day.

But Laura Sawin was different from most women in many respects. She had the best voice, a rich mezzo-soprano, of any person on either side of the family. I loved listening to her solos in church from the time I was a boy to the year before she died. She was an often-requested singer at funerals. She played the piano by ear and could play a tune in about five minutes if you hummed it for her. Although her formal musical training consisted of three, perhaps four lessons, she bought a John Thompson music book and taught my sister and me how to sing and read music.

She and Dad were musical people with good voices who enjoyed singing and playing for Sunday entertainment. Often they would include Marion and me and make it a Mutz family quartet, singing hymns at church. Although Mother had lost a year of her education because of sickness and Dad was two years her senior, she wound up only a year behind him in high school. Their positions relative to their classmates were characteristic of each: Dad, always popular with his peers, was elected class president, and Mom made the other girls jealous. She could fling a retort that made one feel completely dressed down verbally. She laughed a lot and appreciated good jokes, both verbal and nonverbal, but nature and experience had undeniably given Laura Sawin a reserved edge where people were concerned that Harold Mutz did not possess.

It was to this reserve that Kelly Shaw, the night janitor at Peerless so many years later, was referring when his keen family observations startled me in my office.

According to Kelly, I too had that edge.

SOWING AND REAPING

In spite of any family undercurrents of resentment or bitterness over one another's shortcomings, the Sawins were good, honest people. If you bought a dozen eggs from my grandmother Sawin, you always got thirteen. She traded with a grocer, and if she traded eggs for flour, she wanted to make sure he knew he was getting his thirteenth egg so she'd get a little extra flour. It was their way of doing business. Doing unto others as you'd have them do unto you was, after all, a golden rule for my mother's family.

Anna was a very gentle woman who rarely raised her voice. She was firm, however. When you feed thirteen or more threshers in your home, putting on a huge noon meal, and then you go and work until dark, you figure out how to get things done. You go to bed thinking about the milking to be done first thing the next morning.

Long after their daughter, Laura, was grown and married and established in her own home, Asa and Anna still needed help. Throughout my teen years I was frequently loaned to them, particularly during plowing, planting, and harvesting. The benefits were always mutual, however. I learned how to do farm work, and my mother knew I was planted where I couldn't get in much trouble.

Grandma would fix breakfasts fit for a king: cooked cereal (Cream of Wheat or oatmeal), some kind of meat, like pork chops or bacon or a slab of ham, fresh baking-powder biscuits, and a piece of pie or cake from the night before. On first getting up in the morning, my grandfather would build a fire, primarily of corn cobs, in the coal-and-wood range; then we would go out to the barn in the early morning darkness and milk the cows.

There was nothing fun and nothing clean about milking cows, but they had to be milked twice a day. I wasn't expected to produce as much milk as Grandpa's hired hand, Sherm, but my grandfather expected me to produce. Sherm would have the cows in the barn and ready to milk, and by the time the sun broke the horizon, the job would be done. We would run the milk through a strainer and put it in eight gallon cans. Then we would return to Grandma's warm kitchen and fortify ourselves at her table for the rest of the day.

Asa drove straight from breakfast to the dairy. We would load three or four cans of our own milk and stop to pick up other farmers' cans along our way. Once at the dairy, we picked up glass bottles of non-pasteurized milk and delivered them to Mother at our home in town and a selection of other customers en route back to the farm, three and a half miles east of Edinburgh.

The rest of the day depended on the time of year and where we were in the crop rotation—tomatoes, corn, or beans. There is no doubt about it, choring for my maternal grandparents was one of the toughest jobs I ever had. Farming is hard work.

The worst job was picking tomatoes. I didn't mind picking corn so much because I could stand on the wagon and reach for the ears. Riding on a tomato planter to set tomatoes was not so bad either. But sitting and picking them all day? The tomato fuzz would get on my hands and make them so gooey, I periodically had to break a tomato open and wash my hands with it to remove the tomato goo.

I hated picking tomatoes, and I could understand why my grandfather had succumbed to the lure of watermelons.

I could also understand why my parents' generation—even the scions of Indiana's most successful farmers—valued higher education. It was the stepping-stone to a different kind of lifestyle.

Chapter 3

A TIME TO KEEP

Harold Winterberg Mutz and Laura Belle Sawin were married September 30, 1925. My sister, Marion, was born thirteen months later on October 11, 1926, and I made my entrance into this world on February 12, 1928.

Following my parents' high school graduation in 1921, my father entered Coe College in Cedar Rapids, Iowa, and my mother completed twelve weeks of teacher training at Franklin, Indiana. That fall she began teaching at the one-room schoolhouse near the Sawin farm three and a half miles east of Edinburgh, and Dad moved in with an uncle who sold Northwestern Life Insurance in Cedar Rapids. While he obviously enjoyed his tenure as the manager of Coe's Girls' Glee Club, he never finished college. By 1924 he was back in Edinburgh, managing his father's hardware store.

Whatever the factors—whether it was a financial squeeze at home, his brother Frank's departure from the family-owned business, my mother's overriding attractions, or the irresistible combination of all three—Harold was done with school.

His older brother, Frank, had already been managing O. U. Mutz Hardware for several years. Frank had married Florence Rost, the daughter of the Columbus' jeweler, and bought a house just two blocks from his grandparents Winterberg, where his two children, my cousins Tom and Jean, were born.

In the 1920s O. U. Mutz Hardware sold everything from teacups to farm implements. It was also a significant retailer for Peerless Foundry, Inc.

Peerless manufactured replacement parts for a broad variety of potbelly stoves. Typically, the top of most stoves would burn up or the hot blast rings would begin melting after significant use. Peerless would make molds from old parts of the stove and mold pieces to replace them. A "gypsy" (generic) manufacturer, the company had expanded to include a wide variety of stove repairs. Founded by the Williamses, a pair of bachelor brothers, Peerless had just made one of its top salesmen, T. J. Cornwell, its president.

Cornwell needed someone to fill his old position in sales. Apparently, he already planned on tapping the son of one of his best customers. Uncle Frank accepted Cornwell's offer and moved his family to Indianapolis, the company headquarters. Harold took over the management of O. U. Mutz Hardware, married his high school sweetheart, and bought Frank's house in Edinburgh, where his own two children (my sister Marion and I) would make their appearances.

Already the lives of the two Mutz brothers, Frank and Harold, were on parallel tracks. As their sons, born in the same room in the same house, Tom and I were most certainly in for a ride!

Another World

"The past is a foreign country," wrote L. P. Hartley in 1953, looking back at the world of his youth, "they do things differently there." Remembering the Edinburgh, Indiana, of my childhood is like crossing the border into another country in my mind. To say only that we did things differently is to oversimplify the changes that have marked my lifetime. People were different then.

Life was simpler, of course, because we didn't have television, let alone the Internet. I cannot remember a time without radio, but my mother described to me what it was like for her to hear the World Series live for the first time in 1928 (when the Yankees shut out the Cardinals), so my parents must have acquired a radio around the time I was born. We listened to Fibber McGee and Molly, Lum and Abner, Amos and Andy, and newscaster Lowell Thomas in the evenings. But such technological and cultural changes hardly communicate the sea change that has occurred between then and now.

It was not so much a simpler world as a more tranquil world. We didn't live in fear or suspicion.

For example, not a week went past that someone did not knock on our door for food. We lived a few blocks from the tracks, where the trains en route from Indianapolis to Louisville would slow down and it was easy to hop on or off an empty freight car. Mom was never afraid of the straggly hobos who showed up on her doorstep.

She had only one stipulation. "You'll have to do some work first," she would say, "and I will give you some food. Can you chop up that wood?"

Then she would turn her back to the stranger in the doorway.

At six feet two inches my dad was big enough that any hobo, when standing in the door, would take a good hard look at him before deciding to come in. If the man worked, they would feed him a meal. If he didn't, they would give him only a biscuit.

Even as a four-year-old, I understood what had happened when the infant son of Charles Lindbergh was kidnapped in 1932, but that kind of incident was so extraordinary, it had no effect on either my parents or myself a year later when I wandered on my own around the Chicago World's Fair at age five.

When the Depression struck in 1929, selling hardware was really no longer profitable. People repaired possessions because they could no longer afford to replace them. While businesses like O. U. Mutz Hardware struggled to stay solvent, a company like Peerless, whose primary product had always been repair parts, began expanding markets and increasing profit margins. Peerless not only survived the Great Depression; it benefitted from it.

Just as the closure of my grandfather's hardware store became inevitable, events at Peerless provided a job opportunity for my father. In 1930 Harold accepted the offer of his brother's old sales position when Frank was promoted into management. O. U. Mutz Hardware was sold.

So began a new era in the family fortunes of this line of Jacob Mutz's descendants. Dad started work for Peerless with a new car, a 1930 Chevy. Until then we had never owned a car. When driving was necessary, Dad had borrowed O. U.'s. But now a car was essential to his work. Harold Mutz would sometimes leave after church on Sunday evening and not return until a Friday night three weeks later. His territory for Peerless included Alabama, Georgia, the eastern half of Illinois, the western half of Indiana, Kentucky, Tennessee, and North and South Carolina.

He drove around seventy thousand miles a year on dirt roads and was paid twenty-five dollars a week plus expenses and half-rate commissions. He became better and better at his job (Harold Mutz, after all, liked people, especially buyers), and he kept doing business with bigger and bigger customers. By the time the World's Fair opened in Chicago in 1933, Peerless had asked my parents to staff a joint display of the Peerless coal furnace and the Schwitzer-Cummins's STOKOL stoker. We lived in a rented apartment and would take turns covering the exhibit with Peerless one month, STOKOL the next.

I passed out imprinted books of matches until eleven o'clock in the morning. Then Dad would say, "Son, you'd better go and get in line." No one considered it dangerous or neglectful to let a five-year-old loose at the World's Fair. I would head for the soup line supplied by H. J. Heinz and get our meals. That soup line would feed a lot of people. It typically stretched, single file, one to two blocks in length. Nearby, an on-site factory produced Ford motorcars, while another built Chryslers, and a third manufactured Firestone tires. I hadn't started school (my mother had held me back a year), but I was receiving a first-class education.

By the summer of 1934, the airwaves buzzed with the news of John Dillinger's death. We listened to the live reports on the radio in our rented apartment. The infamous lady in red alerted the FBI to his presence at the Biograph Theater and gave him away. Even so, in the headquarters of organized crime, my parents didn't worry. No one considered the Chicago World's Fair an unsafe place for small children to explore.

In those days, someone like President Franklin Roosevelt (in office 1933–1945) exemplified a radical person. Today he would be more representative of the status quo! Two years after the World's Fair's end, when Harold's expanding role at Peerless required our family's relocation to Indianapolis, Mom would give her homesick second grader seven cents to take the streetcar from east Indy to city center to catch the Interurban to Edinburgh so I could spend my weekend with friends.

It's not just the world or the culture that has changed; people have changed.

Just before my dad died in 1995, at the age of ninety-three, he told me, "Son, I would never have chosen to live in any other time in history than I have lived." He was the youngest of O. U. Mutz's four children. When the first automobile came chugging into Edinburgh, he was in a surrey being driven downtown by his mother. The horse spooked, and Emma Mutz couldn't handle him. My dad's jaw, broken when their buggy turned over, remained crooked the rest of his life. Dad had seen the first automobile and then he saw the first man walk on the moon.

But he was ready to go. He believed the best time in history was now over.

SMALL-TOWN MEMORIES

In my earliest memories of Edinburgh, Skippy is always there. For my third birthday, Grandfather Sawin had given her to me. Marion, a little less than five, decided that she wanted a dog too and claimed half of Skippy. My parents had given her a boy's bicycle for Christmas. Dad had sold a lot of bicycles and noticed that the boys kept their bikes much longer than the girls did. He was certainly not going to buy a girl's bike, even for his daughter.

I immediately confiscated her bicycle, but I was no match for Marion then. She could whip me. She came down as I was going up and notched my forehead, but it cost her the end of her tooth. I surrendered an interest in Skippy for an interest in her bike, and we were finally even.

The three Freese boys are permanent residents of that other world of Edinburgh in my mind too. Joseph was the oldest, Tom the middle, and Robert (Bob) the youngest. I was the baby.

They lived four doors down and on the other side of the street. The

Amos family, who owned the veneer mill and were the wealthiest people in town, lived directly across the street from us. The Amoses shipped walnut veneer from Edinburgh around the world for use in fine furniture. Even during the Depression, the demand for Edinburgh veneer never flagged. The Amoses' home was an enormous brick house staffed with several servants and boasting a coffee table in its living room the size of a six-foot dining table. Shirley Amos, who was my sister's age, kept us all well supplied with packs of Chesterfields (in those days, ten cents a package) from the top of that coffee table.

A fence ran down the side of the Amos house with a small space in front of it and a shrubbery line just in front of that space. We nailed rag rugs to the fence and secured them to the ground with bricks, and there we hid and smoked. We would always get some bread to eat afterwards to take the smell of smoke off our breath.

Laura Belle Mutz was the youngest mother of the neighborhood and the most vigilant. One day we couldn't make our way to the bread box, so we hatched an alternative. Robert and I picked up a watermelon from some kids selling them next door and headed for the barn behind our house. We were just passing the back porch of my house when my mother walked out.

Our timing could not have been worse.

Laura saw Robert and me taking the melon and yelled. Petrified on the spot, we dropped it, and watermelon splattered everywhere. Finding our feet again, we took off running and hid.

One can hide for only so long, however, especially if you're only five.

Mom had her apple tree conveniently located at the back door. She selected her switch with great care and used it on both of us.

Right away she knew I had been smoking!

"When your mom got that switch in her hand," Robert recalled years later, "I was ready to go home. You knew she meant business!"

With a stick, I was always a quick learner.

The Freese brothers had horses, and a barn sat behind their house. Our house had a barn behind it too, but our barn contained showcases from Grandpa Mutz's hardware store displaying tools and knives and other sundry items stored there after O. U. Mutz Hardware was sold.

The Freese brothers' barn contained Dandy, a dapple-gray Arabian. I helped take care of him when they were out of town.

The Freese brothers rode a lot, but it was my mother who taught me how to respect a horse, as she had grown up around horses. Beauty had actually been my first introduction to the equestrian world. She was a pinto

Shetland pony acquired by my grandfather Mutz for his eight grandchildren (of which I was the youngest). By the time I got to Beauty, she had been foundered and was not exactly a wild ride.

Grandpa Sawin had "horses" of a different type, and I learned how to drive these horses, sitting in his lap. One was a Model A Ford; the other a Model T pickup truck. The rest of his highly mechanized equipment consisted of a Farmall tractor with steel wheels in front and rear wheels with big steel lugs. Not an ounce of rubber shod that horse's hooves.

Once we were finished with the Chicago World's Fair, I began helping Grandpa and Grandma Sawin on the farm. I might be at Grandpa and Grandma's for a week. Grandfather Mutz was gone by then, and Mother was now gravely ill.

Last Days in Edinburgh

Laura Belle had flunked my Uncle Bill, her youngest brother, in third grade English when she was his teacher, and he had been waiting for his opportunity to get even.

Bill was the gentlest, nicest person of all my uncles. Mother was in St. Vincent's Hospital in Indianapolis, hemorrhaging to death. Her life depended on a blood transfusion, but the only way of typing blood back then was by trial and error. Bill gave his sister a pint of blood, and at first she seemed to respond favorably. Then she grew worse.

Our butcher gave a pint of blood and her condition rapidly deteriorated further. So the doctors tried another pint of Bill's blood, and she began recovering.

Bill had saved Laura Mutz's life.

But Mother continued to be fragile. This meant that Marion and I learned to be self-sufficient at a very tender age. We had to be. Mom taught us how to cook, make beds, and do laundry. Dad continued his work for Peerless, traveling seventy thousand miles a year back and forth from Edinburgh to Indianapolis and making three-week sales tours. It felt as if he were gone constantly.

Consequently, our grandparents took care of Marion and me until a lady was hired who could care for all of us—mother and children—as well as our house.

In return Theresa was given board and a room and seven dollars a week. She slept on a metal cot the size of an army cot in the room where I slept. But as frequently as not, I was at my grandparents' and she had the room to herself.

Grandmother Sawin had me gather eggs every day. More importantly, I was tasked with keeping an eye on their hired man, Sherm.

Sherman Howe lived in a little house the size of a large dining room. It contained a potbellied stove for heat and was attached to the farm's shop, where everything that was broken was waiting to be fixed.

Sherman also had a fixation on gathering eggs. Grandma had me watch him carefully. He'd punch a pinhole in an egg and suck the yolk and egg white out of the hole, leaving the emptied shell intact. I learned to follow him closely, reporting two or three times back to Grandma. In the parlance of the day, Sherm wasn't playing with a full deck.

Saturday night was his night off. He'd get off about five and walk to Edinburgh—a little over three miles distant—because he couldn't drive. Typically, someone would pick him up and give him a ride. Everyone went to town on Saturday night to see the neighbors and get supplies and a shave. Inevitably, the wrong bunch of guys would get Sherm in a tavern and sauce him up. Grandpa would go out and hunt him and often find him in a ditch somewhere. If they didn't hire him, who would? Sherm made a dollar a week—perhaps a little more, but never as much as two dollars. I shadowed him on many of his major activities, but Grandma and Grandpa always knew where I was.

My other important duty was operating the wringer-washer. Mother was home, but weak. Once I was going through the process of switching clothes from one rinse tub to another by feeding the material through the wringer, and my arm suddenly went with the fabric. I hit the spring on the top of the wringer, and the pressure was immediately relieved. They took me to the doctor right away, and he painted the injury with methiolate. Fortunately, only the external skin had been rubbed off.

Some happenings were increasingly difficult to control.

The extended family often gathered for Sunday dinner around Grandma Sawin's table. We were having lunch there one Sunday after church when Dad got a telephone call from the central telephone operator in Edinburgh.

"You'd better hurry home!" warned the voice from the other end of the line. "Your house is on fire!"

My mother became immediately and uncharacteristically frantic, almost hysterical. As we topped the last hill on our charge to home, the city was spread out below us. Mother's hysteria increased. Everything we owned was either in that burning house or sitting in the yard, moved to safety by concerned neighbors. Mother wasn't quite sure which fate was most to be desired.

After all, she was the wife of the chief of the volunteer firemen. She knew what abominable levels of housekeeping previous fires had sometimes revealed. You could not keep shabby home management hidden when the entire neighborhood was running through your rooms, rescuing everything they could lay hands on.

And she just *couldn't* remember whether she had made the beds or not before church that day.

If she hadn't, it was one of the few times in her life she had not done so, and everyone in town would know her beds weren't made.

The car seemed committed to going as slowly as possible. When we finally arrived on the scene, Mother was mortified. There were our beds, sitting out all over the yard, unmade.

Perhaps that was the last straw. Not long after, the decision was made to leave Edinburgh and move to Indianapolis.

TAKE AWAYS

- Financial solvency and sound management provides resources to expand the next generation's opportunities.
- "You can do things with handicaps if the handicaps don't rule you."
- Often the events that most greatly affect the course of our lives and the forging of our destiny are beyond our control and, perhaps more significantly, just beyond the radar of our awareness.
- Pay attention to and appreciate the sacrifices of others.
- Value higher education; it is the stepping-stone to a different experience of life.
- To say things were done differently in the past is to oversimplify; the world, the culture, and even the people were different.
- Just as living in a foreign country can expand our vision, so understanding the past can enlarge our world.

Chapter 4

AT THE CROSSROADS

O N March 2, 1937, the Eightieth Session of the General Assembly of the State of Indiana adopted Joint Resolution #6, designating Indiana as the "Crossroads of America." The creation of this state motto was more than an act of civic pride; it was a three-word snapshot that captured the American movement to superpower. In the grand scheme of things, the contribution of the Mutz family may not appear significant on a national scale, but in our family history—as in the Indiana state motto—this turning point in our nation is caught in a microcosm.

Although the official crossroads of America is commemorated by a historical marker at the intersection of Seventh (north/south Highway 41) and Wabash (east/west Highway 40) in Terre Haute, Indiana, we all knew that the real crossroads were located in downtown Indianapolis where US 40 intersected US 31 at L. S. Ayres Department Store at the corner of Meridian and Washington.

It was to Indianapolis that Dooley's moving van took us, about the same time the Indiana legislature was debating a state motto. Number 822 North Dequincy Street was a high-blue-collar/low-white-collar neighborhood. I was in the second grade and struggling with school. My sister Marion had no trouble at all, but perhaps the transition from the close-knit circle of family and friends in Edinburgh upset me more. If it did, this didn't register in my consciousness. All I knew was that school seemed hard and I wasn't sure I could pass the second grade.

My mother—the woman who had failed her own brother—had no such doubts, of course!

My second grade teacher, Mrs. Fiegel, and her husband and two children attended the Irvington Presbyterian Church with my parents, who had transferred membership from the Edinburgh Presbyterian Church when we moved. Mrs. Fiegel knew Mom was a former schoolteacher and was well aware that she would not be happy if I did not pass second grade. Consequently, I was passed to the third grade, but only on condition that Mother would get me through certain levels of accomplishment over the summer.

And did she get me through them!

Laura Mutz saw her children as anything they wanted to be. All we had to have was the heart and the stamina. She knew no limitations for us. Equally, she brooked no "sissy" stuff. When Laura wanted you to concentrate, you had better concentrate! Day after day that summer she would take me to the front porch of our house, and there we would sit on the glider—Mother and I—from breakfast to lunch. Marion might play in the mornings, but I had to wait until lessons were finished. By the time the school term began in August, however, I was ready for it. I would stick girls' pigtails in the inkwells in the desks and be sent to stand in cloak halls for an hour, but I never had problems with schoolwork again.

In the fall I transitioned to a new school, starting third grade in School #85 with a new teacher, Mrs. Persinger. Midpoint of that year, we moved again, from North Dequincy to 5725 Oak Avenue. This time, however, moving was not an issue. Whatever fears or hesitations might have troubled me over the move from Edinburgh, I had now successfully negotiated the crossroads and was firmly, securely looking straight into the eyes of a promising future.

SCHOOL

Where did Mom get that ability to dream big and motivate others to realize their dreams? Laura Mutz had always been more than a bit in awe of her oldest sister, Nell, who had earned her advanced degree from Indiana University and also been instrumental in the advancement of other family members, especially those who followed in her footsteps at the same school. Both Sawin sisters were undoubtedly motivated by their mother's example, as Anna Riggs Sawin had high educational aspirations for all her children. There was a difference between these two daughters. What Nell set as a goal, her younger sister took as a challenge, determined to achieve something greater.

Mother didn't want to see anything other than A's on our report cards. At the same time, she was quite sure she didn't want either of her children to be educated at a university philosophically aligned with the University of Chicago. She had a very clear vision of what she wanted—high-level performance at a reputable school with a center-line philosophy—and she never once doubted its feasibility.

Heaven save us if we messed up the King's English!

Laura Sawin Mutz had vision, ambition, and force of character. Some of those qualities must have rubbed off on me that summer between my second and third grade years, sitting with her on the porch swing and catching up the previous spring's schoolwork. Certainly my mother sought more in me than educational excellence alone. Many people have dreams, but few have the tenacity and self-discipline to realize them. Laura Mutz sowed both these qualities into her children.

Mom's idea that Marion and I could achieve whatever we wanted turned school into a place of opportunities for our choosing. I began playing the clarinet in the fourth or fifth grade, since the clarinet was what I had decided that I wanted to play. My parents bought one for me, and I took lessons, eventually becoming a member of the School #85 band.

Belden Leonard was the head of the music department at Howe High School and came to #85 on a weekly rotation. Someone had given him money to buy an oboe for the high school orchestra, but Mr. Leonard had no one to play it. He decided to see my parents and ask them to allow me to drop the clarinet and learn oboe, and so I did. Soon I was playing oboe in the school orchestra and receiving music awards, one for best instrumentalist and one for best vocalist.

Finding she had a boy soprano for a son, my mother—herself an excellent vocalist—worked me pretty hard. In sixth and seventh grades, I always sang the soprano solo, especially the Christmas solo. Once my voice changed, I became a baritone but still enjoyed all kinds of solo parts in Christmas programs and other venues. I always and most especially loved singing the Twenty-Third Psalm.

In sixth grade I began my career in the #85 guards. The school had a system for protecting children going to and from its building. An upper-level student clad in a Sam Browne belt and a badge stood on every street corner around the school. By seventh grade I was elected captain of the fifteen guards on duty. Guards had to be at school by 7:30 every morning. As captain, I biked around to make sure everyone was present and accounted for, and as I passed each guard, he would salute me!

School had definitely taken a more positive turn.

BEX REX

After we moved to Indianapolis, my education expanded in other directions outside of school as well. By the time I was ten, I had started taking horse-riding lessons from Mrs. Harry Thomas, whose family maintained a stable in the eastern suburbs of Indianapolis. The riding lessons were probably Mom's idea, but Dad certainly supported them. In fact, it wasn't long afterwards that Harold and Frank Mutz bought a horse together (selected, of course, with help from my mother, who always seemed to become involved in that sort of thing!). While the adults did ride sometimes, Bex Rex was principally my mount, my first (and for some time, only) horse.

We had looked at other horses, of course. A kid at Thomas Stables had a good pleasure horse for sale. His parents were pressuring him to sell it because they wanted a better horse for him to show, so my mom and dad and Uncle Frank came to the stables to see it.

Jim Aikman was crying every step of the way as he rode his horse out for Mom and Dad and Uncle Frank to inspect. The three adults were in complete agreement. None of them was about to break that boy's heart by purchasing his horse!

Then somebody noticed the advertisement in the classified section of the *Indianapolis Star*:

> Horse for sale, Connersville, IN, registered
> American Saddlebred, gelding, 5 years old.

Both Uncle Frank and my dad were sizable men; they were looking for a big, strong horse. Excited, full of fresh expectation, we all climbed into the cars and rode to Connersville to look at this horse. Mom and I and Marion rode with Dad in our blue De Soto sedan, while Frank's family drove their two-toned gray Pontiac. After everyone was thoroughly assured that the animal was sound and the price was fair, Uncle Frank and Dad paid one hundred twenty-five dollars and Bex Rex was shipped home to us.

Rex was loaded onto a horse trailer and transported forty miles to Thomas Stables. I had been taking riding lessons on Mrs. Thomas's horses for a year and was filled with the joy of new ownership. Bex Rex was a beautiful animal, a deep chestnut set off by one white sock and a white star on his forehead.

Whether there lingered a residue of underlying tension between us over the proposed sale of his horse, or whether we were really motivated by boyish pride in our respective mounts, Jim Aikman and I clashed the first time we saw each other after Bex Rex's arrival at Thomas Stables. It began innocently enough: I was visiting my horse and saw Jim hanging around a watering trough, watching us. The next thing I knew, I had pushed him in the water! Laughing and quite pleased with myself, I watched him pull himself out—dripping wet. Jim, however, didn't think it was too funny. Before I realized what was happening, he hauled off and hit me, square in the face, and broke my nose!

It was the first—and last—big fight we ever had. The next day, we officially "met" each other, and Jim has been my closest friend outside of my family ever since. Jim, who went on to become one of the leading horse breeders in the country, started me in the horse business over a dunking in a water trough and a broken nose.

Neither Bex Rex nor I, however, were really very successful in show circles. I was thirteen or fourteen when we entered our first horse show. Grandpa Mutz, who had started me on old Beauty on his farm in Edinburgh, was now long gone. His sons, Frank and Harold, decided to buy their own land, and, as in everything else, they bought it together. Consequently, within a year, Bex Rex was relocated from Thomas Stables to the Mutz brothers' farm, and I was given the responsibility of exercising, grooming, and caring for him.

It was a job I took great pride in doing well.

PROSPERING IN A TIME OF ECONOMIC HARDSHIP

I was learning to take pride in doing a lot of things well.

Being a child of the thirties taught me to take my circumstances on their own terms and look for the opportunities others were missing. My first paid job was cutting grass. I had purchased a lawnmower on credit from my Uncle Ben's hardware store. It was a reel mower, one that had to be pushed. I was paid fifty cents for cutting my next door neighbor's grass. Before I was allowed to collect my wages, I would have to cut the grass, inspect it, cut any missed strips, and then have my mother come and inspect it. Then I had to cut it in the opposite direction. At that point I received fifty cents.

My lawn mowing business expanded, and soon I was cutting several neighbors' grass. Eventually I saved the sixteen dollars needed to repay my Uncle Ben. For the next several years, I grew that business until opportunities opened to make bigger money, working part-time for Peerless.

My lawnmower, however, still occupies a position of privilege in the Mutz basement.

People lived in far greater economic need during those years than anything we have seen manifested since. To give me seven cents to take a streetcar downtown and ride the Interurban to Edinburgh for a weekend—especially as an antidote to homesickness—constituted an extravagance other moms would not, and perhaps could not, afford. I had firsthand experience of soup lines at the Chicago World's Fair by the time I was five. People lived in economic desperation, not just economic difficulty; consequently, they went wherever there was work.

That's how Uncle Bill, Laura Mutz's younger brother, ended up in Tarrytown, New York.

He stood in a hiring line for weeks until the foreman, tasked with preselecting workers, acknowledged his presence and gave him a chance.

"You look a little puny for doing the kind of work we have to do," he finally told my uncle, "but you've been standing in this line so long, I'm going to take you in and give you an application."

Uncle Bill was hired and immediately sent for his betrothed, a first grade teacher in Edinburgh. She packed her wedding dress into a bag and caught the next bus to New York. They promptly married and moved into a rooming house.

Two years later, that job was gone. In the interval, Bill and his bride, Harriet, had acquired a used pickup truck, their sole major asset. Consequently, they loaded it up and drove back to Indiana just to have a place to sleep. We had been in Indianapolis only a year, and the house on North Dequincy was tiny, but we made room.

At the same time, Aunt Marie, my father's oldest sister, had a son out of work and needing lodging, so George Breeding moved in with us too. The house on Dequincy was now bursting at its seams.

Dad started looking for larger accommodations. He found them not too far away in the same general area of town and still close to his brother Frank's home. The house had been built at the start of the Depression and was relatively new and well maintained. Consequently, the owner was quite sure it was worth more than Harold Mutz could afford to pay. However, Harold kept nicking away at the sales agent, plying him with alternatives that grew more and more irresistible.

"Why don't you rent the house to me?" Harold Mutz finally suggested. "And if you sell it, I'll move out as rapidly as I must to satisfy your purchaser."

When he didn't get the response he was after, he sweetened the offer.

"I tell you what. We're in the heating business," he tried again, "and your house needs a new heating system. I'll trade you a new heating system for rent."

Finally, it was a deal!

Dad was away on a long three-week sales trip, fortunately by train this time instead of by car. George and Bill loaded up Bill's pickup and moved all of our furnishings to the new house on Oak Avenue, one pickup truckload at a time. When Dad came home early to surprise the family, the house at 822 North Dequincy was empty. He called to the cab driver to wait, checked to verify no one and nothing was there, and then had the driver take him to Oak Avenue.

When they witnessed a third vehicle pull up and drop off yet another warm body at the front door of 5725, the consensus of the neighborhood was that a band of gypsies had taken over. We soon allayed their fears by explaining to them the source of my parents' prosperity, even during the greatest depression the modern world has known. I lived in that house until my marriage in 1948, almost ten years later.

My father worked for a non-proprietary company. Peerless made its profit by manufacturing whatever parts people needed to keep their old stoves and furnaces burning. While other companies struggled to avoid bankruptcy, Peerless slowly but steadily increased its profits. In times of economic downturn, money is still to be made, but often not by selling new products. Help people maintain what they have, and what money must be spent will be spent on your products.

T. J. Cornwell—who operated Peerless for the three widows who had inherited the company from their bachelor uncles (the Williams brothers)—became ill and died. Frank Mutz became president, and his brother Harold, also a proven company asset, became sales manager. Together the two brothers began running Peerless. So successful was their tenure, those who knew Peerless as a family business assumed the owners were Mutz when instead they were actually three widows named Watts, Wilding, and Spencer. Frank and Harold, however, made sure the women prospered.

TAKE AWAYS

o Goals versus challenge: determine to achieve something greater.

o Vision, ambition, force of character: these characterize quality.

o Many people have dreams; few have the tenacity and self-discipline to realize them.

o Take circumstances on their own terms and look for the opportunities others are missing.

o In economic downturns, money is still to be made, but often not by selling new products. Help people maintain what they have, and what money must be spent will be spent on your products.

Chapter 5

WAR!

WALKED OUT ON the front step of our house to fetch the day's edition of the *Indianapolis Star* that crisp morning in September 1939. Only one word filled the top half of the paper: WAR!

Hitler had marched into Poland. Those of us whose parents were alert to current events recognized the gravity of the situation. Our fathers and young men could soon be drafted. Week by week, month by month, we went to school and turned in our homework and sang in choirs and ran in track...and waited. We waited for news from Dunkirk in June of 1940, feeling it to be a dramatic, traumatic event in the life of the entire world.

Another year passed, and we were still waiting. We knew the government was negotiating a peace treaty with Japan to settle the unrest in the South Pacific, but how could we have known in the midst of those negotiations that Japanese bombers were en route to the Hawaiian Islands?

Now another group of young men were in the sights of the gun. I had classmates whose fathers were immediately drafted. My dad was too old by two years, but I was just about to start high school, and high school had suddenly become a chute that carried you into the draft.

My cousin Tom, Uncle Frank's son, was a student at Indiana University the fall Europe went to war. With American involvement an almost certain eventuality, he joined the Civilian Training Program (CTP) and learned to fly. The CTP was one way the United States began preparing for war as young men were mobilized to buttress the National Guard as part of an internal buildup.

In May 1941, Tom was required to join a summer training program that complemented what he had been doing with the CTP during the winter and spring with the National Guard. Tom joined the V7 program, a college man's training initiative sponsored by the US Navy. One component of V7 was a mandated, one month's cruise on the battleship *Arkansas* departing from Newport News, Virginia, for the Panama Canal.

While on the cruise, the US Navy began moving its V7 recruits to active duty for three- or four-month tours. Consequently, Tom went on active duty upon the *Arkansas*'s return from Panama and was stationed at the Naval Air Station in Pensacola, September 10, 1941. On December 7, 1941, he was on furlough at home in Indianapolis, enjoying a Sunday's rest, when the telephone rang.

Because he was in the top 10 percent of his class at NAS in Pensacola, Tom could choose whether to join the marines or the navy. At six feet four inches, had he stayed in the navy, he knew he would be assigned to a multiengine airplane. Tom didn't want the responsibility for the rest of the crew.

"I love flying," he told me, "and I don't mind being in danger's door, but I don't want to be responsible for other people who have no say in what is going to happen to them."

Anyone on leave or furlough was ordered to report for active duty immediately. Tom got in his car and started driving, with a friend, from Indiana to Pensacola. From there he was transferred to Jacksonville and trained by the marines in the Chance Vought F4U Corsair. Pilots were started on the Wildcat fighters and transferred to the new Corsairs as planes became available. The Corsairs were boxed up and crated and shipped through the Panama Canal to California and from California to the southwest Pacific. Tom was shipped with his plane to Henderson Field on Guadalcanal.

War had already enveloped the Mutz family.

Uncle Frank lived only a few blocks from our house on Dequincy Street. Frank and Harold's close relationship had made us all one close family. All four of us children, my cousins Tom and Jean and Marion and I, had been born in the same room in the same house and delivered by the same doctor. We all attended the same church. And from that moment on, when Tom coughed, the rest of us pulled out our handkerchiefs and blew our noses.

IN THE SOUTH PACIFIC

At Guadalcanal the rookie pilots were taught how to dogfight by battling each other. The marines arrived at Guadalcanal with thirty pilots and eighteen airplanes. Before any of them had seen combat, six to eight pilots and an equal number of planes were lost. Only twelve planes were left when they first saw action. Their training before mobilization had lasted little more than three months; Tom and his squadron were sent to Guadalcanal equipped with more guts than expertise.

Tom was the wingman of fighter ace William E. Crowe. In their most critical action, Crowe as the lead and Tom as his wing attacked 134 Japanese airplanes. Afterwards, Tom was nominated for the Congressional Medal of Honor, but he was quite definite about the real hero of that encounter. "Hell," my cousin insisted later, recounting the story to me, "I wouldn't have done that! I didn't have a choice; I had to follow my squadron leader. I was scared to death!"

During the course of his South Pacific career, Tom's plane was targeted twice. They counted 176 bullet holes in his plane after the first shooting, but not one of them hit him.

The second time he was shot at, only six bullets hit his plane, but all six also hit Tom. Four of the bullets were 50 mm, and two were 20 mm. One hit his thumb and broke it and then lodged in his thigh. Bleeding like mad, Tom's only recourse to stop the flow was to get his Boy Scout knife out and cut strips of uniform to tourniquet his leg. Two of the other bullets stayed in Tom's calf until the day he died in 1992.

Once the Guadalcanal Campaign was over in February of 1943, military strategy in the South Pacific focused on the Solomon Islands. Tom was the first person to touch down at Munda Point Airfield as the New Georgia Campaign unfolded. He landed on a runway made out of pieces of steel the size of a laptop lid, interlocked mechanically to form a surface twenty feet wide and strong enough for planes to land on. The Seabees, the US Navy's Construction Battalion (literally "CB"), faced the most demanding jobs of the war, working day and night building airstrips and docks to transport troops. This was critical work, enabling safe returns for wounded warriors. Paul Greiling, my wife's brother, served as a Seabee in the South Pacific.

Enemy fire once disabled the hydraulic system controlling the flaps and landing gear of Tom's plane. Without the hydraulics, Tom couldn't get his landing gear down, so he leveled his aircraft and fired a 50 caliber bullet at the emergency release chain on the gear. It broke, and he landed his plane on the Seabees' brand-new landing field. Discovering he had no brakes, Tom used the field to keep straight and aim the Corsair at a gap between two trees. Using the trees to sheer off his wings slowed the plane and finally brought him safely to a standstill.

The battle moved from Munda Point to Bougainville Island later in 1943 and did not end until August 1945. Marine pilots would fly up a slot with islands on either side, break between the islands, and reach unprotected Japanese locations by keeping low over the water and using the ridges of the islands' mountains to escape detection.

Bougainville was as far north as Tom was based. Pilots would be sent to Australia for a rest and then returned to Bougainville. When that phase of their duty was completed, Tom and his squadron were transferred back to El Toro Marine Corps Air Base in California, where they began training on Corsairs equipped with rocket armament on each wing. These fighters were the first of their kind.

They practiced a drill that would take them from Cherry Point, North Carolina, to Europe. When training was finished, the new Corsairs were boxed and shipped to Europe, but interservice rivalry intensified, and the ships bearing the pilots' planes were turned around and sent to San Diego for carrier training. The army wanted no marines flying airplanes in the European Theater of Operations.

The one place Tom had most carefully avoided by choosing the marines, he was now on: a navy aircraft carrier.

Tom was on his first thirty-day leave in Indiana in late 1943 when he was transferred from California to Cherry Point. Within months he was back in California. He would have much preferred an assignment to a PBY (Patrol Bomber multi-surface aircraft, often referred to as a "flying boat"). Instead he was transferred to a baby flattop, and on that two things happened.

While Tom was attempting to land after a practice run, the tail hook on his plane bounced off the ship's deck and back into the plane and stuck there. Fast-moving aircraft are safely landed on carriers by using four cables stretched across the ship's deck to catch a hook dropped from the plane's tail (this keeps the nose of the plane in the air). Tom was left to land the plane with no hook. He crashed off the deck of the ship into a cable arresting net off its side. Miraculously the plane did not burst into flame, and Tom scrambled out of it without so much as a scratch.

He had survived his greatest fear as a carrier pilot.

Another event that marked itself indelibly on Tom's memory was the mobilization of US forces for the occupation of Japan just days before General MacArthur signed the peace treaty on the *USS Missouri* in early September 1945. Tom's squadron was among those dispatched to oversee the rendezvous of Allied forces from over twenty thousand feet high in the sky.

"As far as I could see," Tom reminisced later, "there was nothing but US ships and aircraft. The sky was alive with our aircraft and the water alive with our ships. I couldn't help but think about how we started with twelve planes at Guadalcanal."

I, however, had spent the war years much differently.

THE HOME FRONT

Knowing the leverage an education could have with the military, my mother persuaded the superintendent of Howe High School to permit me to finish high school in three years. I started my freshman year in September of

1942. I was fourteen and dead certain to be in the military, along with all my cousins, friends, and buddies, within four years. If I wanted to hurry to finish before that critical eighteenth birthday, Mother said she'd help me.

So she promised the principal that the only time I would be out of school over the next three years was to plant and cultivate Grandpa's farm in the spring and bring in the crops in the fall. In wartime, agriculture places high in national priorities, and the school officials offered no serious objections.

This arrangement did not exclude extracurricular activities connected with school. I lettered in football and ran the mile in track as well, but I was a slow runner and not particularly good. I also did the high jump, although I was barely competitive at that too. Still, even though I was not so great, I pushed my way through.

So did my teammate, Dave DeWitt. Like me, Dave was not a particularly good runner, but he worked out every day and practiced harder than any of the rest of us. I beat him a few times in high school, but Dave kept running after he graduated from Howe and enrolled at Indiana University. There he won the Big Ten Mile Championship in 1947–48.

The alumni magazine of IU featured a picture of three generations of DeWitts: Dave, his son, and his grandson, each a winner of a Big Ten Mile championship.

Dave is the perfect example of a person with average talent but the determination to stretch that talent as far as it can possibly be stretched. As you grow older, you realize how many people have hope in their hearts related to something they want to do or be. What many lack is confidence in the value of their own efforts.

It builds our confidence, of course, when we have someone else believing in us, and our mother very much believed in Marion and me.

The day I started at Howe, the administration started the Victory Council, and I was appointed the freshman delegate. The duties of this position included mobilizing bond drives, representing my classmates at meetings, and making public speeches.

My first speech was in front of a gym full of people. My knees shook. The piece of paper in my hands shook, and if I hadn't had a podium to cling to, I'd have fallen down. But by the end of that speech I knew how to get the papers to calm down. I was so elated, I was certain I was on my way to becoming a Supreme Court Justice. In fact, by the time I had finished my second speech, the settling of the paper in my hands was quite focused: I had absolutely convinced myself that I could manage my way through law

school. In fact, I knew I was capable of managing my way through anything I wanted to conquer!

Laura Mutz was equally certain her son's opportunities were bounded
only by his will. He was, after all, her son!

I still sang throughout high school and earned an occasional five dollars
singing at the local funeral home. I would slip in behind a two-way screen
in my high school togs and sing Bach/Gounod's "Ave Maria" or "Fairest
Lord Jesus" or "Panis Angelicus." The funeral home primarily served the
Catholic community of the area, and in those days these were the only
three songs one could sing at a Catholic funeral.

By the time June of 1945 rolled around, I was seventeen years old and
ready to graduate after only six semesters of high school. I shared the honor
of being valedictorian with Roy Horton. Actually, Roy was valedictorian of
the graduating class, but my grades were just as good as his, and I had done
it in a year less. A compromise was struck: Roy, who was uncomfortable at
the thought of public speaking, was recognized as the "official" valedictorian; I, however, gave the valedictorian's speech!

By August 1945, World War II was over. The nation had not required my
service, and it no longer even required pre-college civilian military training.
The war years had, however, seen my tour of duty with Peerless begin.

HIGH NOON

Frank and Harold Mutz were making Peerless go in two directions at the
same time. The furnace and stove parts business was continuing profitably,
but Harold had discovered that wars—like depressions—could generate
unique opportunities for growth.

Early in the war he had secured a military contract to build auxiliary
bilge pumps for duck trucks—amphibious trucks designed and manufactured by General Motors to facilitate troop landings as the navy moved up
the chain of islands in the South Pacific. Simultaneously, men were being
housed by thousands in new barracks, and those barracks needed heating.
Along with some other furnace manufacturers, Harold put together a pro-
totype of a furnace that would keep barracks adequately heated and began
bidding on contracts to manufacture them for the US government. He
secured enough of these contracts that, along with building bilge pumps
for the military, Peerless kept busy.

All that almost came to a screeching halt during the middle of my second
year in high school. I got up one chilly February morning and headed for
school. Someone knocked on the door of one of my classes and brought

an urgent message: my father's business was burning down! Somehow—I think a school employee took me—I went straight to the location. We could see the smoke from a long way off. We passed the grocery store at the beginning of the block, and then the Peerless plant came into full view. Rolling up to a barricade, beyond which we could see the fire trucks, we got out of the car and pleaded with the guards. Finally, I convinced them that I had a right to be with my dad and provide him moral support until he and the other managers went home.

Dad was startled to see me. "What are you doing here?" he began.

But the fire and the smoke quickly drew our attention back to the burning building straddling two-thirds of the block on which we were standing.

The fire had started at high noon. This timing was a significant factor in the FBI investigation that followed. To burn down a facility of that size, located just two blocks from a fire station, at noon in broad daylight required planning and forethought. The FBI found wet, oily rags and suspected it was arson, but it was wartime and the concerned parties connected with Peerless were not significant enough to warrant an extended investigation.

The experience was as traumatic for me as anything connected with the war. It recalled memories of our home burning in Edinburgh when I was a child—vivid memories still etched in my mind. The fire also jeopardized the renewal of our government contracts for bilge pumps and barrack furnaces. Perhaps most significantly, because of the limited availability of manpower on the home front during war, I found myself drafted for something very different from military service.

Someone had to pick up the marbles and put those machines back together. I started the next day, assembling a bunch of my buddies who weren't running track that week. We could work only during daylight hours because there was no electricity. No bulldozers could be allocated to that kind of cleanup activity. They were needed where Tom was: at Munda Point in the South Pacific. We cleaned up the mess with shovels, picks, wheelbarrows, and boxes. Fortunately, the building, although it covered about two-thirds of the block, was not particularly large, only about thirty thousand square feet.

Stewart Warner was my best friend in the cleanup group. By the end of two weeks we had the area cleared. The machinery and equipment were fenced in and a tarp put over the top, stretching from the part of the building that had survived the fire to the grocery store at the end of the block.

In two weeks production resumed. We had to keep faith with our contracts or the government had the right to cancel them, so we literally built bilge pumps under trees as long as it didn't rain. The foundry itself was rebuilt as quickly as possible from the kinds of materials used in the building's original construction, as stipulated by local codes. The new wooden posts, struts, and rafters were fire resistant but still wood, and wood could burn again. We were still vulnerable to arson.

By the next fall, Peerless was back together and I was negotiating my last year in high school. A year later, in September of 1945, instead of enlisting in the US Marines, I found myself enrolled as a freshman at Indiana University.

And Tom was back.

Chapter 6

NEW BEGINNINGS

WHEN I BEGAN my studies at Indiana University that first semester in 1945, my parents gave me one piece of advice that perhaps more than any other shaped my financial future.

"Get to class early," I was told, "and make friends with any students who are there early too."

I made sure I was early to my first Principles of Accounting class. Someone else had beaten me there, a skinny guy sitting in the middle of the front row. I sat next to him and introduced myself.

His name, he told me, was Fred Risk. It wasn't long before I knew Fred was one of the smartest guys at IU and I wanted to keep up the friendship.

At that time, however, I would never have guessed that over the course of our lifetimes Fred and I would form a partnership that would buy and/ or sell over 278 companies for ourselves and our employers. Our association proved to be one of the most significant of our respective business careers.

But Fred was not the most important person I met at IU. Her name was Jean Greiling. I ran into her during the first few weeks of school, but our paths did not really cross until two years later.

HOOSIER DAYS

My mother was quite happy sending me to Indiana, a quality institution that coupled her rigorous academic standards with a strictly center-line political philosophy. I was a business major, of course, with an eye toward law school. In the 1940s IU had a program that allowed selected students to fulfill their baccalaureate requirements by taking major courses their first three years and then fulfilling remaining elective and general education core requirements with their first year of law school. Students would receive their BS degree after a year of law school with the option of studying two more years for the LLB–JD (Juris Doctor).

Marion was already on campus, a second-year Spanish education major. She was trying out for a part in the chorus of the Jordan River Revue, IU's annual variety show, written and produced by IU students, and she wanted me to try out too. As always (ever since Skippy), Marion's persuasive powers prevailed. I tried out and received a callback from the student in charge, asking if I would consider auditioning for the male lead. In the end, I was given the lead and a fair amount of publicity, and with the help of Dr. Lee Norvelle, the head of the drama, music, and arts department, I performed the part in front of many full-house audiences in the IU Little Theater and other venues.

Consequently, I did a whole lot more singing as a student at IU than I had ever planned to do.

I owed three dollars and seventy-five cents for my first semester's tuition after two scholarships—one for twenty-five dollars and the second for thirty-five dollars—had been applied to my account. Tuition was covered, but I was still faced with buying books and meals at the beginning of the semester, so I hired myself out to my fraternity, Kappa Sigma. I arranged with another fraternity brother to make the dorm beds, and made seventy beds every other day, alternating turns. My only other choice for generating a meal ticket was to wait tables. I preferred making the beds because I could determine my schedule.

Toward the end of my freshman year, feeling like I was ready for anything with a year of Principles of Accounting behind me, I answered an ad by Hoosier Tarpaulin for a summer accountant. That summer I discovered that I was not an accountant, since I certainly did not enjoy doing accounting all day. Irene Golden was my supervisor at Hoosier Tarpaulin and had been a bookkeeper there for years. Much later, she would be one of the first people to move into a retirement center that we developed and built and which my very capable daughter, Marcy, managed. I was delighted to have Irene there as a resident, as I knew she would support me with other residents later should the need arise.

By the end of my summer keeping books for Hoosier Tarpaulin, I was ready to return to Peerless.

Christmas breaks, spring breaks—over any kind of break—I worked for Peerless. I made sheet metal elbows, I boxed goods for shipment, I did shipping. A truck driver seemed always ready for a vacation, and I could drive a truck, which generated lots of "fill-in time." Wherever there was a job for me to do, I did it, but I was always careful not to push someone else out of work.

By that time Peerless was a gray iron foundry. Gray iron is a type of cast iron containing graphite, which gives the product made from it high thermal conductivity and a characteristic gray color. Frank and Harold had located the gray iron foundry adjacent to the rest of the business. It required molders who were reasonably skilled labor. Over summers I would some-times work in the foundry, which was an unpleasant place, hot and smoky.

On Mondays, the skill set I had developed trailing my grandparents' hired hand, Sherm Howe, came in handy when I was dispatched to round up missing molders. After getting their pay on Fridays, some workers would head straight for the taverns. It was often my lot to find them on Monday mornings.

O. K. Davis was a pretty good molder, but he hadn't shown up for work one morning, and I had a check for him. I walked into a store where molders typically hung out and asked the man running it, "Do you know O. K. Davis?"

"O. K. Davis?" He shook his head in reply. "I don't know no O. K. Davis. Do you know O. K. Davis?" This was directed at another guy lounging in the store.

"No, I don't know no O. K. Davis."

I didn't bat an eye. "Well, that's too bad," I said, turning as if to leave, "because I have a check for him, and I was trying to find him to give it to him."

"Oh!" the two men echoed together.

"You mean *that* O. K. Davis!" exclaimed the man behind the counter. "Well, sure we know O. K. Davis! He's just behind that door!"

I pushed the indicated door open and there was O. K. Davis in the back room, still sauced from the night before.

My job for the summer of 1947 was sales. Dad started me on my sales career selling stove repairs and outdoor grills throughout southwestern Indiana, from Kokomo on Highway 31 across to the Illinois border and south to Kentucky. The area boasted only two cities of any consequence: Evansville and Terre Haute. Most manufacturers considered it marginal ter-ritory at best. The southwestern quartile of Indiana was a less affluent part of the state. There, statistics showing projected sales were grim. Perhaps part of my success that summer could be attributed to my youth, because at nineteen, I was less impressed by the statistics and full of confidence in my own ability. At any rate, I did well enough to know that it was possible to earn a living as a Peerless salesman in southwestern Indiana.

But the most important business lesson of the summer of '47 was not about selling; it was about buying.

ROUND OAK

By that time, Dad and Uncle Frank had negotiated a purchase of an interest in Peerless stock from the widowed nieces who owned the foundry and were ready to venture on their first acquisition. The Round Oak Stove Company, based in Dowagiac, Michigan, had once been the nation's premier manufacturer of heating stoves. Kaiser-Frazer Corporation had purchased the defunct company to acquire manufacturing capacity for the production of their engine blocks.

Henry J. Kaiser had acquired a reputation as the father of modern American shipbuilding with the establishment of the Kaiser Shipyard in Richmond, California, during World War II. He drew the world's attention when his teams produced a cargo ship—nicknamed a Liberty ship— in four days. After the war Kaiser partnered with automotive executive Joe Frazer to establish the Kaiser-Frazer Corporation and manufacture automobiles. The purchase of Round Oak had provided a place to manufacture their engine blocks, but they needed *all* of Round Oak's equipment cleared out before they could begin full-scale production.

Frank and Harold Mutz were interested.

I witnessed my first business purchase at my father's side. Harold Mutz (God bless him!) wanted his son to go with him because he was trying to train him, even though Harold had never purchased a business of that size before.

It took Dad the entire day to negotiate the purchase of Round Oak. I listened and learned. By the end of the day, two things were perfectly clear: first, I was going to need money to pay my own way to college that year; and second, I was not going back to school in the fall.

Dad considered it a marvelous opportunity for me to gain experience, moving Round Oak from the Kaiser-Frazer location in Dowagiac, Michigan, to a different facility fifty miles farther south. It was work any strong-backed person could have done, but Harold Mutz was certain it would teach his son how to manage people and details. So I stayed out of school that fall and moved Peerless's first acquisition to its new home.

As things turned out, the assignment was not quite as complex as Dad originally thought. Peerless ended up buying an optimal building to house Round Oak from Kaiser-Frazer in Dowagiac, so I did not have to coordinate a long-distance relocation project.

Ultimately, the result of my semester off was to help catapult me into management long before I would otherwise have been ready. I learned two lessons I could never have learned in school:

1. The most important management decisions are made in the selection of people to staff an operation. I was responsible only for hiring temporary employees to mechanize the Round Oak move, but that was enough to demonstrate the decisive edge the right people in the right positions give any endeavor.

2. People can be managed effectively and successfully, even under stressful conditions (although at this early juncture in my life, I was intuiting how to do this more than developing and following proven principles).

I was always in a hurry. No matter what I was doing or where I was going, it was always better to be there sooner than later. In this case, sooner was better. I never had to move to Dowagiac, for which I have always been grateful. If Harold Mutz had required it of me, I undoubtedly would have moved there, but the choice to miss a semester of school was mine, and one I made willingly. My parents certainly had a voice in the matter. I heard the idea first from my father, but it did not originate with him; it originated with Faye O. Ellis, a director of Peerless and the son-in-law of one of the widows who owned majority control.

Ellis arrived in Dowagiac just as Dad and I were beginning to grasp the extent of the project we'd undertaken. He came at Dad's request to make his personal assessments of how many truckloads of material it was going to take to vacate the old Round Oak site (Ellis owned and operated his own trucking company). No one had yet suggested to me that I should miss school to personally oversee the completion of the task.

"Why don't you just let Oz stay here and do this job?" he suggested to Harold.

"Well," Dad replied slowly, "Oz is in school."

"That doesn't make any difference," Ellis insisted. "He'll learn more doing this than he will in school."

Dad generally believed that too, and I think he was right.

What appeared to be a sacrifice, leaving college at the beginning of my junior year, ended up being to my advantage. I had to live a little differently from my peers at the time, but the semester off constituted more of a social than an educational sacrifice on my part. It did not put me behind educationally and definitely moved me forward in management experience.

JEAN GREILING MUTZ

I returned to Indiana University in January 1948. Perhaps I was making up for lost time, but the IU fraternities and sororities sponsored a program of tea dances and joint dinners, and after my tenure at Dowagiac, I was ready for some socialization. And it was at my second tea dance that I ran into this girl, a Chi Omega.

I had actually met her on a previous occasion. I certainly knew her name: Jean Greiling. Before my Round Oak sabbatical, she had been the double-date of a Kappa Sigma fraternity brother when he and I had gone to a dance. Now she had my full attention. I wanted to spend time with her.

We went on our first date on February 17, 1948, and began to discover how many interests we shared. I loved to sing, and Jean was a piano major. Frequently, she accompanied me when I sang. Music helped draw us together, and I was quite certain I never wanted us to be apart.

The quandary immediately facing me was saving the money to buy an engagement ring. That was perhaps my first lesson in saving. I did not want to pay for Jean's ring in installments; I wanted to buy it, pay for it, and give it to her as soon as possible. As it turned out, I had just enough money to buy it outright the day before I asked her to be my bride.

We were married six months after our first date, on August 22, 1948. She was a stunning bride just as she was later to be a stunning model. In the years that followed, she was featured in a myriad of style shows.

That fall, a year after my sojourn with Round Oak Company in Dowagiac, I returned to Indiana University for my final year of schooling as a married man. Jean and I completed our senior years and graduated together the following June.

I knew from my summer job at age nineteen that there was an excellent living to be made from commissions on Peerless stove repairs and outdoor grills, and I knew that successfully marketing Peerless in the "Dead Man's Gulch" area of western Indiana was an important task for me to perform for my father. It seemed the obvious next step. So in June of 1949, after receiving my baccalaureate degree from Indiana University, I began working full time as a commissioned salesman for Peerless Foundry, Inc.

During our second year of marriage, from June 10 through December 31, 1949, I finished my first six months in full-time sales for Peerless with an income of ten thousand dollars. Jean had secured a position teaching music in the Indianapolis school system, and her salary for a nine-month teaching contract was $2,465. She had been such a gifted musician that her primary professor in piano at Indiana University had tried to talk her out of marriage in favor of a career as a pianist.

She taught one full year, and we had enough money by the end of our second year of marriage in 1950 to build a house, a very nice house, in northeastern Indianapolis. Then, in 1951 she gave birth to a beautiful baby girl, our daughter, Marcy.

GHOSTS AND BABIES

When we were confident Jean was pregnant with our first child, I went to the family doctor I had known from childhood and asked him which obstetrician we should contact.

"You don't need to go to an obstetrician," Dr. Dorman responded. "I can still deliver a baby."

That suited me because I trusted him.

Jean was eight months and one week pregnant when I decided that I needed to paint the basement of the duplex we lived in to prepare for the baby. We had three rooms. A baby grand piano dominated the living room, and it was impossible to get through the front door without moving the piano bench. We also had a bathroom and a bedroom, which we shared with a boxer dog named C. O. (for Commanding Officer). We had bought him from a man just returned from Europe, where he had flown fifty missions as an air force pilot. C. O. was small enough that Jean could put him in her coat pocket, which she often did.

I was painting with a spray because at Peerless, we had some capability of paint spraying. The house had a full basement that had the potential of being a playroom. As I was spraying, with white paint, Jean came to the head of the basement stairway, which had no railing, to view my progress. She looked down at me and I looked up at her, and my face was as white as her blouse. The sight so shocked her, she lost her balance and tumbled down the stairs, hitting her head on the sill cock valve of the water heater, cutting a ribbon across her forehead that started bleeding copiously. On top of that, she caused the valve drain on the water heater to gush water. I was certain Marcy's arrival was imminent. Jean was unconscious, and I was about as helpless as a human being could be. I sped upstairs and ran next door. The dentist and his wife who lived there were equally shocked at my ghostly appearance. I had not realized that I was covered in white spray paint.

The dentist raced to my rescue. We ran up, down, and back around, and by the time we were back in the adjoining basement, Jean had become conscious again. The dentist bandaged her wound, and the "ghost" put her to bed.

A few weeks later, she woke me up in the middle of the night.

"Ozzie, I think the baby's coming!"

I supported her with my arm as she slid into the car, and I took her to the Methodist hospital, pulling up to the emergency entrance to check her in.

"My wife's about to have a baby!" I explained helpfully.

They seemed unconcerned. "You'll have to check in with the hospital first."

"Where do I check in?" I asked.

"You'll have to go upstairs to the business office and pay first."

We had no hospitalization insurance—no one did then—and I didn't carry checks.

"Oh!" the clerk replied matter-of-factly. "In that case you'll have to go to the city hospital."

I was determined. "I'll go upstairs!" I assured her. "You just take care of my wife and I'll talk to your business office!"

To my surprise, when I reached the business office, I found one of my fraternity brothers there late, finishing his work, so I was able to persuade him to give me a counter check. I paid, and they took Jean to the labor room. Then they parked me down the hall and down the stairs, and I waited for them to call my name and inform me whether we had a baby boy or a girl.

We had left for the hospital at two in the morning. By eight o'clock that evening, Dr. Dorman accosted me in the waiting room.

"You might as well go home, Oz," he advised. "There's not going to be any baby tonight. You are just losing sleep. They'll call me if she starts to deliver."

"Well, I'll stay another hour or so," I replied. I was wearing my good clothes and I carried my briefcase, which I had been working out of all day, as I headed up to what I thought was the labor room.

"Can I help you find someone, Doctor?" a polite nurse asked.

I decided to play along. "Yes, I am looking for Mrs. Mutz."

The nurse led me to Jean's room. She was wringing wet with perspiration. I didn't know any better but to assume that was what "mild" labor looked like, so I followed the doctor's orders. I packed up and drove home. Thirty minutes later Dr. Dorman telephoned.

"Well, Oz, you have a daughter!" he announced.

A PRESENT FOR JEAN

Not long after Jean and I were married, I had joined the naval reserves. I volunteered with an eye toward a commission because I had a college degree and whatever other credentials they were looking for. I had passed the academic test without problems, but to qualify for a commission, I also had to pass a physical.

"You have flat feet," said the man as he signed the form. "If you'd been called up during the war, you'd have been 4F: turned down, flunked. You'll have to apply for something in the navy."

The navy permitted me to serve in the reserves. Now, the Korean War was in full swing, and I was quite certain I was about to be called to active duty. I held a unique position as a member of a reserve unit for the US Navy Surface Division. I was the only one in the division who knew how to type and the only one besides our commanding officer who was a college graduate, so I served as his secretary. I knew my CO was away. Rumor held that he had gone to Washington, DC, to volunteer us.

I didn't want to leave my wife with a used car. The day Marcy was born, I walked straight from the hospital to the car dealer and purchased a new Oldsmobile 88, the first one delivered in the state of Indiana. After closing the sale, I drove it to my parents' house and set it on blocks in the garage so the tires would be off the floor. Jean didn't drive it until we had paid for it. Once in a while, we'd take Marcy and go look at it when we visited my parents.

Four or five months later, my commanding officer, Joseph W. Barr, came into the office and ordered me to type a letter.

"Yes, sir." I snapped to attention.

"Type a letter, Mr. Mutz, and say that after serious evaluation of your situation, I have determined that it works a real hardship on your family to work for the navy and hereby am applying for your discharge."

I was shocked, but I typed the letter. A month later, I was honorably discharged.

Joe Barr later became the Secretary of Treasury under Lyndon B. Johnson and president of the American Security and Trust Company in Washington, DC. He was first a congressman before serving in the latter two positions.

Our son, Bill, was born two years later in Coleman Hospital. Jean would not have gone back to Methodist if it had been the only hospital left in the state. Neither would she tolerate going back to Dr. Dorman, having been less than adequately attended.

When we knew she was pregnant the second time, we investigated and identified the man reputed to be the best OB-GYN in Indianapolis. When we checked in Coleman Hospital, I discovered yet another fraternity brother, who was our doctor's resident physician. Bill was a breech birth. I had been waiting an hour when my fraternity brother came out to reassure me.

"You're lucky, Oz, that you have Dr. Smith. This is going to take some skill." He sat down beside me. "You have a breech baby, and the umbilical cord is wrapped around his neck somehow or other. It's going to take some real skill to avoid a problem." He needn't have repeated himself. I had understood that part of it well enough from the beginning.

"Sit down and relax," he continued. "Dr. Smith and I are going to deliver that baby. You're not! I'll make sure Jean is adequately cared for!"

An hour later he returned with a grin on his face. "It's a boy!" he announced. I had wanted two children: a girl and a boy. I was ecstatic!

Two Are Better Than One

I had married an exceptional, elegant woman who has enriched my life for sixty-six years. Jean is the finest human being I have ever known. A master nurturer, her genuine interest in those around her inevitably encourages them to lift their sights to the something greater that life can be.

During those early years at Peerless, Jean was asked to model for the largest department stores in Indianapolis, including L. S. Ayres and William H. Block. She did so to raise money for an array of Indianapolis charities. Every May she worked tirelessly for the benefit of the Indianapolis 500. She personally introduced herself to the drivers while working with their wives on fundraisers. Benefit dances were hosted at the Indiana Roof, a twelve-story building in downtown Indianapolis. Speedway managements and support staff worked with the women, providing for the availability of the dance floor at little or no cost.

As our much-loved children, Marcy and Bill, grew older, they attended the Fall Creek Elementary School. The Parent-Teacher Organization (PTO) at Fall Creek decided to separate from the national Parent Teacher Association. They wanted a female president and invited Jean to run. Following her election, she served the Fall Creek chapter of the PTO as president for several years.

My wife's life has been lived in a steady stream of service to others. She has always been ready to stand in the gap when asked. She has led numerous Bible studies, served as chairperson of Stansfield Circle (an Indianapolis service organization meeting the needs of the elderly), worked tirelessly for the State Board of Republican Women's Clubs, served as president of the

Columbus Service League, served as a member of Tri Kappa, a philanthropical sorority, and as chairperson of the Indianapolis Anti-Crime Crusade.

Her love for music and the piano had begun at an early age. She had spent hours at the keyboard, perfecting her gift for music while other girls her age engaged in more trivial pursuits. Her primary piano professor at Indiana University encouraged her to pursue a career as a concert pianist. Now she filled our home with wonderful sounds, playing the classics. Others benefitted from her musical passions, including the Indianapolis Symphony, the Columbus Symphony (she served as president of their support group), and later the Imperial Symphony Orchestra of Lakeland, Florida, where she served on the board. Jean's pursuit of the arts has provided education, inspiration, and entertainment to patrons of all ages wherever we have lived.

We had worked hard to save a substantial down payment for our first home; there was little left over for furnishings. To set up housekeeping, we installed a pull-out sofa that provided limited seating and a bedroom set. I was more concerned with paying off the home than decorating the interior. Jean felt otherwise. She understood the importance of beauty in nourishing the soul. She convinced me that beautiful lamps could be fashioned from two large, unfinished George and Martha Washington statues. Her gift for design and attention to details were unerring. The lamps were duly refurbished and greatly enhanced the beauty and comfort of our new home.

Jean also has a gift for hospitality. At the peak of our Virginia development, she hosted twenty-three guests, inviting them to share the enjoyment of our Court Manor home. One of her greatest virtues is that of persistence. Time and time again, I was able to accomplish personal goals like completing my bachelor degree in IU's business school because of her unwavering support. Her careful, steady direction challenged our children and all those associated with our home life, from Indianapolis to Virginia and back to Indiana and Court Manor West, to reach their full potential.

My wife is also a perfectionist, and I have particularly benefitted from this virtue. As I labor over this memoir, she continues to keep me focused and centered, asking me the hard questions and reminding me that "You want this to be your best."

Even after sixty-seven years, her presence at my side makes me feel special. I take pride in her poise, her graciousness, her careful attention to detail. One evening in New York, I escorted her to dinner at a fine restaurant. Jean was elegantly dressed. Apologizing to the *maître de* for the absence of a reservation, I asked about a table.

"No problem, sir." He dismissed my concern airily. "For you and Miss Fontaine, there is always a table!"

I corrected him immediately. "But this is my wife, Jean Mutz!"

"If you say so, sir."

He was quite convinced that Jean was the popular movie star Joan Fontaine. It wasn't unusual for dinners out to be interrupted by other diners asking for autographs!

But my wife has given me more than beauty, confidence, encouragement, and two wonderful children. Each day Jean begins with *coram Deo*, a Latin term that literally means "in the face of God."

"Let me live a *coram Deo* life today, Father," she prays. "I want to live it in Your presence, under Your authority, and to Your glory!"

Her life keeps Christ at the center of everything and in the forefront of the mind. Jean says this is how she can "pray without ceasing" (1 Thess. 5:17) because she is cognizant that He is with her *all* the time.

"Your thoughts and decisions are guided by His wisdom," says Jean, "and not by your own thoughts, which can tend to be much more worldly."

"Two are better than one," the Book of Ecclesiastes insists, "because they have a good reward for their labor" (4:9, NIV). What I have accomplished in life, I could not have achieved without Jean at my side. And, most of all, I love her.

FINANCIAL FOUNDATIONS FOR A FUTURE

I knew my parents avoided going into debt, and the only significant long-term debt they incurred was medical bills. They also kept their charge accounts current. If a payment had to be delayed, it was for medical expenses. Their money management undoubtedly started me trying to figure out how to save, but the first time I really concentrated on putting money back was the year my sister Marion was married.

I wanted to buy her and her husband-to-be a really spectacular small, portable radio. In the late 1940s, few college students spent that much money on a wedding present. I knew I had to get the money first, so I saved so I could buy that radio for them before they were married.

Still, my parents had set an example. If anything, my parents were less frugal than Jean's. My mom had always wanted a new house, as had Jean's mother. By the time Jean and I had been out of school fifteen months, we had saved fifteen thousand dollars to build a new house, but the new house we wanted cost twenty-five thousand dollars. I didn't want to owe a lot of money on a house (or on anything else, for that matter), and I still don't. Money management options were clear to me. You either fly now and pay later, or pay now. I wanted to fly later and pay for my trip expenses on the front end.

So we made more money and saved more money, and a little over six months later, at the end of our second year of marriage, we built a new house. It was twenty-five miles from my parents' home on Oak Avenue and barely in the same county as my sister Marion's house. Jean's family were almost two hundred miles and three hours north in La Porte, Indiana.

By the time Bill was born in 1953, I had been promoted to vice president of wholesale sales at Peerless, and Jean and I had built and moved into our new home. We purchased our second new car in 1954: a maroon Buick Super with a white top and red upholstery. It was one of the prettiest cars I have owned. The next year we drove it from Indianapolis to New York and back, taking a day to make the 890-mile journey each way. Jean's father had died and her mother needed encouragement. Her brother, who was just below the vice president at AT&T, lived in Ramsey, New Jersey, so Jean's mother rode with us to visit him and to attend a convention in New York City with us.

These two ladies taught me how to drive my new Buick from the back and the front seat. I was even arrested for speeding on the Turnpike at Summit, Pennsylvania! The convention we attended was hosted in the Governor Clinton hotel in New York City, so that is where we stayed. It was anything but the nicest hotel in New York. However, there we saw our first color television program, the Army-Navy game for 1955. Neither Jean, her mother, nor I had seen a color TV program before, and its effect on us was quite dramatic.

The future was beginning to look very bright!

TAKE AWAYS

- A person of average talent with determination can stretch that talent as far as it can possibly be stretched.
- Many people have hope in their hearts related to something they want to do or be, but they lack confidence in the value of their own efforts.

- Our confidence grows when someone else believes in us.
- "Get to class early and make friends with any students who are early too."
- Business is not about selling; it's about buying.
- The most important management decisions are made in the selection of people to staff an operation. The right people in the right positions give any endeavor the decisive edge.
- People can be managed effectively and successfully, even under stress.
- You fly now and pay later, or you pay now.

PART TWO

THE

CORPORATE

LADDER

Chapter 7

SMALL BEGINNINGS

WHEN WILL IRWIN visited Edinburgh during my childhood, it was a town event. Many of us children would follow him down the street as though he were the Pied Piper. My mother made sure I was dressed very, very crisply, sharply, and correctly. It was a big deal when Will Irwin came to town, even if he were there for only a few hours. Occasionally, as the chair of the Interurban, he would arrive in town in a private car on the train. More infrequently his chauffeur, Clessie L. Cummins, would drive Will Irwin from his home in Columbus to Edinburgh. Although Irwin had been born and raised in Columbus, his local family and business connections justified our claiming him as a native son.

In 1917 Cummins had obtained permission to turn the garage of his home in Columbus into a machine shop. Undoubtedly, Will himself had financed this sortie into the realm of manufacturing, but Cummins was an investment that would one day pay a very handsome return. During World War I, he manufactured cannon hubs and began experimenting with diesel engines. In 1919, shortly after the war and the demand for cannon hubs had ceased, Will and Clessie founded the Cummins Engine Company. By the time I was born in 1928, Will Irwin was aggressively expanding the family's banking interests by merging his father's bank with the Union Trust Company to create the Irwin Union Bank and Trust Company, in Columbus, Indiana. He was also, reservedly, keeping his chauffeur's engine company afloat.

It took Cummins almost fifteen years to really find his market, but such was the height of Will's esteem for him that the Irwins maintained their financial commitment to Cummins's enterprise. The Irwins' faith in his engines was perhaps not quite as certain, but in 1933, with the introduction of its Model H diesel engine, the Cummins Engine Company began taking off and Clessie L. Cummins found his market in the diesel truck.

By 1934 Will Irwin had turned over the management of the family concerns to his grandnephew, J. Irwin Miller. Under Miller's directorship Cummins developed a unique approach to selling high quality products with service, and by 1937 the company began turning a profit. With the advent of war in the forties and the construction of the interstate highway system in the fifties, Cummins's profits soared and J. Irwin Miller found himself the head of a Fortune 500 company.

However, he had been my business hero long before that.

HEROES AND ROLE MODELS

J. Irwin Miller ran the family enterprises until his death in 2004. He was recognized internationally as a philanthropist, a businessman, and a Christian. He was worth hearing. If he was giving a speech somewhere nearby and I could sit in a chair and listen, I would always leave knowing my time had been wisely invested and I was richer for having heard him.

While a student at IU, I attended a series of his lectures. From then on, when I had a business problem, I knew at least one person who could explain it to me.

For example, in the early seventies, I had undertaken to help some physicians establish a computerized medical history system that would allow anyone to walk into any medical office, stick a card into a printer, and have a complete medical history printed on it in minutes. The doctors, pioneering the system, were so intensely motivated that they had given up successful medical practices to finance development, but they were running out of money and had come to me for help.

At the time, I was working in Columbus in an office near Miller and could arrange a visit.

"You are working on the wrong problem, son," J. Irwin told me. "The problem is not the lack of medical history or the system. It's the lack of access to the system. Until people of limited means can get access to medical records, this venture is going nowhere."

I had the problem focused, but I was trying to solve it in the wrong way. Our solution was overkill. It wasn't a wrong solution; it was just the wrong solution for the times.

Perhaps the Cummins' diesel engine had taught him this lesson. It had taken fifteen years and the advent of truck high technology to create the "right" market for Cummins engines.

From a different angle, an Apple can do today what an IBM 370/150 could do years ago. Even if the 370/150 is a bargain, you are better off buying the Apple computer.

A second chestnut I pulled out of J. Irwin Miller's fire, as I sat there listening to him, concerned calculating start-up costs. The Cummins engine plants took a huge input of capital to build and be successful.

"If you are going to develop a business that needs a factory," J. Irwin told me, "figure out how much land you need, buy twice as much, double that, and buy some more around it."

Forum Group put his theory into practice a substantial number of times. We applied that principle in a start-up. Irwin's advice was particularly profitable when we bought something that had been started with the intention of doing the development ourselves. The times we were stingy—thinking, "We only need ten...why are we buying thirty and wishing we could buy sixty?"—we inevitably regretted it. Applying Miller's advice has been responsible for substantial development profits in my business experience.

As influential as Miller was in my life, many advisors were just as important, not the least of whom was my own father.

Anyone who couldn't work well with Harold Mutz couldn't get along with people. Frank Mutz was as volatile as anyone on the Peerless management team, but he was never a difficult person. The two brothers presented a study in a successful business partnership. When I started at Peerless full-time, I was essentially working for my uncle, who was the company president, and my father, the executive vice president.

Two things made their relationship work. The older brother was willing to share the glory, as well as the work, with the younger, and the younger brother was willing to defer to the older while carrying the heaviest part of the load. I never saw them fight. If there were disagreements, more than likely it would be between me and my dad. Harold and Laura Mutz encouraged family discussion at meals. If Marion or I disagreed with either of them while eating dinner and talking about some subject, we were granted full freedom in expressing our divergent points of view. Around Frank Mutz's dinner table, no one disagreed much. Tom, even though he retired as a major in the Marine Corps, always deferred to his father.

But Frank and Harold got along together famously. I probably had lunch with them at least a thousand times and never heard them argue once. I was the only one ever likely to disagree!

My father was a detailist. When Peerless entered the air conditioning business, an air conditioner being a much more complicated device than a furnace, Harold Mutz knew where every nut, bolt, or screw went. His older brother didn't have a clue.

"Why doesn't Uncle Frank know some of this?" I asked Dad once, early in my full-time career with Peerless. "Why do I have to always come and ask you?"

"Oh, he doesn't have time for that kind of foolishness," he replied nonchalantly.

Later, when I had more experience working with the two brothers, I learned that when Frank asked me or my dad, "Well, what kind of screw do you think it would take?," he was really telling us to look for the solution ourselves. He was an excellent delegator.

Dad appreciated this idiosyncrasy as a matter of efficiency; they both knew he was the knowledgeable one. Anyone who worked for Peerless respected Dad as the person who knew about the product and how it was put together.

The two brothers respected each other in a way that allowed that respect to flow from one to the other and back again, and everyone under them benefitted from that.

ON THE ROAD

At Peerless we made the cast iron core of an outdoor grill, which customers could put in their backyards on a concrete pad. I sold the cast iron grill frame for nineteen dollars and ninety-five cents. My assignment was to pioneer sales in that quartile of Indiana, which was considered the marketing "Dead Man's Gulch." However, since I had begun working that area the summer before my junior year at IU, I was less than daunted. I knew my territory.

My first sale as a full-time employee of Peerless was to Schnaiter Lumber Company in Martinsville, Indiana. I had sold them some outdoor grills and whatever they needed for stove repairs during my summer stint with Peerless in 1947. I had been a kid then, and Russ Schnaiter had gotten a "kick" out of buying things from me. Now I was supporting a wife and was more focused. If it humored Russ to let him treat me like a kid selling stove parts as a school fundraiser, his attitude didn't bother me as long as he bought from me.

For the following three years, I led the sales force every month except one. I started selling the cast iron grills and then added furnaces in the early fifties. Those first furnaces were steel clad, and from there I went to gas-fired and oil-fired automatic furnaces, and then added furnaces augmented with air-conditioning to my inventory. In 1953, Peerless promoted me to manager of wholesale sales and services.

Of course, it didn't hurt that my uncle was president and my father vice president. That helped, but Tom and I had to force their hands some. Frank and Harold had been expanding Peerless since the end of World War II. Tom had come on full-time before me, and we did our jobs well and served the interests of Peerless well, but we certainly inherited both position and responsibility from our fathers, although it took substantial effort on our part.

Tom had been making his living via Peerless's retail sales, service, and installation business. This branch of the company installed and serviced

HVAC equipment. Tom had been leading retail sales just as I had been leading wholesale sales to dealers. The four of us lunched together as often as three times a week, and at lunch, we'd talk Peerless.

Luncheon conversations typically focused on long-range, strategic planning, but we were not sophisticated enough to call it that. By 1952, Frank and Harold were getting weary. Dad was fifty, Uncle Frank perhaps a little over fifty-six. Both had been through a period of dramatic adjustment during the war and a somewhat less but still stressful readjustment when it ended. Both wanted help, and so the two brothers had decided to hire a sales manager.

Tom and I each knew that we could work for the other, but we weren't so sure we wanted to work for someone else.

This wasn't the first time Frank's and Harold's sons had gotten together and agreed on a plan of action related to Peerless, and made it happen, but this was the first time we'd linked our fortunes as our fathers had linked theirs.

It became the pattern: I was the spokesperson for the two of us, and I backdoored the deal.

"If you won't hire one of us to be sales manager, Tom and I will know that we don't have a future here." I confronted the two fathers. "We don't care which one of us gets it, but one of us needs to."

Faye Ellis was still on the Board of Directors for Peerless, and Frank and Harold went to him with our request.

"It seems to me you're cutting off your nose to spite your face," Ellis responded. "Separate the two businesses and turn one over to Tom and one over to Oz, and you'll have two growth entities to profit from instead of one."

The two Mutz brothers followed his advice. Tom was given the retail business to run and became Vice President of Sales and Services, Retail. I was made Vice President of Sales and Services, Wholesale. We assumed our new responsibilities for Peerless in 1953 in exchange for a salary plus commissions plus a percentage of profits. The year came and went, and the two of us made substantial incomes—in fact, more than we had anticipated and certainly much more than our fathers had thought we would make.

I was keeping track. I knew we were doing much better than anyone had expected, thirty thousand dollars plus a percentage of profits.

My dad began waffling.

"We're going to need to make some adjustments," he wavered.

In the end he took 25 percent of our income away from us.

I was angry. "You can do anything you want to me and you can do anything you want to Tom," I objected bitterly, "but not after-the-fact adjustments, or else you are going to be looking for new sales managers." Tom was upset too, but I was, as usual, the spokesperson.

I was crying and my father was crying too. We both knew I was in the right. We also both knew that Tom and I were making a whole lot more money than most other young men our ages. Finally, we four reached an agreement on increased wage bases.

Tom and I began expanding Peerless in several different directions. We initiated the move into air-conditioning, and Peerless entered the HVAC (Heating, Ventilating, and Air Conditioning) market. In 1954–55, I could sell a three-ton air conditioner wholesale at three hundred fifty-six dollars, add on an A coil and outdoor condensing unit, and sell a packaged unit that combined heating and cooling, powered by oil or gas. Today the equivalent unit would cost approximately eight hundred dollars.

THE LADDER OF SUCCESS IN SALES

Like many significant elements in our enclosed spaces, air conditioners are generally sold one at a time. When Peerless entered the residential air conditioner industry, all I could think of was the Fuller Brush salespeople who canvassed our homes door-to-door in Edinburgh and Indianapolis. The salesman knocked on the door as a "cold call," carrying a large trunk full of Fuller Brush products and selling them on a one-at-a-time basis. It was a selling lesson those of us who matured during the thirties and forties could not overlook. Why couldn't we use it to sell air conditioners?

We could not until we polished our approach and adjusted it for a two-or-three-step sales process instead of a sales/collection process on a single contract. Using our own sales installation and service capabilities, we canvassed both sides of a street with two people, a block at a time. This approach yielded us an average of one good prospective customer for every two blocks we canvassed. Our target was to change the lifestyle in every family's home.

First sales are very important. Experience soon taught us that the sale and installation of one air-conditioning system within a city block would result in an average of three sales within two years in that same block as Mrs. Jones "caught up" with Mrs. Smith. The same technique worked on selling air-conditioned automobiles, but the results were faster.

When Mr. Jones came home from working in an air-conditioned office all day and found his living room in use as the neighborhood air-conditioned theater featuring the evening news, inevitably Mr. Smith would say, "Jones, how much does one of these things cost?" The real problem was to get the mechanic off his seat and in the street working at selling instead of spending his energies on aspects of his business that could be handled by a much less talented employee.

Air-conditioning sales began soaring.

Dad and Frank negotiated with the widows who owned Peerless for the opportunity for Tom and me to buy stock in the company. As our salaries began to reflect the evolution of our management responsibilities, they grew to fifty thousand dollars and sixty thousand dollars per annum. The Mutzes were never officially partners. Uncle Frank was always Dad's boss—but not really. The two brothers were actually corporate officers who also functioned as partners, and Tom and I were an extension of their relationship. Tom and I were also corporate officers and functioned like partners. Our management model at Peerless was one of the most effective it has been my privilege to help develop. But it is a style of team management that would be very hard to replicate. It depends on precisely the right mix of people. I could not have done it with anyone but Tom. He'd have been more able to work without me than I without him.

Tom would have said that he worked hard and I worked hard but with a difference: I also delegated more effectively.

I suppose, since neither of us had a brother, the reality behind our management success in Peerless is that, like Frank and Harold, we were something more than partners and corporate officers: we were family first.

TAKE AWAYS

- It took Clessie Cummins years to find the right market for the Cummins engine.
- Trying to solve the problem in the wrong way doesn't mean you haven't figured out the problem. It doesn't mean you have the wrong solution; it just may be the wrong solution for the times.
- "If you are going to develop a business that needs a factory, figure out how much land you need, buy twice as much, double that, and buy some more around it."

○ The recipe for making a relationship work: be willing to share the glory as well as the work; defer to the other while carrying the heaviest part of the load; respect each other in a way that allows respect to flow one to the other and back again. Everyone benefits from this kind of relationship.

○ Polishing a sales approach may mean adjusting it for a two-or-three-step sales process, not just sales and collection.

○ The Peerless management model was one of the most effective it has been my privilege to help develop, but it is a style of team management that depends on precisely the right mix of people and personalities; corporate officers can function as partners.

Chapter 8

MONCRIEF, 1959

SON," THE HEAVYSET man lounging before me drawled, "yer a nice-lookin' young man and I enjoyed your presentation, but yer mixed up pretty bad."

This was not an auspicious beginning. I had just launched my best sales pitch to the biggest builder in Miami. Tom and I were expanding Peerless into air-conditioning. I had already taken Peerless into Iowa and begun manufacturing heating and air-conditioning units for Thermogas, Inc., although initial sales were a bit sluggish. Florida seemed a pretty safe bet to try my luck next.

"In Florida," the man continued to explain, leaning back lazily on his chair, "we got da sea and we got da shade and we got da *breeze*." He emphasized "breeze" by gesturing with a pudgy hand toward the window. "When you got doze things, you don't need no air-conditioning. You just go back up north to all those cities around the Mississippi. Dey got lots of humidity around doze rivers and you cain sell yer air-conditioning there."

I took him at his word. I took my air-conditioning and my sales pitch back north and targeted the humid river cities of the Mississippi River basin. HVAC sales, including installation accessories, exploded!

Our effective market suddenly increased. We did not have the sales force to manage the new private label accounts like Thermogas and Wickes Corporation that began coming in. I had to manage them as "house" accounts because we couldn't afford to pay sales personnel. We used management to take care of the private label accounts, and I was that management.

I was busy. But I still had time for Marcy and Bill, and Jean and I sang in the church choir. In fact, I sang most of the male solos. I loved to sing. The singing, however, was about to come to an abrupt end.

EXPANDING PEERLESS

I was keeping extremely busy marketing HVAC wholesale sales and services, but Tom wanted to build a chain of retail sales, service, and installation businesses under the Peerless brand. If he couldn't get this accomplished under the Peerless name, he was ready to do it under some other name. I was tasked to find such an entity because, in spite of my cool reception in Florida, I was now responsible for national sales and services. In 1959, I thought I had found exactly what Tom was seeking.

Since I had been the contact point, Tom considered it logical that I broker the purchase, and I concurred. In 1959, Peerless purchased Moncrief, Incorporated, based in Atlanta, Georgia. I negotiated the purchase and turned Moncrief over to Tom to manage.

Of course, owning a company in Atlanta meant that Tom had to invest a large amount of his time there, at least during the initial changeover. I had always assumed that would be Tom, but he soon had enough of time away from home. I had two very young children, and Tom had three in high school.

"Oz, let's take turns in Atlanta," he suggested.

I was game; I wanted to make Moncrief work as much as he did, so we tried it. But things went from bad to worse.

No one at Moncrief knew who their boss was. Inadvertently, Tom and I had put too many cooks in the kitchen. One of us was going to have to take full responsibility for our new acquisition. I just didn't quite realize yet that it was going to be me.

THE WRITING ON THE WALL

Peerless had owned Moncrief for just short of six months. Tom and I were sharing managerial duties, but Moncrief was a troubled company when we bought it and it wasn't getting fixed.

One Monday morning my father called me into his office. When Harold had something heavy on his mind, it was easy to tell. The atmosphere in the office thickened.

"What are you doing the rest of the week?" he asked me.

I would be in my office, obviously. I assumed he wanted the details of the work ahead of me.

"Could you change your plans without too much disruption?" he continued.

"Sure," I replied. "What do you have in mind?"

"Son, I want you to go to Georgia and check into Moncrief. And I don't want you to come back until that business is making money."

Silence lay heavy between us.

I knew better than to say anything. There was something more coming.

"That business hasn't made money for fifty-nine months in a row," Dad spoke slowly.

"I know."

"You and Tom were the ones who wanted to buy it, weren't you?"

I paused. "Yes, sir, we did," I agreed.

"Well, *we* bought it. *You* fix it!"

The stress on the pronouns was unmistakable. I wasn't quite so sure I followed his meaning.

"We've been trying to do that," I returned.

"I didn't say that, Oz." Dad's eyes never left mine. "I said *you* fix it. Tom doesn't have enough experience in manufacturing to fix this. You do. Fix it!"

By the end of that fateful morning, we had negotiated a plan for turning Moncrief around, a plan that started with my leaving my wife and two children in Indianapolis while I lived in Atlanta, Georgia. Dad agreed I could come back every other weekend once things at Moncrief began turning around. I would give the next thirteen months of my family's lives to making Moncrief profitable.

Marcy, who was eight when I left for Atlanta, would get in the clothes chute and sit in the laundry hamper to smell my clothes, reminding herself that she did have a father.

Had I been an independent employee, had the executive at Peerless been only an employer and not my father, I would have quit or been fired. We had an executive vice president at Peerless then who was well qualified and a very decent person, but who was also very jealous of my position and reputation in the company. He seemed convinced that Harold Mutz was showing his son favoritism.

"Well, Jack," I snapped finally, after he had made an insinuating remark, "anytime you want to go, just let me know, and I'll hand you my bag and let you leave your children on a Sunday night. We can see how you feel about that!"

Jean wouldn't have let me do this later, and I wouldn't have done it. Nor would I have allowed the separation to continue so long. Some weeks, when the weather was bad, it was close to impossible to leave my children and wife on a Sunday evening and fly to Atlanta, knowing it would be at least another two weeks before I would see them again—and perhaps longer.

For the next thirteen months, after Harold confronted me in his office and ordered me there, I flew to Atlanta every other Sunday night and didn't return until the Friday almost two weeks later. I flew back to Indianapolis every other Friday night and was in my office at Peerless Saturday morning. I worked in the Peerless office until Saturday night when I returned to Jean, Bill, and Marcy. We would spend Saturday night and Sunday trying to act like a family, and then Sunday night, I was on my way back to Atlanta.

Small wonder the singing stopped.

By the time I left Moncrief thirteen long months later, I had learned the importance of making a profit. This was a lesson I would never forget. I had also experienced firsthand one of the most obvious differences between the human relations practices of manufacturing in the north (i.e., Peerless) and those of the south (Moncrief).

Our Atlanta factory designated a men's room for "colored." I shared the use of it with our one African American employee, Will, who served us well as janitor and clean-up man. Will and I also shared a drinking fountain that was not used by any other employees.

We had our own.

THE KEY TO PROFITABILITY

In the midfifties, management was not yet a science, but it was certainly headed in that direction. After earning my degree from IU, I continued to develop my business expertise through advanced education programs, seminars, and conferences. I learned lessons more effectively during my thirteen-month sojourn at Moncrief than any teacher or conference speaker could have imparted to me, but if my previous training had not provided the necessary foundations, these lessons would have taken twice the time to learn. Some of the most important ones I may never have absorbed.

Business management was effectively approached as a science only after the introduction of the computer. The multitude of logistical problems, the exponential growth in amount and kind of available data, and the subsequent burgeoning need for new ways of data processing defined the parameters of business as a science. People, however, cannot be quite so effectively quantified or predicted.

And people, as I realized at Moncrief, are the most important key to profitability.

I had discovered as I moved up the management ladder at Peerless from sales manager to vice president of wholesale sales and service to vice president that I could help make a salesperson out of almost anyone.

When I was around twenty-five years old and first promoted to wholesale sales manager, one of my salesmen from Cincinnati, Ohio, gave me a book by a man named Frank Bettger entitled *How I Raised Myself from Failure to Success in Selling*. The book was a bit of a revelation to me. I found the application of its principles immediately rewarding and naturally assumed that what had been good for me would surely be good for anyone else on my team. Consequently, I required everyone to read it.

Eventually, I added some other titles to my required reading list. When someone began working with me, I would require him to read each book on the list and give me a short synopsis of it, telling me what he had learned. My goals for these assignments were quite straightforward. I wanted to develop every employee working for us as a salesperson. I've had the difference between marketing and sales explained to me several times but never quite convincingly—but I do know that I have never led a business that had enough well-trained salespeople. I discovered that if someone could be taught how to sell, he or she could be taught a variety of skills.

In the seventies, those on the front edge of business administration in the United States would have identified my practices of twenty years prior as innovative (perhaps even visionary!) and called them "mentoring." I was not concerned with what I was doing; I was focused on the outcome.

I especially wanted even our engineers to be able to sell.

The University of Chicago's School of Business pioneered the study of business management in the United States. It was only the second school of its kind when it opened its doors to students in 1898 and the first to offer an executive master's degree in business administration in 1943. My years as a student at Indiana University paralleled Chicago's strategic development of its MBA program. When the chance to participate in research with the school through Indianapolis University arose, I jumped at it.

Perhaps I owe this edge in my business career to my mother too. Her family had always valued education, and her sister Nell had a long-standing relationship with the University of Chicago. My mother had been adamant that I take my own education seriously. Consequently, I was not just open to what business professionals in the area of higher education might have to say, I actively sought them out.

At any rate, I began working with the group at Indianapolis University (it was Indiana Central College then) who were affiliated with the University of Chicago team, researching criteria for management selection and development. I worked in a little cell with a few other mid-level or high-level managers. I had a couple of salesmen besides myself when I was promoted to sales manager at Peerless, and I was expected to go out and recruit a sales organization in an industry that almost didn't exist—air-conditioning!

It was a virgin problem, and that is probably what caught the researchers' attention. They worked with me to develop the criteria for what we were seeking in sales force personnel. Such criteria would give me a tool for assessing a candidate's chances of success in our sales before I hired him or her.

With what I had learned from my trainees, coupled with my reading program and what I had observed and learned on the field, I could tell almost the day I hired a person for Peerless whether or not he or she were likely to be successful in sales. By then I had developed my own working thesis that the most important decision a manager ever makes is the hiring decision. Everything else is secondary. If I fail on the hiring side, no amount of corrective action will ever overcome the problem I create.

The University of Chicago's research had provided a profile of what we thought would be a successful salesperson. Business profitability, they had shown, does not come from engineers or accountants, and improving engineering staff or accounting is of limited benefit to a company's overall margins. The research team's numbers did not support that. But increasing the effectiveness of a marketing team was found to give the edge to any business. Peerless became the direct benefactor of this business/education partnership. We had an edge in the HVAC industry.

The challenge facing us in Atlanta was how to bring that edge to a company already headed in the wrong direction.

FINDING THE RIGHT PERSON: THE ART OF FIRING AND HIRING

The first critical step any manager must take is to accurately diagnose the need. Moncrief had lost money for fifty-nine months. It was a leak, not a geyser. They had been losing very small amounts of money at a rate that would not have threatened bankruptcy, but the fact remained that Peerless's new acquisition was not profitable.

What was causing this drain?

Identifying the cause is the first step in finding the cure. Where money is a problem, the cure is most often a management overhaul. Most CEOs, including me, don't like to face that fact. Managers can do all the snake dances they like, but success inevitably comes down to this: if you don't get all your management put together in a "can-do," "want-to-win" fashion, money will always be a problem.

Tom and I began studying our managers on our first arrival at Moncrief. We started at the top.

We had negotiated Moncrief's purchase from its owner and CEO, Lawrence Kent Jr., and had allowed Kent to remain corporate president. Kent had inherited Moncrief from his father, Lawrence Kent Sr., who, in turn, had worked for the company's founder, Stephen Moncrief, and purchased it from him on his retirement. The company had an impressive track record of pioneering the heating and air-conditioning industry in Atlanta, engaging the services of Georgia Tech-trained engineers in its product development. The edge it had in air-conditioning technology is what drew Tom's and my attention when looking for a place to expand Peerless interests in that industry sector. Why a company that had cornered the HVAC market in Atlanta and developed a competitive product like the Temperature Control Central Air Conditioner should be losing money was a bit of a puzzle. This could not be only a matter of having the wrong salespeople.

It was, however, very much a personnel problem.

I was unsure of Lawrence Kent Jr. from the first, but for the first three or four weeks that I spent in Atlanta, I thought he might step up to the plate and become the real leader Moncrief so obviously needed. Then, one Monday morning, he didn't show up for work.

I'd been there all weekend, working in my lonely apartment overlooking the main expressway in downtown Atlanta. It was so small I could barely turn full circle in it.

Kent didn't show up Monday. He didn't show up Tuesday or Wednesday, and I didn't get a call or a note or a telegram. Thursday morning I received a telegram from somewhere in Mexico:

"Kingfish running stop. Be home next Monday stop."

True to his previous pattern of action, as I learned, he had decided it was time to go fishing for a week and didn't tell anyone. He had an airplane of his own and had flown to Mexico.

I was absolutely stunned that a guy could be that irresponsible regarding his vocation. His father had started at Moncrief, had bought into it and stayed with it and taken care of it, and as he developed it, he had brought his son along. Harold Mutz had done the same thing with his son.

What I didn't know then and heard later was that both Lawrence Kents, father and son, were alcoholics.

When Kent managed to return the next Monday, we had a brief conversation. I told him I'd be happy to monitor his progress throughout the following week and then discuss what the remedy might be. I had not the slightest idea he was drinking or had any problem of that sort. I was a "damned Yankee," and Moncrief's employees did not squeal on their management, especially to Yankees.

By the following Monday (I'd been at home in Indianapolis that weekend), I knew I had found the biggest problem with Moncrief. This was not a problem that could be fixed without a change of personnel.

I told Lawrence Kent Jr. he needed to pack up and be ready to go by Friday night, as his position at Moncrief was terminated.

Kent did not protest. His laundry was dirtier than I suspected at the time, and he knew it was not a question of *if* but *when* I would find out. HVAC companies were considered clean, and in that era, drinking on the job was not something to be overlooked.

Of course, when we started the search for Kent's replacement, we were looking for a marketing type: someone with good sales potential. For Moncrief to succeed in marketing, we needed its head to be someone who could succeed in marketing. If the retail side of Moncrief could start working profitably, we knew that we could make the manufacturing side work. If necessary, we were prepared to recruit personnel from Peerless's Indianapolis operation.

In assessing a candidate's marketing potential, we wanted firm benchmarks, not just a list of projects he or she had dabbled with. If a candidate said he had led something, we wanted to know from where to what. We knew what we wanted, and we turned our attention to where we might find such an individual.

Five major companies formed the backbone of the fledgling air-conditioning industry at that time: Carrier, Chrysler Air Temp, York, Frigidaire, and Trane. Of those, Air Temp and Frigidaire, who were subsidiaries of major companies, were by far the weakest. They seemed the logical place to look for a manager with marketing potential who wanted an opportunity to move upward at a different speed.

I found Bill Denton in Dayton, Ohio, working for Chrysler Air Temp as the sales manager of the packaged goods division ("packaged" referring to air conditioners, such as window units, that delivered cool air directly without the use of ducts). His credentials were good, his marketing education was from Rutgers University, he had solid marketing experience with a verifiable record of having led sales from a start to a strong finish, and I sensed he was teachable. The initial hiring decision was made, but there had to follow a time of test-flying the new person to make sure I had discovered what I thought I had found.

After that, I immediately involved Denton in the hiring process as we began creating a management structure he could effectually administer. It needed to be his team if he were going to do the job we needed him to do. As counterintuitive or illogical as it may appear, the management structure is a pyramid that must be built from the top down if it is to have a strong foundation. My most important job at Moncrief was assessing that structure and the location of its weaknesses. In Denton I had found the top of my pyramid, but he needed some help identifying and replacing the stress points in the structure beneath him. In other words, I had hired a man who could lead Moncrief but who was still inexperienced at strengthening the overall management structure by selecting and positioning the right people beneath him. With my support, Bill got it right.

A month after Bill and his family had moved and settled in Atlanta, Bill was comfortable in the office, and we began recruiting the next tier of managers. Bill functioned as my screener, exposing him to how we approached the hire, and it freed us.

The first two layers of recruiting are critical from top down or from bottom up. You have to build on what you have, and you have to have good people or you cannot carry on good business.

We followed a policy of one-over-one recruiting and promotion: Denton (with my oversight) hired Foster Law as vice president of manufacturing. Then Law (with Denton's and my oversight) hired manufacturing foremen, supervisors, and metal benders. That, after all, was Law's job. It was Denton's job to enable Law to do his job, and it was my job to make sure Denton could do his.

Anything concerned with the hierarchy of management had to be recommended by the manager who supervised the person and approved by the person above that manager. If Foster Law wanted to promote Johnny Foreman to senior group leader, he had to go to Denton and provide the paperwork. After Denton looked it over and gave his approval, the move would go forward. Salary and any other concerns would be included in that one document, which was Law's authorization to promote Johnny Foreman: a one-over-one paperwork system complementing the one-over-one recruiting and promotion process.

The process may seem self-evident, but I have been amazed at the number of businesses without a formalized written structure. We put the structure in place as part of Moncrief's *Policy and Procedure Manual* and eventually used our written protocol to formalize the same structure in almost a hundred other businesses. It was a basic management model that could strengthen the management structure of any business anywhere.

Forty-five days after I started at Moncrief, I made a surreptitious trip home, even though, according to the terms set with my father, I hadn't earned it. My dad knew that; my uncle knew that. They both turned their heads and pretended they didn't see. They knew I was working hard. Change was in the air in Atlanta.

TAKE AWAYS

o Making a profit is important.

o People are the most important key to profitability.

o Develop every associate as a salesperson.

o Develop a criteria for sales force personnel:
   this is the tool for assessing a candidate's
   chances of success before employment.

o "The most important decision a
   manager makes is the hiring decision" should be your working thesis;
   everything else is secondary.

o To find the right person, you must accurately diagnose the need. This is your
   first critical step in the hiring process.

o Identifying the cause of a problem is
   the first step in finding the cure.

o Where money is a problem, the cure is
   most often a management overhaul.

o If all your management is not put together
   in a "can do," "want to win" mind-
   set, money will always be a problem.

o Use firm benchmarks when
   assessing a candidate's marketing
   potential; if a candidate led something, learn from where to what.

o Know what you want in an associate
   and where to look for him/her.

o As counterintuitive as it seems, the
   management structure is a pyramid
   that must be built from the top down
   if it is to have a strong foundation.

o Assess this structure and identify and replace stress points.

- Practice one-over-one recruiting and promotion as a policy: hierarchal changes are recommended by the manager supervising the person and approved by the person above that manager.

- Practice a one-over-one paperwork system that complements the one-over-one recruiting and promotion process. Written protocols strengthen the management structure of a business.

Chapter 9

VACATION

During the tour of duty that followed, the thought of a vacation never crossed my mind. I began coming home for half a weekend, which was hardly fair to my family, but it was more than I had been allowed during those first few months at Moncrief.

I made an attempt at remedying this situation by planning a week's vacation with Jean, Bill, and Marcy the following summer. They were to come to Atlanta for a week and stay in my "luxurious," pea-sized apartment (about as big and accommodating as a very small bedroom). At the end of the week, we had scheduled a trip to Jekyll Island just off the coast of southern Georgia.

By car, the drive to Jekyll Island from Atlanta was almost five hours, one way. I had one weekend to enjoy my family, an airplane stored at Lockheed Martin in Marietta, with Jean as my copilot. The choices were obvious. Jean, Bill, and Marcy spent the first part of their week touring Atlanta from the eleventh floor of my apartment building. On Friday at noon, we loaded our luggage into my Cessna 175 at Marietta and began our journey to Jekyll Island.

A Love Affair with Flying

When I was about three or four years old, I was sitting in a sand pile in the backyard of our home in Edinburgh and, hearing the drone of an engine above me, looked up and saw my first plane.

"Marion!" I tugged at my sister's elbow next to me, pointing skyward. "Look! It's a Ford!"

Perhaps if a Ford had wings, it would have resembled the biplane, flying less than a thousand feet above us. I could not have been more mesmerized at the sight.

Not long after, my grandfather Sawin paid for my first flight. The man was selling rides from a pasture east of Edinburgh, about halfway to Asa's farm. For the rather large sum of two dollars (this was the Depression era), Marion and I had our first view of Edinburgh from the sky. This biplane was a three-seated tail dragger. The pilot steered from the single seat behind us while Marion and I sat in front of him and scanned in awe the little corner of Indiana we loved so much.

The bug was in my blood. If there was an opportunity to get in an airplane, I took it. In the 1930s, Midway in Chicago (known as Chicago's Municipal Airport) was the busiest airport in the world, with its four cinder runways intersecting to form one very small cross. The grass runways of Chicago Heights Airport were located southeast of Midway near Gary, Indiana. While Harold and Laura worked the Peerless booth at the Chicago World's Fair, I would bribe the college boys to entertain me with a trip to Midway, enticing them with the chance of driving my parents' car. There I would stand and watch in fascination as planes landed and took off. When I started flying my own planes to make business trips, I would have to land at Chicago Heights because air traffic control would not let me land anywhere else.

Eventually, I was allowed to fly in and out of O'Hare and Midway and used all three Chicago airports as circumstances dictated.

My family and associates thought I was crazy to fly a single engine airplane into O'Hare, which was second only to Atlanta in the rankings for busiest airport in the world.

But people in love do crazy things!

TOM'S AIR SHOW

Tom's war experiences as a pilot coupled with my fascination with airplanes could lead to only one thing. I pestered him until he agreed to take me up in an airplane one Sunday afternoon and show me some of the stuff he had done in the bigger, heavier, more powerful planes during the war. The only aircraft we could find to rent was a Cessna 180. Frank Mutz did not encourage Tom to fly after the war. Tom's young wife, Joyce, was pregnant with their first child, and it was important to Frank that he have an heir.

My father was not excited at the prospect of having a pilot for a son, but Tom was rather confident that Dad would have paid for flying lessons if we had asked him. I hadn't yet asked, but I was determined to have Tom take me for a ride.

At first Tom was just having a good time, flying chandelles and seeing how far he could get my stomach up my throat. Then suddenly everything changed. A loop started at the top in high power; once the plane turned upward from the bottom of the loop, around seven o'clock, its velocity carried us to the top again. The best way to come down again was to have very little power on. As we went down, Tom shoved the throttle forward to repower the plane and take us up and out of the loop. Only, when he throttled up, nothing happened.

We were directly above downtown Indianapolis and less than five hundred vertical feet above the tallest building in the area. We were breaking the law. I was also quite sure we were about to break our necks.

Tom scouted out a place to land. The Naval Ordinance Plant was then famous among armament manufacturers around the world as the site that produced a legendary weapon, the Norden Bombsight. It was a huge factory, but the only thing we could see was a strip of grass down the side of the site. We recognized where we were immediately, and Tom knew just where to land. He didn't have to land short but used up half the greenway with the plant directly on our left. By the time the little Cessna had quit rolling, we had a jeep offside each wing loaded with military police.

Fortunately, Tom had his pilot's release license with him, identifying him as a major in the Marine Air Corps. With a fair amount of fast talking with the military commandant, he negotiated our release. Then we reboarded our plane, turned around, and took off. The only damage we had caused was the doubling of our airport rental.

"If the engine turns on, I fly it," Tom shrugged, unmoved. "On Guadalcanal I didn't inspect my airplane either."

Neither Frank nor Harold Mutz was so calm about the incident. The idea of flying lessons for me was squelched permanently, and Tom and I were under a prohibition: the Mutz sons were not to fly together again. The scare had almost put me off flying, but when I saw an opportunity for low cost lessons several years later, I approached Tom to teach me again.

"Oz, you know we are not supposed to do that," Tom reprimanded me, acting like an older brother. "You promised and I promised, and I am not going to break that promise."

FIRST LESSONS

My pilot's license documented that I did eventually learn how to fly in 1959, but I had begun several years before that. Jean and I had been married long enough to have Bill and Marcy but not much longer than that. Consequently, my flying career had several false starts. Every time I began lessons, my wife would approach my boss (who was, to the detriment of my plans, also her father-in-law and the grandfather of her children) to pressure me to give up such a lunatic idea. And when your boss makes a request, it has all the power of an order. I stopped my lessons.

Then I discovered I could learn how to fly in half-hour segments. Sky Harbor was a small training airport conveniently placed a few miles from both my office at Peerless and my home. Two or three days a week, someone began scheduling my lunch meetings there.

By the time I had lunched at Sky Harbor sixteen times, with a total of eight hours air time, my flight instructor turned to me in the cockpit and said, "When you make this next landing, stop. I'm going to get out."

"Why?" I asked.

"You're going to solo," he announced.

I could feel myself turning pink. His confidence scared me, as I did not feel ready.

But he got out and I soloed.

I didn't know enough about flying to be scared when I taxied the plane and began my takeoff. Takeoff is the most dangerous leg of any journey, but after only eight hours of "lunch," I was still ignorant of that. When I turned the plane and began my descent for landing, however, I was afraid.

But the landing was uneventful, and the lessons continued. I would solo and my instructor would get in and out of the plane, letting me know what I'd done right and what I'd done wrong. After eight more hours (sixteen additional meals), I considered myself a pretty decent pilot and decided it was time to stop playing hide-and-seek over the lunch table.

So I told Jean and Harold what I had been doing. I showed them my log book where my instructor had signed me off for flying across country.

Harold was upset.

"Oz, you promised me!" he began.

"I promised you I'd quit taking the lessons on my way home from work, Dad," I interjected quickly, heading him off at the pass.

Jean had remained ominously quiet. She only had one question, and her eyes never left my face as she asked it.

"Do you plan on taking our children up in that thing with you?"

"Yes, ma'am, I do," I replied, returning her look steadily.

"Then, Oz, you are not going to be the only one who knows how to fly it. If you are taking the children, you are taking me too."

So Jean began lessons and before long, she had learned how to solo. If the day were sunny and the forecast clear, I could say, "Jean, take me to Springfield today," and she would get me there. At first, I would be the one to land us once we arrived at Springfield, but soon it didn't make any difference.

That's how Jean had become a weather and safety expert by the time we took our trip to Jekyll Island.

Trials and Errors

My first plane was a Beech Bonanza, the longest-produced single engine four-seater in aviation history. It had a V-tail configuration, which made it a little tricky to fly by the standards of its day. The Bonanza was not a forgiving airplane. I had to pay attention to it all the time. When Leland Gunn provided me with a Cessna, I immediately appreciated the advantages of the top wing. I could use my knees to steer it, even though I still had to watch what I was doing.

Leland's company in Little Rock, Arkansas, was a customer of Peerless—an important customer—and my enthusiasm over my newly acquired pilot's license apparently rubbed off on him. His office was five minutes from the Little Rock airport, where I would land when visiting him. He began flying two to three hours a day, and soon he had surpassed my skill level as a pilot.

It was just natural, when he won a sales contest among Peerless distributors for a week at the Americana Hotel on Miami Beach, to plan on flying my airplane to Miami. Adding the fun of flying to the fun of the vacation, Jean and I flew to Little Rock and picked up Leland and his wife, Nancy. Then we flew from Little Rock to Stuart, Florida, just north of West Palm Beach and next to Port Saint Lucie on the Atlantic coast.

Suddenly, the weather soured. Two non-instrument pilots were flying according to VFR (visual flight rules) and it was raining like cats and dogs. Rather than risk killing our wives and orphaning our four children, we landed in Stuart and spent the night. The next morning we resumed our journey to Miami.

Within minutes we'd flown no further than Lantana Airport (a mere forty miles away) when a shade was pulled across the sky. We could not see more than a quarter of a mile. I was navigating the concrete beam of Interstate 95 just visible outside my window. The rain from the previous day had intensified. Suddenly—whoosh!—another airplane crossed our nose, a house-width away from us!

That was too much for me. I made a one hundred eighty degree turn and headed back up the concrete beam. I had noticed a very large airport near Palm Beach, which seemed the perfect place to land our plane and wait out the storm.

I tuned my radio to tower frequency. They were calling me, telling me to abort my landing. I acted as if I couldn't hear them and landed.

By the time we were stopped on the runway, young men with guns were emerging from the shore patrols surrounding us. I had landed on a naval training base.

Leland and I talked them into allowing us to taxi to a building where the number of officers surrounding us increased. Eventually I found myself sitting across from the base commander in his office, listening to him lecture me and wondering how I was going to get my passengers to Miami. At length, the commander finished venting his spleen and told me my airplane would be chained to the station's water tower while he decided what to do with us.

"I want to thank you for being so hospitable," I replied drily, after he had crushed my query about overnight accommodations with a terse "We don't have any place to take care of women here." Leland and I escorted our wives off the base, located a hotel (with some difficulty), and spent a restless night awaiting the commander's decision.

The next morning he cleared our departure, and within the hour, we were in Miami, the edge of our week's enjoyment a bit flattened but not blunted.

THE AIRPLANE BUSINESS

About a year later, I wanted to buy a twin engine airplane from the people who sold me the Bonanza. They had a twin engine for sale and acted as if they didn't give fifty cents whether they sold it to me or not.

Of course, they knew I had the down payment.

"When I think about how hard we work to sell air conditioners to people who don't even know they want one," I remarked casually to Leland, nonplussed by their indifference, "airplanes must be easy to sell."

Consequently, he and I began looking around at airplane distributorships in the Miami area. Two months later, my telephone rang in the middle of a busy morning.

"Were you serious about getting into the airplane business?" Leland asked from the other end.

"Well, yes, Leland, I think I am." I was distracted and listening with only half an ear.

"I am sure glad to hear that, Oz, because I've just bought us an airplane distributorship!"

I almost fell off my chair. He certainly had my full attention now. "Whoa, there!" I countered, Moncrief flashing through my mind in all of its unfolding, gory mess. "If we are going to buy a business, I should at least look at it first, Leland!"

Leland was very bright and knew a lot about many things, but I was not sure aircraft distributorships was one of those. "Well, you'd better get down here soon because I am about to close," he announced, and hung up.

The next morning I was in Little Rock.

Private business owners often inflate the size of their income to impress potential buyers. With some consistency, a careful buyer will find they did not have the income they alleged they had historically. I insisted on looking at the seller's income tax returns.

"I don't have to show you these things," he balked. "Gunn's already bought the business."

If Leland Gunn had not been my partner, I would have never touched this business. Selling airplanes is tough. There is only one sure way to generate a million dollar net worth in the aircraft business: start with two million.

I was already serving time in Atlanta for having acquired Moncrief for Harold Mutz, and it wasn't long before I just wanted out of the airplane business. One small obstacle prevented me, a very small obstacle: the 1 percent of shares that Leland Gunn owned and I didn't.

It wasn't long before I knew that anyone who wanted me as a partner would have to be willing to sell me 51 percent of the ownership. After my stint in the airplane business, I knew that if I and my associates didn't own 51 percent of the shares, I didn't need a partnership.

Leland was my friend, but that didn't alter the fact that he wanted an aircraft distributorship, and I soon found out that I did not. While there are exceptions (like Fred Risk), they are few and far between. Where partnerships are concerned, it is better to have a big piece or no piece at all. If you can't control it, stay out.

Winging It

Starnes Aviation at Little Rock, Arkansas, was the Cessna wholesale distributor for Arkansas, Mississippi, and western Tennessee. We renamed it Sky Travel and added my Beech Bonanza as additional capital investment. Then Leland and I began trying to figure out how to market airplanes.

We discovered that the surest way to market airplanes was to teach somebody to fly. By providing flying lessons and convincing the prospective customer to sponsor flying lessons for his wife, we dramatically increased our opportunities to sell an airplane.

Learning to handle an airplane was like conquering a mountain for our female customers. Soon Leland and I had our operating plan written up in great detail.

Once our operating plan had been tested, tweaked, and fully documented, we contacted Dwane Wallace, the CEO of Cessna and founder Clyde Cessna's nephew. Wallace was a medical doctor who had given up his practice to oversee his uncle's company, which was otherwise run by white-silk-scarf-and-goggle pilots. I knew on first meeting him that he was one very smart man.

We showed him our facility in Little Rock, the new radio shop we had added, and our merchandising plan. Wallace seemed impressed. He invited us to present our marketing model to the next tier of management at Cessna headquarters in Wichita. To ensure Wallace was still in the sales stream with us, we reviewed the plan with him a second time the night before our scheduled presentation to his company executives.

Both Leland and I had been in businesses where survival depended on creativity and aggressive marketing. We hired an attractive, instructor-certified saleswoman who made the cold calls for us in Little Rock because most of the time she could at least get her foot in the door. While Leland or I would have to make two or three appearances before someone would notice we were real, she was noticed on the first call.

"Mr. Smith," a secretary would buzz the boss, "there is someone from an airplane business here to see you."

"I don't have time to talk to someone about an airplane," he would bark back.

"Mr. Smith, she's a very attractive young woman..."

Not only would Mr. Smith's curiosity open the door, he was almost sure to schedule a trip to the airport for a demonstration ride. Two, maybe three times out of ten, our salesperson would persuade the man in the office to get in a plane. Once she had him in the plane, the rest was quite predictable.

After a fifteen to twenty minute demonstration on the stability and reliability of the Cessna product, the lady instructor in the left seat would purr, "Why don't you take over?"

The male ego immediately joins our sales force. "Anything that woman can do," thinks Mr. Smith, "I can do better," and in five minutes, he's flying our Cessna.

But getting Mr. Smith introduced to the thrill of flying was not our salesperson's goal. Her mission—our objective—was to sign up Mrs. Smith as our student. If Mr. Smith's wife would join him and fly the airplane and become our student, we could begin writing out the sales order.

This kind of marketing is a slow, steady, difficult job that requires a substantial investment of money to finance it. Dwane Wallace thought it was a good idea, but selling airplanes is hard work in the most optimal environments.

His lieutenants disagreed. I could see the lay of the land on their faces. The vice president of marketing, an aging pilot with a crop duster history, plainly resented Wallace's bringing us in. Possibly the reason was because the plan was NIH (not invented here).

We asked for 50 percent of the cost of running our sales program for the first year as discount on additional sales. We had already solved any Federal Trade Commission problems. Both Leland and I were quite sure Wallace didn't have any other two people as well informed as we were on the limits and possibilities of marketing an airplane.

We were put into a room after our presentation while they discussed it. Half an hour later, Dwane Wallace walked through the door with his head down.

"A program like this is too expensive to run nationwide," he began apologetically. "My men are all agreed, so I guess we'll have to pass."

"You don't have to run it nationwide, Mr. Wallace," I replied, reminding him politely of the Federal Trade Commission regulations.

His head remained bowed.

My frustration made me curt. "Well, you just saved me a lot of time!"

"Why's that?" For the first time Wallace looked up.

"Because night after night, I've spent precious time putting this program together with Mr. Gunn, and your people didn't give it a fair chance. But more than that—more than just refusing to give us a test just to help sustain our business—you haven't given us any alternative. You don't have anything to suggest to help us sell airplanes. We don't have any other sales program."

Wallace clearly did not like my tone, and I probably should have restrained myself, but Leland and I had worked too hard figuring out a way to sell Wallace's airplanes.

"If you had come back to us and said, 'We won't do this, but we'll help you guys do that,' I'd have been OK with this," I continued, truly angry. "But if you are that flat on your back with marketing your airplanes, then I am through and this free executive is no longer available!"

Cessna's corporate response to our firing line experience typifies big company reasoning. A savvy corporate headquarters response invites practical input from the frontlines and tests it before making decisions.

From that moment on, I knew, even if I did not communicate it to Leland, that the airplane business and I were soon parting company.

FLYING HIGH

In return for the investment of my Beechcraft Bonanza into the company, Sky Travel provided a Cessna 175 for my use.

Its first (and almost my last) voyage started one late Sunday afternoon from Indianapolis. I was flying at eleven or twelve thousand feet and had just said good-bye to Chattanooga, Tennessee, below me when the plane sputtered and died. No matter how much I fiddled with the starting system, I could not get the engine back in operation. Oz Mutz was "dead stick" in the sky, twenty to thirty minutes shy of his landing field in Marietta, Georgia.

Hills rolled out below me. There was no place to land and my only choice was to head back to the Chattanooga airport and hope I could glide in for a good, power-free landing. Over the airwaves, commercial pilots, fearful of a collision, were asking where I was. I focused single-mindedly on one thing: I needed to make an absolutely perfect landing. And I did— rolling to a halt right in the middle of the intersection of all four runways, tying up the entire airport.

A mechanic arrived at the runway intersection and hit my starter button one last time. To my embarrassment and confusion, the engine turned over and the plane started to run. I couldn't figure out what had happened. One fuel gauge read empty, but the other showed full.

My airplane had siphoned itself dry. The fuel bladder in one wing had collapsed, spewing fuel out of the bleeder port and across the top of the wing.

Once I had taxied to a ramp, I telephoned to Little Rock and told them we had a problem.

"Oh, yeah, we forgot to tell you that when we brought you the plane in Indianapolis, Mr. Mutz," the man on the line drawled. "We were having some trouble with that one before."

"Don't ever bring me another one that isn't fixed!" I snapped.

Apparently, no one at Sky Travel was listening. The pilots who brought me my replacement craft paid no attention to the information I gave them. They were on the final stage of their journey back to Little Rock, just over the Memphis Downtown Airport on Mud Island, when the engine quit running again. Mud Island had only one runway, and the pilots' attempt to stretch the landing glide across the Mississippi and reach the runway failed. A little boat from the shore fished the pilots out of the water, and as they stood safely watching on its deck, our Cessna 175 slowly sank into the river. For once Sky Travel made a quick sale; the insurance company bought that plane.

I told Leland that it was time for me to get out, but he didn't agree. I was scheduled for my semiannual flight physical, and my doctor was in Indianapolis, so I booked an appointment with an airline physician in Atlanta who had administered flight physicals to pilots from Delta and Eastern airlines. We finished the physical and he began to comment on this and that condition to me, but I shut him down quickly.

"I don't need to come back to see you," I calmly explained. "I only need to come back if I have a problem."

A week later his nurse called me. Patiently I explained the ground rules again: "You don't understand; he doesn't need to call me."

"Mr. Mutz," replied the nurse, equally patient and unmoved, "You don't understand. He needs to see you."

The doctor lost no time in getting down to business. "Mr. Mutz, you have Bright's disease," he announced soberly.

In those days, nephritis was a fatal kidney disease involving at least one kidney and maybe two. I would need dialysis, but the only state where dialysis was available was Washington. It had cornered the rights to all dialysis equipment as part of a business deal.

"I am going to have to give you more tests," the doctor went on.

"Can we do them at night?" I asked.

He looked at me quizzically. "That's a rather unusual request, Mr. Mutz," he said. "Why nights?"

I cleared my throat. "I just don't want to get my family all excited about something that is probably not going to amount to anything anyway," I explained. The stress of living apart was enough.

Happily, the urologist who first diagnosed my condition was incorrect. I completed additional tests at night and was assured that I did not have Bright's disease. One thing, however, had become clear: the last thing I wanted to do was leave my wife with an aircraft business. Should I get caught at eleven thousand feet in a sick Cessna again and not make it back to the ground safely, I was not going to leave Jean with that albatross around her neck. I had to get out.

Leland understood. He found a lawyer in Little Rock interested in the aircraft business and opened negotiations with him. John Haley was one of three lawyers working on corporate transactions for the Rose Law Firm.

I sold my share of Sky Travel to Leland, and Leland sold it to John. Although I would never market another plane, my flying days were far from over.

A WEEKEND OUTING WITH THE FAMILY

On that fateful day on my way to Jekyll Island with my wife and children, I was still in the early throes of sorting out Moncrief and just beginning to figure out how to market airplanes for Sky Travel. We were in a Cessna 175, courtesy of Sky Travel, and headed for our first family vacation in over a year.

I had Jekyll Island in sight to the left and a thunderstorm in sight to the right. My copilot was glued to the swiftly closing distance between the two.

"Ozzie," she finally burst out in disbelief, "you're not planning to land *there*?"

"Yes," I replied with equanimity, "I am."

"You can't land there!" Jean insisted, her voice rising. "There's a thunderstorm moving in on that airport!"

"I think I'll beat the thunderstorm, Jean," I replied calmly. We didn't have transponders in cockpits then, or I would have known immediately how far from safety I was.

The two children in the seats behind us had grown quiet and still. I kept the nose of the plane pointed toward the airport on Jekyll Island, but the closer we came, the louder Jean's objections. Bill had the aviation bug as well and was quite sure if his dad said it was OK to land, it was OK. His mother was the amateur.

Marcy was equally convinced her mother's superior track record should be honored.

The battle lines were drawn. The tension mounted. Eventually I had no choice but to do a 180 degree turn and head back to Atlanta, several hundred miles behind us. We flew back to the Lockheed Martin airstrip at Marietta, parked the Cessna, climbed into the car, and drove to Jekyll Island.

We arrived around eleven o'clock that night, having foregone dinner for the sake of expediency. I had secured reservations. In fact, I had prepaid with my credit card by telephone for two rooms. The young clerk at the desk squared off bravely if quite apologetically: there were no rooms available.

After I expressed my disappointment to him without success, I asked him for the nearest alternative.

"It's back in Brunswick," he answered, obviously relieved that he could offer positive input. "I'd be glad to call for you, if you want to go there."

He called. They had one room. Defeated, I retraced our journey back across the causeway to mainland Georgia, where we stumbled into two crowded beds and went to sleep.

A terrible odor in the room awakened us the next morning. None of us had noticed it the night before, but the stench from a nearby chemical plant was overwhelming. The wind had changed overnight and blew the odor toward us. Hastily we repacked the car and drove back to our motel on Jekyll Island. I checked in and they apologized. We decided the best way to get over the disappointments of the previous day was to rent two tandem bicycles and explore the island.

Jean steered one bicycle and I the other, each with a child on the back.

The decision seemed a wise one for two reasons. Both Jean and I wanted to get the kids down to a more earthy adventure, and I didn't want tar from the freshly tarred island streets on my new Cadillac automobile.

But fresh tar on tandem bicycles is not such a good idea either.

I kept us out for the absolute minimal amount of time it would take for Bill and Marcy to feel like they had enjoyed a long bike ride. When we arrived back at the motel, we found its lobby flooded.

The elevators were not working, because of the flood, so we waded through six or seven inches of water to get to the stairs and access our rooms.

"You're not to worry, Mr. Mutz," the front desk clerk reassured me. "We'll have it pumped out in a couple of hours!"

Jean and I looked at each other. I groaned.

Food had been relatively sparse so far, so Jean and I decided the best strategy was to get a decent meal and stall until the water had disappeared, along with whatever else might be in it.

The front desk clerk referred us to Morrison's Cafeteria. We started the children, spattered with tar from the bike ride on the streets, down the serving line, ready to give our two troopers anything they wanted. Had Bill asked me for chateaubriand, I'd have given it to him and urged him to take more. As it was, we all decided on fried chicken.

We settled down at a table and cleared the trays, and I, perhaps understandably a bit hungrier than the rest, bit into my chicken.

It was delightfully rare. In fact, it was not cooked.

My one free weekend. My only vacation with my family. I'd had it.

Once again we trooped back to the motel. The water had not drained, but the helpful clerk at the front desk suggested another place to eat. I herded everyone into the car and we drove to that restaurant, splattering big drops of tar all over the sides of our beautiful new car. By that time, I didn't care, as my sole objective was to complete that vacation as quickly as possible.

Early the next morning, we left Jekyll Island for Atlanta. By noon the next day, Jean, Bill, and Marcy were on their way home to Indianapolis. I was left behind in Atlanta, trying to figure out how to make money with Moncrief.

I needed to figure out how to sell airplanes, too.

Rest at Last

It would still take me a year to finish the job at Moncrief. Replacing Lawrence Kent Jr. was my first and most important step in fixing Moncrief's problems.

On the alternate weekends when I wasn't back in Indianapolis, I attended the North Avenue Presbyterian Church in Atlanta. Some might not consider church the source of important business information, but when it comes to making key personnel decisions, church contacts can be very helpful.

I was chatting with Dr. Vernon Broyles, the senior pastor of North Avenue Presbyterian Church, about a few things on my mind. Foremost was the fact that the former president of Moncrief was an alcoholic, even while serving on the church's official board. I gently upbraided Dr. Broyles for allowing him to serve, knowing the nature of his addiction.

"Sir," the pastor retorted, peering over his glasses, "I'd rather have had Lawrence Kent Sr.'s opinion on a business decision when he was inebriated than most people's opinion stone sober."

To identify the management problem with Lawrence Kent Jr. as an alcohol problem is to miss the point. His father had functioned effectively before him, although the father and son shared the same addiction. The critical point is that management *was* the problem.

Most profit problems stem from people problems. A company's people are its most important key to profitability. You can look under the chairs and under the stairs and a lot of other places for the magic potion that makes earning money easy, but if you don't accurately identify, address, and monitor the problems with your people, you are wasting your time and your money.

At the end of thirteen months, I had replaced every senior manager at Moncrief with someone more capable. I was going home on a confident basis, knowing things would work without me.

From that juncture on, I was based back in Indianapolis. Every four or five weeks I would do a liaison trip and check on Moncrief's people to ensure there were no problems developing that they were not handling, and certainly at the end of every quarter I would be in Atlanta. But the long ordeal was finally over. Moncrief was making money and I was home.

I could sing again.

Chapter 10

ELECTRONIC SPECIALTY COMPANY

PEERLESS NEEDED TO raise the long term capital to pay off short term funds used in buying Moncrief, and I knew where to go in quest of it. Fred Risk and I had met the first day of our first class at Indiana University. During college, while I spent breaks working for Hoosier Tarpaulin and Peerless, Fred worked for Harris Trust Company and W. T. Grimm and Company, a merger and acquisitions facilitator/broker that specialized in private debt placements. We both opted to finish our last year of undergraduate work by taking our first year of law school. I knew by the second semester of law school that I wasn't finishing. I was tired of going to the bathroom with a book in my hand. Fred Risk, however, graduated from IU's law school in 1951 and started to work.

In that capacity, he suddenly showed up in my office at Peerless, using old school ties to hustle some business. In addition to being an old friend and someone whose abilities I admired, Fred had the knack for gaining the respect of older people quickly because he was not intimidated by them. Neither was I; this was one of many traits we shared.

I had gone to Fred before for a private debt placement for Peerless, and in the process, he had negotiated with our lead banker at Indiana National, Pat Flynn. A few days later, Pat called us.

"Who was that young man you sent down to talk to me?"

I inquired politely as to his motives for needing this information.

"We have a position to fill," the banker replied, "and I'd like to talk to him some more because we are looking for a man like him."

"I believe, sir," I cautioned him respectfully, "you won't have much success in hiring Fred Risk. He's spoken for."

He did, however, manage to hire Fred, who was young, newly married, and probably wanting to live a little closer to home. Fred began his tenure at Indiana National, the oldest and largest bank in the state at that time. He became the star trainee of their recently created executive management program, just as I began working with the University of Chicago and Indianapolis University on researching hiring criteria for salespeople.

Fred became our financial advisor as well as our banker. After we had bought Moncrief, I took Peerless's capital need to him.

And when Electronic Specialty Company came knocking on our door, Tom and I went straight to Fred.

We had a plan.

THE BEGINNING OF THE END

Having just restaffed and unraveled Moncrief and made it productive, Peerless was starting to go where Tom and I wanted it to go. We had no thought of selling anything, but Harold and Frank were no longer quite so trusting about the future.

Many companies start out as family enterprises, but few families have brought to a corporate management structure the blend of shared respect, hard work, and genuine feeling that characterized the Mutzes. When my mother died in 1963, the stability of the whole structure no longer seemed so certain.

Our family circle had experienced loss before then. Tragedy had repeatedly struck my sister Marion. Her first husband, whom she had met as an undergraduate education major at IU, went on to graduate from Indiana's School of Law and begin practicing as an attorney in Wabash, Indiana. Three years after their marriage, he was killed in an automobile accident.

Marion would lose two more husbands. The second succumbed to a heart attack after thirty-four years of marriage. The third she found dead after only a year of marriage. They had sung in the church choir together. She came home from school one afternoon and he was gone.

Grandma Mutz was living in an apartment halfway between our house on Oak Avenue and Uncle Frank's house. The family lived close in Indianapolis. They shared her loss.

In 1956, Laura Mutz was ready to live in the country again. Frank Mutz bought out his younger brother's interest in the farm they had purchased jointly (Bex Rex's home), and Mom and Dad bought the farm next to it. Its house was the original building constructed by the land grant owner, a Scotsman named MacGregor, who had owned all the land in the area at one time. As usual, we had to load up all of our families and go inspect the new purchase.

Marion's second husband, Bill, was living then. I noticed him eyeing askance the lightbulb on the end of an electrical cord dangling from the ceiling. My brother-in-law was a city slicker. I couldn't help but bait him.

"Well, Bill," I asked, "what do you think?"

"Oz," Bill returned, "anything they do to this place will be an improvement!"

Mother loved that house. Immediately she began restoring it to its original grandeur.

Her death six short years later diminished us all. We had been preparing for that event all of our lives (she had never been healthy) but we never really expected it.

Our family was still processing the loss of my mother when Electronic Specialty Company proposed a merger with Peerless. Whether knowingly or not, they had chosen a strategic moment to approach Frank and Harold. Tom and I were caught completely off guard.

When Electronic Specialty came knocking on the Peerless door, they introduced themselves as a merger candidate, but their intent from the first was to acquire us. Tom and I had no experience in selling a company, but we knew someone who did.

However, asking Fred Risk to broker the sale was Plan B. We first approached him with the offer of a presidency.

"Fred," I began, with Tom at my side, "Tom and I are just a couple of peddlers trying to get a bit bigger. We know what opportunity looks like in the HVAC industry. If you'd take the presidency of Peerless and let us work as your vice presidents, we can build a company with real meat on it."

This proposal was our only alternative to being acquired.

Fred's response was noncommittal. "Let me have forty-eight hours to think about it," he responded.

Thinking (correctly, as it turned out) that he would go directly to his boss, the chair of Indiana National's board, we began discussing money. He was making twenty-eight or twenty-nine thousand dollars a year, so we began talking about forty-five thousand dollars for each of the three of us. In those days, that was the price of a bank chair.

"I'm sorry," he began, and we knew what was coming, "I can't make a change now. They've just raised my salary."

Frank and Harold left the final decision to their sons. In the end the decision to sell Peerless to Electronic Specialty was made by Tom and me. That should not have been the way it worked. Who in a company makes the decision to sell? Uncle Frank was the chair of the board of directors, and my father was the company president, but neither of them seemed fully present at that moment.

Harold Mutz had just lost his wife of over thirty-five years. Both men now knew what death taxes looked like. That aspect of the future looked grim.

Tom and I had to decide what we wanted to do with the rest of our lives, and we had to make that decision quickly.

As part of a larger company, Tom and I could still have a good time with our work and make a lot of money. We had never worked for a large company before. The time and the offer seemed opportune, as our fathers were willing to swing whichever way we wanted them to swing. They had realized for some time that Tom and I were the reason for their accelerated growth at Peerless, and they were transitioning toward retirement.

So, in the fall of 1963, Peerless became the newest subsidiary of Electronic Specialty Company.

When the deed was completed—when it was all over and done with— it didn't feel good to me. The sale of Peerless to Electronic Specialty was a watershed moment in the lives of the Mutz cousins. If I could do it over, would I sell? No; I'd reverse that bit of my history. It might have saved me some considerable grief later. Perhaps I'm still suffering from seller's remorse. We were having a successful time by then, Tom and I, making a lot of money. In hindsight, we could have done just as well by ourselves. We didn't really need to become part of a larger company.

Instead, we joined Electronic Specialty Company.

Virginia

In the end, it was a stock-for-stock merger. ESC owned six HVAC manu-facturing businesses, and we made the seventh. Tom and I had traversed the other six entities as a condition of the consolidation, but we had to agree on the location of the new plant. This stipulation meant that we were not going to move Peerless to one of the existing bases.

That tour of inspection revealed two things to Tom and me. First, every-thing new that Electronic Specialty Company was building was good—and that included several factories. Second, almost every business they bought was substandard. They needed management badly. The only way to get rid of the hot baton was by passing it to someone else. ESC wasn't just acquiring Peerless; they were after managers.

The challenge we faced in accepting their offer was to help them upgrade their management to match their developing production facilities.

The Key to Profitability Revisited

Electronic Specialty Company was doing and saying the normal things a buyer does in the context of a merger.

"You guys will be running the show," they promised. "We have a big plant being constructed in Virginia, and Oz can work on that manufac-turing business. Tom can buy a bunch of retail businesses."

We believed them, and we should have believed them because that was exactly what they did, as it was in their best interests to do so.

When they told me, "Oz can work on that manufacturing business," I didn't quite grasp their full intent. They would need someone to move one hundred thirty-eight families and eight hundred truckloads of equipment seven hundred miles from eight different locations to the Shenandoah Valley of Virginia.

That someone would have to be responsible for building a 660,000 square foot building, equal to twelve football fields in size, and staff it with nearly a thousand agriculturally oriented people who must first be put through a rigorous manufacturing training program. This person would have to transform an entire semi-agricultural community into a manufacturing base.

In fact, Electronic Specialty Company had no one they could move to Virginia who had the experience necessary to ensure the success of this kind of operation. They didn't even have anyone with experience to sweep floors in their management structure. I had experience doing both. They had already targeted me for this job.

Electronic Specialty had a Policies and Procedures manual—even though it wasn't a very good one—and I reviewed the qualifications for officers very carefully. ESC's chair, William Burgess, who was also the chair of Young Presidents Organization (YPO) International, could appreciate those qualifications too.

"Mr. Mutz, I can't promise you that if you complete this merger you will end up in a specific chair," he began, dangling the prospect of future greatness in front of my nose, "but I think you know where you are going."

"I take it, sir," I replied evenly, keeping my eyes fixed on his, "you don't want a specific management contract with us?"

"I'd be inducing you with an unequal inducement, Mr. Mutz."

"You don't want to give us management contracts." I paused, considering those future prospects he was dangling quite pragmatically. "That's OK. We don't want one. If you don't like us, we'll be gone. If we don't like you, we'll be gone."

By that time, Tom had arrived at the same conclusion. Immediately following the merger in 1963, my office moved to Cleveland, Ohio, the corporate headquarters of Iron Fireman, where I was initially positioned as their director of marketing. Electronic Specialty Company owned Iron Fireman, Petro, and Warren Webster, Inc., in Trenton, New Jersey. Our merger resulted in a new entity, Space Conditioning Systems, which incorporated Iron Fireman with Peerless, Round Oak, and Moncrief. Tom and his wife moved to St. Louis where ESC had purchased a sales, installation, and service outlet.

Iron Fireman was the largest coal stoker company in the world at that time. Its president, Lewis Cox, had been the male secretary of the chairman of the Iron Fireman board, a bit prissy but an OK performer. He was still in Cleveland, but he needed to get Iron Fireman moved (shut down and the money-bleeding stopped) to Harrisonburg, Virginia.

Ray Harmon, the president of Electronic Specialty, knew Cox would not have accomplished that job in a lifetime. That made it a little easier for me.

By 1964, I had been promoted to vice president and general manager of Space Conditioning Systems, Inc. My working relationships had begun shifting when I supervised the Round Oak move and had grown increasingly apparent as a result of Moncrief. This shift was now formalized when, as VP/GM of Space Conditioning, I was placed at the helm of the Peerless Division as well.

I was back on the road again. This time, however, there was a definite end in sight, even though it would take almost eighteen months to get there.

TAKE AWAYS

- If you don't have ownership of 51 percent of the shares, you shouldn't be in the partnership.
- Give a program a fair chance rather than refuse to test it. If declining a program, offer alternatives.
- A savvy corporate headquarters response invites practical input from the frontlines and tests it before making decisions.
- A company's people are its most important key to profitability.
- Accurately identify, address, and monitor problems with your people.
- Many companies start out as family enterprises, but few families bring to a corporate management structure the blend of shared respect, hard work, and genuine concern for each other that creates a successful future.

Chapter 11

LINE UPON LINE

WE DEVELOP EXPERTISE by building a little bit of experience on a little bit of experience on a little bit of experience. Whatever the risks or rewards, that is the hill we have to climb to be good at anything.

I knew I was going to have to build a manufacturing business from the ground up, so I began visiting every place that had any kind of HVAC business. I had experience moving a company with Round Oak, and I had experienced turning a leaky company around and making it profitable with Moncrief. But I knew those experiences together were only my jumping off place at Harrisonburg.

And this was no skipping-rope kind of jump. I had to take Space Conditioning from a concept to a set of plans to construction. Then I had to open this new facility with people who had no previous training but were competent enough by then to make the plant fully operational in a short period of time.

I began where my past experiences had taken me. In the beginning of my career, I hadn't known a sound way to pick people, but the process had taught me that the most important decision I ever made as a manager was the hiring decision. Let me reemphasize this: the hiring decision of any high-level subordinate is the *most* important business decision. If I were right in my choice of hire and had set the new hire up correctly, my business would succeed for a long time. If I hired the wrong person, I had set it up for short-term failure.

By the time I was with Space Conditioning, I knew that most businessmen take far too little time in making their selections of managers.

For example, Frank and Harold Mutz never hired anyone with an alcohol problem. If such a problem surfaced in secondary investigations of a candidate, it was all over. They had a zero tolerance policy for alcohol. My father and uncle had set that up as a guidepost, and I didn't deviate from it.

To this I had added the screening process developed in conjunction with the University of Chicago, and at Moncrief I had started applying that type of screening to other elements of a business. As a result of this, I already knew who I wanted as my chief manufacturing officer in Virginia.

Bob Houck had been two years ahead of me in high school. He was an exceptional basketball player in a basketball state, attending Purdue on an athletic scholarship. We knew in high school he was going to Purdue eventually, but given the state of world affairs in the midforties, Houck went directly into military service. His basketball was good enough to qualify him for an all-service basketball team.

I knew Bob was the kind of person you could throw into a problem who would not require supervision. He was a starter-upper by nature.

I sought him out for Peerless after returning to Indianapolis from Atlanta. I knew he had gone from Purdue to a manufacturing supervisory role with Bryant Heating and Air Conditioning. I knew him to be tough, and the kind of person who could take the long walk to success. He was on the payroll at Peerless when we sold to Electronic Specialty Company, and he was exactly the man I wanted to support the layout and design of our manufacturing facility in Virginia.

This assignment was a huge job that required someone huge to fulfill it. I could not risk finding out after six months that I'd hired the wrong person for the job. Starting up Space Conditioning was not the time to mess around trying to teach rookies. I needed as many known producers in my chain of command and activity as I could recruit. Before moving to Peerless in 1961, Houck had accrued five or six years of experience at Bryant. When I went to Virginia, I made sure Bob was transferred there from Indianapolis. He was one of a handful of key people that I took by transferring them from other management teams.

Ray Harmon, the president of Electronic Specialty Company, was intensely interested in our segment of his total business and was ready to put more money in Space Conditioning than in the rest of the corporation put together. Lewis Cox had shifted from the presidency of Iron Fireman to the presidency of Space Conditioning. Technically, I reported to Cox, but most things were openly copied to Harmon because I really answered to him.

Harmon practiced a style of leadership that relies on what I call "management intrigue." I didn't really like this management style too well, especially when doing a consolidation job where you must keep looking at the pieces to see if you can put the puzzle together. You need all the pieces on the board, facing up, so you can find the one you need next quickly. When you need to find a team to play this afternoon, recruiting needs skill and care, but not mystique.

I had my Policies and Procedures manual from Moncrief. I had the selection criteria and job specifications for a salesperson, but not for a director of engineering. Richard Wright was the man I was evaluating for vice president of product development. I could at least get inside the box by checking him against the job criteria we had identified for sales. Some of those would be the same criteria for director of engineering, so I could at least find out if Wright had those.

But where was I going to find someone with the experience of moving a factory from seven locations with eight hundred truckloads of machinery, equipment, and inventory? Where was I going to find the person to design and build a 660,000 square foot factory to centralize all of that?

Ironically, it was Harmon with his "management intrigue" style of leadership who found the most strategic member of my team. Harmon introduced me to a chain of people who knew Critical Path Method technology. PERT (Program Evaluation and Review Technique) had already been developed by the US Navy to design, manufacture, and mobilize the atomic submarine and was being used in the sixties to put a man on the moon. CPM (Critical Path Methodology) was a related technology, begun as an experimental project modeling technique by DuPont in conjunction with the Manhattan Project. Harmon had discovered enough about PERT and CPM through his connections in Los Angeles, where Electronic Specialty was headquartered, to discuss them and was confident one or the other would speed our progress. He also knew anything that could facilitate us would be money in the bank.

Consequently, Harmon located a man trained in CPM working on a specialty project for Litton Industries in California. He was a member of a group of people trained in CPM who were only one step behind Ford's "whiz kids."

Actually, Harmon had found the man through William Burgess. I reported to Harmon, and Harmon reported to Burgess. As international president of YPO, Burgess had valuable connections. He located two or three second-level operators doing CPM at Litton through his friends there. Harmon passed a name on to me, and I recruited him.

Or tried to.

I felt like I was trying to coax a prima donna from the Russian Bolshoi. First there was the Jaguar to negotiate. He owned a Jaguar convertible. Nothing would do but to agree to ship that convertible from California to Virginia on a moving van. A car transport just wouldn't do. He wanted that car inside a moving van because the car had to be safe. He negotiated for that moving van.

Somewhere in Oklahoma the moving van caught fire and the car burned up. If he'd only let me put it on a regular car transport! I had him in the palm of my hand. We quickly purchased a new Jaguar for him, but because we had produced in that regard, he worked thirty-two hours a day for me!

He was, in the final analysis, worth everything we put into him. My office was so large that we eventually turned it into the executive dining hall. The diagrams that charted our critical path from design to construction to full operation began and ended in the same corner of that office, stretching around all four walls to get there. We consulted that chart daily. I knew that when I arrived at a certain point in the room, we were going to hit a brick wall if I didn't have my paint spray booth in place. The paint spray booth might not be in place because the Ransburg Company owned the patents on it. I knew such contingencies months in advance, and I knew I had to have many critical components, like the paint spray booth, long before their suppliers solicited our business. At every step of the way, I had to make people believe we were going to accomplish something that hadn't yet been accomplished.

Our management team was the critical element in the corporation's success or failure. Ralph Freeman had been in charge of heavy equipment manufacturing for Iron Fireman in Cleveland for twenty years. I placed him in that position in Virginia. We were developing a miniaturized, modularized HVAC system that went into a package about the size of a four-drawer filing cabinet. Corning Glass Company was building the heating elements for us, and Columbia Gas Systems, Incorporated, was building the burner systems to go into it. Charles Reichelderfer supervised this full-time project. While we were moving and building a factory, Freeman was overseeing this same kind of development activity in Virginia. As vice president of product engineering, he was the head of that function.

Herschel Snodgrass was manager of transportation, just one step lower than a vice president. He oversaw more than just shipping and receiving. Snodgrass was responsible for bringing in the early product components from Japan. Other HVAC companies hadn't entered that trade yet. Electronic Specialty was working on the Japanese imports as part of its total corporate development.

Bill Wepfer was probably the most important man working for me because of his unique experience in sales. I knew when I started this recruitment process we would have to find our vice president of sales in Arkansas. Bill was the vice president of sales for the Arkansas Louisiana Gas Company (ARKLA), the only manufacturer of gas-powered air-conditioning equipment. I knew I had to tap into ARKLA's marketing experience to make

Space Conditioning competitive, and I wanted the most important marketing person in the industry.

It was a recruiting move that needed the utmost delicacy and skill. I began by calling Bill directly.

"Hi, Mr. Wepfer, I'm Oz Mutz from Space Conditioning," I introduced myself. "As you probably already know, we are developing a product to compete with a product that you sell. I'd like to have a good relationship with you and with your company, and I'd like to hire someone from your company to maintain that relationship. Actually, Mr. Wepfer, I have no choice but to hire someone from your company because we need their experience. I was wondering if you might know of someone who might be interested in an opportunity with our company. They would eventually be replacing me."

Had Wepfer not taken the bait, I would have dropped down a level and contacted the next guy.

But he did.

"Well, I'll be glad to talk with you, Mr. Mutz," he replied with a pronounced Southern drawl. "I could meet you in Memphis or Little Rock. Memphis would be fine for me. My mother's there."

So we met in Memphis. After preliminary introductions, Wepfer asked the question I was hoping he'd ask.

"Mr. Mutz," he began, looking at me steadily. "Would you be interested in hiring someone with as much experience as I have?"

Bill Wepfer definitely understood sales.

HARRISONBURG

When Tom was opening retail stores, he'd go into a town like Northbrook, Illinois, and hang out until he found a good retailer. After the third or fourth town, he'd shake them all until he'd sifted out everything but the three or four best, and then, together, we'd go check those out. He'd negotiate the deal we'd agreed on, and we'd go from there to finishing the purchase.

In Milwaukee, we had no business, but Iron Fireman did. It was a building-block program that we could develop. The two of us had come far enough down the road to know what had to be done to build a business. We had certainly built Space Conditioning, literally, from the ground up.

It had taken us almost to the middle of 1965 to get a paper system in place so we could generate eight or nine copies of an order at one time. At that juncture we could write an order and ship it quickly! The sheer size of the consolidation we had achieved had taken its toll on me. I was in my office at six-thirty in the morning and there until nine-thirty at night, seven days a week with time out for church. We had put seven companies under one roof. Just negotiating the different philosophies behind each of those companies had added immeasurably to the complexity of the task.

In addition, management systems were not in place for the larger computers coming into use at that time. We needed an area spacious enough to house an elevated 370/156 mainframe computer with its cooling system. Up until then, I had dealt only with manual accounting systems. We were living in the dark ages of information technology.

As if that were not enough, we needed to acquire, service, and maintain a fleet of trucks to alleviate our dependency on cross-country haulers. In the HVAC business, transportation is always an issue because you have to build your product in one place and install it elsewhere.

Meanwhile, Tom and I were always hunting other manufacturing businesses to buy, although there was a difference in what we were buying for Tom and for me. Lewis Cox, who was now reporting to William Burgess, would look for purchases and go to Burgess in California.

However, Tom and I negotiated the purchase of International Heater in Utica, New York (one of our weekend assignments). We had it completed, save for closing, and then something happened that blew it apart—the fish got away. In the mergers and acquisitions business, for every deal you complete, you probably negotiate two or three; there is rarely a one-for-one ratio. For every proposal we completed four or five were not. International Heater is one we didn't get completed because we didn't get the money transferred.

I loved that facet of my work at Space Conditioning, but I was just so tired all the time, I could hardly move.

Although I had my family with me, I might as well have been in Atlanta with Moncrief. On Thanksgiving Day, 1964, I arrived home in time to carve the turkey, eat my share, and then go back to work.

Nevertheless, I was learning what I was going to be doing for the rest of my life, even though I didn't know it then. I was enjoying what I was doing; I just needed to get some sleep now and then!

COURT MANOR

Six months from the time my office moved to Cleveland, Ohio, Jean and I were ready to move to Harrisonburg, Virginia, taking two truckloads of furniture with us. Jean had never seen the house, which I had leased for two years from the owners, who were big time cattle owners/producers. Our residence sat on one thousand five hundred acres of land with twenty-six barns and other houses on it. Although I had viewed it for only an hour with the owners, at least I had found a home for my family and a barn for my newly purchased mares.

The entrance was gracious, if a bit imposing. The driveway led to five miles of private paved road and board fence presenting an impressive façade.

The people of Harrisonburg wanted our plant there badly. James Madison University and everyone else remotely interested in our success had helped me lease this house. Court Manor had belonged to Willis Sharpe Kilmer, the heir to the Swamp Root fortune. Kilmer's uncle, a doctor, had developed the Swamp Root formula and started peddling it as a patent medicine around 1878. According to Kilmer, during Prohibition, Swamp Root, which was 20 percent alcohol, was "good for two million dollars a year after taxes."

Kilmer had invested his money wisely in thoroughbred racehorses, and he was the world's leading money-winning horse breeder. Exterminator ("Old Bones") was the upset winner of the Kentucky Derby in 1918 and went on to become American Horse of the Year in 1922. Kilmer's horse, Reigh Count, won the Derby in 1928, but it was Sun Beau, the largest money maker in racing until Seabiscuit in 1939, who made Court Manor the premier American thoroughbred breeder until Calumet Farm in Lexington, Kentucky, eclipsed it in 1941.

After Kilmer's death in 1940, his heirs turned Court Manor into a dude ranch. The main residence had taken a bit of a beating, but I had made it a condition of the lease that I could do anything I needed to improve it (subject to their line item approval) and apply the costs to my rent. By the time the owners saw what Jean had done with the kitchen and the dining room (without spending fifty thousand dollars), they were ready to give me a blank check.

"Let her fix it up the way she wants it," they agreed, "and we'll pay for it." I never sent them a rent check during our entire tenancy; they sent me checks.

The moment we pulled up to the front door, I knew we needed help if Court Manor were to become a home for Marcy and Bill. Jean and I had anticipated their concern when I first announced the move, but they surprised us. Before agreeing to relocate with Electronic Specialty Company, I had flown the whole family to check out Harrisonburg. Every response from Marcy and Bill communicated only enthusiasm for the move.

Once back in Indianapolis, Jean had planned the ultimate test of their fervor. We had never turned the basement of our house into a game room, although it had always been our intention.

"If you paint the basement," Jean suggested to them, "we can probably move, but if you don't, we may not be able to sell this house and we will have to stay here."

Marcy and Bill set to work immediately. They worked long hours, and tirelessly, painting that basement. It appeared that their initial excitement about moving to Virginia was not waning, even though they, and their mother, had never lived in the country.

Eventually the house sold, our worldly goods were sent out before us in two moving vans, and the children made their momentous journey to Virginia in a light blue 1963 Cadillac. Not too many hours later we had followed the trucks down the drive and up to the front door of Court Manor.

I was a bit dismayed. The owners had agreed to turn the property over to me in good condition, and it wasn't. Farmhands were cutting grass and making an effort to trim the yards, but the house itself seemed untouched.

The movers had gotten out of their trucks, eyeing the size of the house. "Uh, is a lot of this stuff going upstairs?" asked one.

"Yes, most of it," I confirmed to his evident sorrow. Marcy and Bill had already clambered out of the backseat of the Cadillac and were tearing up the front steps and around the back of the house, exploring.

Jean and I began making our way toward the front door, when suddenly I felt a hand tugging on my pants.

I looked down and there was Bill. "Dad," he asked, "how do we open the pool?"

"Pool?" His question caught me off guard. I had noticed a covered area at the back of the house, but the presence of a pool had never occurred to me. I paused just long enough to collect my thoughts. "Your mother and I will have to think about whether we want to open it or not"—I paused again, looking Bill straight in the eye—"but if we do, you will have to take care of it. The first time I have to take five minutes to mess with it, it's finished!"

Bill was around eleven at the time, but he knew better than to mistake my words for an idle threat. We opened the pool, and he shouldered the responsibility for its upkeep.

Although Jean had not complained, I could see she was very concerned. I opened the door so she could step into the two-story front hall ahead of me. There, above us, was the sky, gloriously visible through a circular hole in the ceiling where the roof had been wet.

I had been impressed with the history of the place because it was a historic landmark during the Civil War. Court Manor had been a field hospital used by both Yankees and Confederates. It boasted fifteen bedrooms with baths and a commercial kitchen complete with walk-in cooler.

Jean didn't appear to care much about Court Manor's history. She stood immovable, staring at the hole in the roof above her.

If ever a woman had a battle to make a house into a home, Jean did. But within sixty days she had Court Manor living up to its name. In that little town of fifteen thousand people, Space Conditioning was to become the largest employer, and Jean was badly wanted there. Some backs were broken for her. It wasn't all one way.

I would come home at night so tired I could barely put one foot in front of the other, and she would take me through the house, showing me this thing or that thing that had been done during the day, and I would be laughing by the time she'd finished!

Then our water well went bad, all 1,827 feet deep of it. It took us six months to get the parts to repair it. We learned to drink vast amounts of RC Cola and boil water.

Although Bill lived up to his promise to maintain our pool, Jean and I needed more help. She would take the kids to school in Harrisonburg seventeen miles away, return home and supervise the work on the house, then go back and pick the kids up at the end of the day—a round trip of sixty-eight miles every day. Jean didn't complain even though she had reason to.

"Keep your eyes peeled for a man with a fast walk," I asked a couple of my supervisors. It turned out no one had a faster stride than Lee Young.

So I moved Lee Young from one of our construction crews at Space Conditioning to help Jean with the house. Our daily ritual was soon established. I'd drive to work in the morning and get out of my car in front of the office, and Lee would get in it and drive it back to the farm, where he would turn it over to Jean. After that, he would take care of whatever needed to be done next at Court Manor, either on the house, in the yard, or, perhaps most importantly for me, down at the horse barns, before driving my car back at eight or nine at night. That's when I'd get off work and come home.

When the work was heavy or the cleaning major, Lee would put together a crew of five or six people to help him. By the end of our first year, it seemed anyone that we ever knew wanted to visit the Shenandoah Valley and had turned up on our doorstep. One night in 1965, we had twenty-three guests, all at the same time! The room rates were free.

We still had to complete the move for Space Conditioning. All over the United States, employees were functioning the way they were intended to function three years from then, but our business control systems were not yet in place.

Court Manor, however, was beginning to feel like home. Bill was learning to drive. US Highway 11 cut straight across the farm. Part of our property was on the north side of the highway and part on its south side with a huge tube through the underpass connecting the two sections. Bill would drive his jeep right under the road and pull into the driveway on the other side. The police respected the fact that, though underage, he was still on private property. Besides, they probably feared that Jean would quit sending them homemade chocolate chip cookies if they did anything to Bill!

Our first winter saw big snows, and the second saw even bigger snows. One day it began snowing at eleven in the morning, and by eleven o'clock the next morning we had accumulated five to seven inches of snow. I had an exhibition in Louisville, Kentucky, scheduled for the next week. The governor had declared an emergency and ordered everyone off the highways, but I had anticipated his action and rented a car from Avis. I had to drive to Washington to catch my plane to Louisville, and I didn't much care to have my own car out on that road. I drove on closed roads and passed only one car on my way. The police seemed always to be headed in the opposite direction. They didn't even slow down as they approached me.

Airport access from Harrisonburg was an issue. I had to take flights from DC to Charlottesville or to Atlanta to fly anywhere. The company had offered to look into buying or leasing an airplane for me so I could be more mobile. They made good on that promise, to the extent that they let me work out a deal with a local trucker, Jake Smith. Jake was an over-the-road trucker who also had a very nice airplane and took excellent care of it. He also employed an outstanding pilot, and I preferred having him fly me to owning my own airplane.

After thirteen months of my living out of a suitcase in Atlanta and traveling for Peerless more than any father ought, we were happy at Court Manor and satisfied with the move. Were we to stay in Virginia, I knew we would be building a house or finding a different home at the end of our lease. It never occurred to me that I might buy Court Manor. I had actually worked out a plan with the board of trustees of James Madison College to purchase the property and make a gift of the part we leased to the college for a faculty club with a tax option. However, they decided at the last minute it was too luxurious to be a part of faculty benefits.

I was still under the illusion, encouraged by my IU training, that we were going to have another depression, and I was too concerned about the economic stability of the future to entertain any idea of buying Court Manor for my family as an option. I was not concerned about being dismissed from Electronic Specialty, but I was increasingly uncomfortable with the ethics of their style of management and unsure of the depth of my own commitment to the company.

If it had not been for that, we would probably have stayed in Virginia for the rest of our lives.

TAKE AWAYS

- Expertise develops slowly when a little bit of experience on a little bit of experience on a little bit of experience. Whatever the risks or rewards, that is the hill we have to climb to be good at anything.
- The hiring decision of any high-level subordinate is the most important business decision we make.
- For every deal you complete in the mergers and acquisitions business, you negotiate two or three. Don't expect a one-for-one result.
- If you are acquiring companies, you are acquiring opportunities. Capitalizing on these opportunities is the key to success. Failing to seize your opportunities before the window closes can be devastating.

PART THREE

AT THE
CROSSROADS

Chapter 12

HAMILTON-COSCO, INC.

WHEN ARE YOU coming home, Oz?"

I assumed Fred Risk was asking about the next weekend or holiday we had free to visit Indiana. Mutz Corporation business and mutual friends kept us in touch. His salary increase at Indiana National had been followed with job promotions, and his star was rising on the Indiana horizon.

Jean and I, on the other hand, were feeling increasingly restless and uprooted. As much as we enjoyed Court Manor, a critical decision time was fast approaching. Do we build a home for our children and our horses in Virginia and dig our stakes in? One nagging reservation constrained me, and I called Fred to talk it over.

As long as I was at Space Conditioning, putting roots down wasn't a problem. But I was increasingly uncomfortable about staying with Electronic Specialty Company. The ethical boundaries of decisions and practices were not being set by me, and I was required to work within the ethical guidelines provided from above. My chief financial officer functioned more like a guard dog than an employee. He reported directly to the CFO in Los Angeles. In the beginning, he was there to make certain I didn't go off any rails. ESC had entrusted a very substantial business concern to me and they were wise to watch it—and me—closely.

If I were forty years old and offered the job of establishing a Chinese copy of Space Conditioning this afternoon, I wouldn't hesitate in turning it down flat. "You need someone else," I'd urge.

It was a very, very tough job and would be almost as tough now as then. This side of the merger/acquisitions business has no pattern to follow. If you are acquiring companies, you are acquiring opportunities. Capitalizing on these opportunities is the key to success. Failing to seize your opportunities before the window closes can be devastating.

I had done a fair job of making the most of the opportunities Space Conditioning had given me, but I was disenchanted with the ethical environment in which I worked. My guard dog was not keeping books and records crystal clear as I directed him. No one was doing anything illegal, but I knew he was following directives from Los Angeles that made me uncomfortable. He simply ignored my remonstrations.

If we built our home in Virginia, I would be stuck at ESC and Space Conditioning. No other place in the Shenandoah Valley would pay me a salary of sixty thousand dollars. Fred was one person whose counsel I was certain would be sound.

"That's simple enough," Fred replied after I had continued to bemoan my prospects in Virginia. His manner characteristically abrupt and to the point, Fred repeated the question. "When are you coming home?"

I began to get the drift that there was something more on Fred's mind than my future in the Shenandoah Valley. I hedged a bit, but he wasn't biting.

"When you set a date, call me, Oz," he said and hung up.

Not long after, I found myself sitting down across from Fred in his office in downtown Indianapolis.

"I have a date set for you to talk to someone about a job," he began, cutting to the chase. "They've been trying to hire me, and I told them you were the one to do it."

He had my full attention. I asked the big question: "Who?"

"Hamilton-Cosco, here in Columbus. It was founded by three brothers: Bill, Earl, and Clarence Hamilton. The older two want to retire, and Clarence is ready to move up from being president to CEO and let someone else do the running. What do you think, Oz?"

Much as I had traveled, I was personally very homesick. Columbus, Indiana, was only a little over ten miles from Edinburgh. It sounded like home to me.

Bound Away

Electronic Specialty Company was flattering in its anxiety to keep me on deck, but I'd had enough of that ethical climate. I was getting out. My cousin Tom and my father, however, were still with ESC, although in very different capacities. The best thing I could do for the Mutzes as a family upon exiting was to position both Tom and Dad for something they might want to do later.

Harold Mutz had continued running the HVAC parts and pieces business that had been a segment of Peerless. When I left ESC it was with the understanding that he had first refusal on that business, should they ever decide to divest it.

But the luster of buying and selling had dulled some for Harold Mutz.

Seller's remorse and buyer's remorse is the same sickness. The only happy day in the life of a merger-oriented business is when a business is bought or sold. But when the business sold is one, as in Dad's case, that you have spent years building, there is no acquisition that can possibly take its place. The decision was the right thing to do—right for estate planning, right for family tax planning, and right for Harold Mutz, who was in his sixties and not used to saying "Yes, sir" to many people, especially the boss who also happened to be his son.

My departure from Electronic Specialty Company made Tom indispensable to them. I kept him informed of every detail as I negotiated my exit, and he was left with a number of businesses that were his ongoing priority to develop for Space Conditioning. As in Harold's case, Tom was ensured the right of first refusal should ESC decide to divest itself of any of those entities.

Subsequently, Electronic Specialty did divest the Iron Fireman locations in St. Louis, Chicago, Milwaukee, and Cleveland, and all of these fitted together with what Tom was doing. When I took over Iron Fireman with Space Conditioning, I had also wound up with Timken Silent Automatic. The heating business had been owned by the Mellon family (who also owned the Pittsburgh National Bank, currently PNC) and had been a part of the Timken Bearing Company. In other words, the heating business Timken Bearing had acquired had been sold to Iron Fireman and was part of the three packages of business ESC had merged into Space Conditioning. Each of these packages had four or five subsidiaries—like Timken—that had to be parceled out. The right of first refusal meant that, depending on where it was and whose it was, Dad, Tom, and I had been building on that premise.

After I stepped out, both Harold and Tom Mutz were left in excellent condition, fully occupied with very profitable endeavors. But now the Mutzes had pulled apart, developing their interests separately and independently.

Of course, we were still family, and we were all always conscious and informed of what the others were doing.

Tom eventually left Electronic Specialty Company too, but not before he had acquired Moncrief along with the Iron Fireman locations. At his death, he owned a total of twenty-two businesses, none of them particularly large, but all of them very profitable. Tom was a profit hawk. He only bought a business after he had already figured out how to make more money with it. His belief that leadership needed to be in place and be visible moved him from Indianapolis to St. Louis, again to Milwaukee, and finally to Chicago, as he purchased new entities and relocated his family to be on site.

I shared Tom's conviction that leadership must be visible, accessible, and involved, but with some significant reservations. To be present does not necessitate relocation. The manufacturing business requires even greater on-site managerial visibility than the marketing or distribution businesses that Tom developed, but I was not prepared to uproot my family with every manufacturing acquisition we made.

I chose instead to bring them home.

Cosco

In 1965 I accepted the position of chief financial officer of Cosco. Jean and I brought our children and our horses back to Indiana and built our home on a farm near Columbus. We called it Court Manor West. A little bit of Virginia was moving to Indiana with us.

Although Clarence Hamilton had hired me to be Cosco's president, he first brought me on board as CFO. My early dislike of accounting in college came back to me full force. I hadn't spent significant time at double entry bookkeeping for years, so I was very ill at ease. My role as CFO was to reshape the company—to take some pieces out and to put some pieces in, all of which had been identified prior to my hiring. Cosco was a very good manufacturer because they kept things simple and did them well.

The Hamiltons had hired some "young Turks" who were a lot better with numbers than I, but who had proven a lot less able with management. They had purchased the Cal-Dak Manufacturing Company in Little Rock, Arkansas, a manufacturer and marketer of TV trays. If I lived long enough, I could have made money with Cal-Dak, but I wasn't counting on living that long.

Getting rid of Cal-Dak was the first thing I did at Cosco.

Then I worked on acquiring Ransburg. Cosco needed reshaping, and the Harper J. Ransburg Company was my means of doing just that.

Ransburg manufactured kitchen and bathroom accessory items that complemented the bridge furniture Cosco manufactured. The president-founder, Harper J. Ransburg, had devised and patented a painting system used to decorate everything from salt and pepper shakers to canisters and serving platters. Ransburg's electronic dispersion painting system saved literally tons of paint and did a better painting job by eliminating the need for an overspray system. This innovation produced a better result at lower cost.

Their painting system was perhaps the most valuable asset of Ransburg. When we purchased the company, we did not get the patents, but we did require the rights to sell the auxiliary systems. Ransburg was a very valuable, well-known acquisition.

One of Ransburg's employees created a gypsy system for manufacturing these systems under a different name at a lower price. Then he began marketing his products to Westinghouse, General Motors, General Electric, and other large concerns. It was critical to act proactively to secure our manufacturing frontiers. Ransburg sued GM because they were using its system without paying royalties.

Recognizing the painting system's patents as Ransburg's most valuable company assets, Cosco positioned itself to protect them. The effort was successful. Maintaining the prerogatives that Ransburg's patents had given us was an essential step in realizing the plan for reshaping Cosco. Buying and selling Tucker Plastics was another.

ESTABLISHING CRITICAL MASS IN ACQUISITIONS AND MERGERS

The Ford "Whiz Kids" were some of the smartest businesspeople in America, strategically transforming the management models that would guide American business for several generations, but it was Henry Ford II's example that had always attracted my attention. I couldn't help but fix on the man who was wise enough to gather this talent pool around him. Ford had a realistic grasp of his own strengths and weaknesses. He recognized the need for a leadership *team,* people who were smarter or more experienced than he and who brought leadership to the Ford Company in areas beyond his personal expertise.

I had experienced the results of this management style—an approach that releases the benefits of genuine leadership, not just sound management, into the life of a company. Tex Thornton was the head of Ford's Whiz Kids. I encountered him as the CEO of Litton Industries when I worked for Electronic Specialty Company.

Watching this mix of very bright people running companies that, generally speaking, had some sickness and needed them to sort it out taught me how to do some of the same myself. I had approached my task at Space Conditioning from this perspective, purposefully recruiting and positioning key players in our management team to optimize all of our leadership potential.

Some of these people I brought with me to Cosco. Bob Houck served in effect as the chief operating officer at Ransburg. If I had a business needing help on the manufacturing side, I knew Bob was the one to send to fix it. On the sales side, I could count on a man like Walt Enoch to bring the level of ethics that was important to me. I had hired him as the field sales manager at Space Conditioning, where his gentility and Christian commitment countered the strong autocratic leadership style of his boss, Bill Webfer, an Annapolis graduate. Enoch was eventually a founder of the St. Louis huddle of the Fellowship of Christian Athletes.

Good ethics in the people you deal with is exceedingly important. You must know they are telling you the truth, especially when you are gathering the critical information related to a potential acquisition.

A wise decision regarding any acquisition depends on a reliable assessment of the following four key points:

1. The technical analysis of the business. You must have audited financials from a creditable auditor. The auditor does not have to be one of the "Big Four" accounting firms (in my day the "Big Eight"), but it must be ethical and reliable.

2. On-site verification of analysis by looking. The ability of those "young turks" (who typically push an acquisition) to manage a company should not be assumed. The methods by which they conduct their analyses often do not reflect a managerial point of view, and their assessments may consequently fail to identify critical factors in the business's potential success or failure.

3. A future operating plan to be implemented after the acquisition operating plan. This must include a projected budget and the numerical results flowing from it.

4. A plan for recruiting and positioning key managerial personnel. This is the single most important factor if the success of the future operating plan is to be realized. Leadership must be identified and available, either on the payroll or accessible.

When I was promoted to executive vice president of Cosco after six months as its chief financial officer, I began negotiating the acquisition of Tucker Manufacturing Company, using these four key tests. The purchase of Tucker was perhaps my greatest contribution to Cosco— the proposed sale of it my undoing.

FILO TOCCI AND TUCKER MANUFACTURING

I had hired a former FBI agent to investigate Filo Tocci by the time I was in the third or fourth negotiation to buy his business. I was convinced the man had to be affiliated with the Mafia. The information coming back to me on all my key points was simply too good to be true.

Although I was looking for something negative, the detective came back with only positives.

"You have a unique man and a unique situation here, Mr. Mutz," he assured me. "This man's word is truly his bond. He's sold millions of dollars of housewares to Wal-Mart without a contract. He does it on a handshake."

Over my lifetime I have negotiated hundreds of deals, ranging from the purchase of large tracts of land to the sale of a substantial business enterprise, but my dealings with Filo Tocci were in a class by themselves.

In a business climate where anyone or anything that appears too good is suspect, I would want my grandchildren (and anyone else for that matter) to know that there are people out there who are unique because they are good. The ability to recognize and value the difference between an operator who is unique and ethical from one who is unique but unethical can itself be a rare quality in a business manager.

If there is something significant on the negative side of a seller, the public record will generally alert you to it. With the seller's permission, you may talk with his or her banker and inquire about their relationships. Bankers will inevitably give you some kind of signal if a relationship is sour. They will, of course, be careful. They will not want to torpedo the sale, but if they are thinking of you as being a potential client, or if you are already their client, they will understand the advantages of honesty.

We probably got the lead on Filo Tocci from a bank in the beginning. My only regret in my dealings with him is that I failed to attend his funeral.

During Cosco's negotiations to acquire Tucker, I would sit in the small office across from Filo with our lawyers and suddenly a lawyer would interrupt with a "No, we can't agree to that."

I would wait for Filo to look at me. I wouldn't say anything until I had seen his eyeballs. I knew and he knew that we had already agreed on that point.

"You're here to make sure we haven't done anything illegal," Filo admonished the attorney. "Don't interrupt us by trying to change the substance. If I want your advice, I'll ask for it."

Filo had begun in the plastics injection-molding business, working on the frames for Foster Grant eyewear in Lexington, Massachusetts, and then migrated from one injection-molding business to another until he founded Tucker. When he started Tucker, he ran the plastic injection-molding machines himself. He knew from the ground up how to make plastic parts of credible value at the lowest cost.

By 1966 Filo was ready to retire, but his son was not ready to take over the business from him. We bought Tucker with a loan from Indiana National via Fred Risk. We hired only one man with the acquisition of Tucker, an MIT graduate named David Webster. Like all MIT grads we had hired, Dave was an excellent businessman. Filo, however, didn't like him. All of Filo's employees were Italian American, and he considered an Italian last name the prerequisite for operating a molding machine well.

They were unquestionably some of the best manufacturing people I have ever encountered. Cosco didn't have a right to that quality of management, because they didn't pay them that well.

Filo retired to Florida, but he was always available when we needed him, always helpful. His son Lenny became our sales manager and eventually ran Tucker for Cosco. He continued in that position after Cosco was later acquired by Lameloc, which was subsequently acquired by Rubbermaid.

I had tried to consolidate Tucker and Rubbermaid in the early seventies, but the powers that be at Rubbermaid did not consider Tucker's quality worthy of the Rubbermaid brand. Tucker's main customer, Wal-Mart, was expanding.

In fact, Wal-Mart was making Rubbermaid look like a toy.

I had acquired Tucker for Cosco in 1967 for $3,380,000. Three years later I was negotiating its sale to KKR for Bear Stearns for $11,800,000.

Clarence Hamilton should have been happy with me.

THE PIVOTAL ROLE OF LEADERSHIP

My biggest weakness as a businessman and as a manager is my impatience, always being in too big a hurry, and always wanting to sell early instead of late.

I'd look through a CPM (Critical Path Method) and think I understood it, asking three or four critical questions and then signing off with a "That's good enough." I'd have forgotten that the team who has to execute the plan doesn't have the same skill set, prior knowledge, or past experiences as we did. Instead, I'd project how we would do it and fail to see what additional resources or support someone else might require if they were to get the same results. This kind of blindness was true across my spectrum of management abilities and skills.

I intentionally corrected my managerial weaknesses when I put together a management team or partnered in a business deal. Clarence Hamilton was unaware that he had need to correct anything, and therein lay his and Cosco's eventual demise.

Cosco's strength lay in being a style-oriented business. We manufactured baby furniture and bridge sets and marketed them on the strength of their steel tube construction and the colors and patterns on the high chairs and play yards. For me, these decisions were simple, direct decisions and not difficult to make.

Clarence Hamilton's greatest weakness as a manager was his indecision. A straightforward yes or no was almost beyond his ability. He would delay making a decision, not realizing that to delay a decision is often to make no decision. Instead, Cosco's CEO would belabor every facet of the point as if it were critical. Five people on a committee had to look at a display room and help decide which pattern or which design or which color we could use. Nothing was ever simply voted on and finished.

After the committee had surveyed the options, we had a list. The next step was to have Mrs. Clarence Hamilton look at the list. She was as close to a design decision maker as we had. In my opinion, Earl Hamilton, the middle brother, had been the most important factor in Cosco's design success, and he was certainly the one with good taste. Earl had been wise enough to know when to quit and rich enough to stop caring. Clarence was never that self-aware.

As with everything Clarence managed, Cosco's Human Resources were an example of overkill. They had developed a personnel review plan almost sophisticated enough to run General Motors. An annual fitness review is usually sufficient, but Cosco conducted one every six months and on the anniversary of your hire. My first fitness review was a taste of what was to come.

Clarence looked dire. I had been at Cosco only six months.

"I hate to have to do this with you, Oz," he began, "but there is something I have to discuss with you."

I was on the edge of my seat. "Yes, sir, go ahead."

"Oz," he sighed, "you just have to get some nicer clothes to wear."

I was floored, but I returned his look with a level eye. "What did you have in mind, sir?"

"You just don't dress up well enough."

"Mr. Hamilton," I replied quietly, "I don't know what you would like me to do."

"Hickey Freeman," Clarence ordered. "Buy more tailored suits."

I think I was wearing a Hickey Freeman suit at the review. I know the last suits I had purchased were Hickey Freeman.

"I'd like you to go to Capper and Capper in Chicago," he finished. "I have a friend who works there who will fix you up."

Having "fixed" my wardrobe, Clarence promoted me to executive vice president.

Six to eight months later, I was formally made the president of Cosco. As such, I was invited to speak to a men's group in Hope, Indiana, and, probably looking for some kind of recognition, I accepted. My subject was the spread of Communism and the necessity of stemming the tide if we were not going to have a serious problem in the Free World.

The next morning, Clarence Hamilton suddenly appeared beside my desk and laid a newspaper down in front of me.

"What is this?" he demanded.

"Looks like a newspaper to me," I replied, not disrespectfully.

An article recapped the speech I had made in Hope the previous night.

"I didn't see this before you gave it," Clarence scolded me. "You are not to make any speeches which could be construed as company policy that I haven't approved first. You will conform to that directive!"

"Sir," I promised him, "I just won't make any speeches."

Later, I realized what had happened. Columbus, Indiana, was the international headquarters of the Cummins Engine Company, and the people of Columbus thought that J. Irwin Miller could walk on water. I had already learned as the Chief Operating Officer at Cosco of an unwritten agreement between Arvin Industries, Hamilton-Cosco, and Cummins to avoid proselytizing or hiring executives from each other. Such a ceiling on executive marketability was not in the community's best interests, I thought, but the doctrine ruled supreme in Columbus.

And when Clarence Hamilton saw the article in the newspaper, he was immediately afraid that I might have offended Arvin or Cummins.

I knew then it would be a challenge working for him.

TAKE AWAYS

o Leadership must be visible, accessible, and involved, but to be present
   does not necessitate relocation.

o Henry Ford II gathered a talent pool of
   "Whiz Kids" because he had a realistic
   grasp of his own strengths and weaknesses
   and recognized the need for a leadership team: people who were smarter or
   more experienced than he and brought
   leadership to the Ford Motor Company
   in areas beyond his personal expertise.

o Ford's management style released the benefits of genuine leadership, not just sound
   management, into the life of his company.

o Dealing with ethical people is exceedingly important; you must know you
   are being told the truth, especially
   when gathering information critical
   to making a wise acquisition.

o Four keys to a wise, reliable assessment of a potential acquisition:

   • Audited financials from a credit-
      able auditor providing a tech-
      nical analysis of the business

   • On-site verification of the anal-
      ysis by visually looking at it

   • A future operating plan to be
      implemented after acquisition

   • A plan for recruiting and posi-
      tioning key managerial personnel

o The ability to recognize and value the
   difference between an operator who

is unique and ethical and one who is
unique but unethical can itself be a
rare quality in a business manager.

○ Impatience is always a weakness; a manager will be in too big
a hurry and want to sell early.

○ Delaying a decision often means
making no decision.

Chapter 13

CONTRACT NEGOTIATIONS

MY INITIAL INTRODUCTION to Cosco was as vice president of finance and included no responsibilities for labor relations. Clinton Frank held that position, and had served in the hierarchy of labor relations at Genesco, which had originated as a shoe company in Nashville, Tennessee. Cosco had been organized by the carpenters and joiners segment of the AFL-CIO and acquired a significant history with them by the time I arrived.

That I would be sitting in a Cosco board meeting with Clint Frank discussing what to do with the union contract staring us straight in the face was inevitable. It just happened sooner rather than later, as the old contract was expiring within two months. We had the union's new "alpha and omega" before us and knew if we just signed it, business would continue as usual.

Management had come close to "just signing" it more than once in Cosco's history. Cummins employed two thousand workers, Arvin around fifteen hundred. Cosco payrolled eight hundred and fifty people at Columbus, Indiana. As I studied the contract in my hands, I knew how it had been developed.

Cummins' labor manager had negotiated their contract with the United Auto Workers in Detroit, who had a relationship with General Motors. They had reached an agreement over insurance clauses, vacation benefits, and everything else that GM might have to do with hourly labor but which we would not normally consider in Cosco contracts. For example, sick leave was a new element, picked up in Detroit contracts in the late sixties.

Once Cummins' labor manager settled on the basis of GM's negotiations, Arvin settled for a buck less, and we would settle for a dollar less than Arvin. In effect, we had been invariably two dollars off whatever was the going rate in Detroit.

Someone I couldn't have identified in a police lineup was negotiating our contracts for us.

Clint Frank was a politician. Like me, he was a relatively new employee who had never yet negotiated a contract with Carpenters and Joiners. Clarence Hamilton and his two brothers had.

I was in my first year at Cosco. Cummins and Arvin had already settled their contracts. The task ahead of us was considered straightforward and obvious. Copies of the Arvin and Cummins contracts had been circulated two or three days prior. My name had been among those on the list of addressees. I was expected to have read the contract and be prepared to comment on it at the meeting.

I chose not to comment, deciding to just sit and listen. It did not take long for me to understand from Clint Frank's comments that he was a peacemaker.

I sat and listened, ground my teeth, and kept silent. I am not generally a peacemaker where labor unions are concerned because I had firsthand experience, several times over, of the cost of being a peacemaker.

I had just come to Cosco from a battlefield in Virginia and understood the huge dislocation of people and processes when companies ran from labor unions in order to grow.

RESPONDING TO ORGANIZED LABOR

Moncrief was a small potential client for the Teamsters, but Jimmy Hoffa's people had been interested in organizing its labor force. One of my connections in Washington, DC, occasionally worked with Hoffa. I had asked him to simply communicate to Hoffa what he knew to be true of Oz Mutz: that I was a man of my word; that if I said I would take a strike rather than yield on a point being negotiated, he could count on a strike.

Jimmy Hoffa called me on the telephone, and no strike materialized at Moncrief in Atlanta.

My experience with labor unionization predated my position at Moncrief. I had worked at the Peerless foundry in high school and throughout college. As a result, I had been solicited—and harassed—by the first attempt at organizing labor in the company's fifty-two-year history.

Some of the people harassing me were men with whom I had been working summers and weekends for years. When the union organizer appeared and made his inroad into our labor force, stirring up ill will between company labor and management, those relationships—even friendships—with people in the bargaining unit seemed suddenly for sale.

I learned firsthand why labor unions gain a toehold in a company. In the final analysis, management did not do its job.

As far as any worker knows, the first level of management above them is the "company." In a smaller company like Peerless, at least at that point in history, there was a real relationship between top management and worker-level manpower. Frontline employees knew that the top management's names were Harold and Frank and their immediate boss was Ed Hearn, who functioned as a foreman of the foundry where most people worked. How Ed Hearn related to them reflected the management of Harold and Frank Mutz in their eyes. If Ed Hearn did his job poorly, the seedbed for labor organizers would be ready for sowing. If Ed Hearn did his job well, with honesty, integrity, and backbone, unionized labor would find its path into the workforce more difficult.

The process of unionization was not always as clearly understood by management as it should have been. It would begin with a union official notifying the National Labor Relations Board (NLRB) of the union's plan to solicit the workforce of a particular company for affiliation with their union. Postcard-type notices were then sent to all employees requiring signatures if they wanted to elect a union representative. If a third of that workforce returned their notices signed, the NLRB would verify the accuracy of representation and schedule an election date to determine the union representative of the hourly employees.

Typically, the hourly employees all voted for representation, and the management knew they now had a unified workforce opposing them.

In 1952, after more than fifty years of successful business, Peerless was certified by the NLRB for a representation election.

I had been out of college three years, Jean and I were married, and Marcy had joined our household. I was just beginning to earn a good salary at Peerless, and Tom was making an even better living. He and I were concerned about the impending election, but our fathers were devastated, as they understood it represented a failure in their leadership.

What had they done wrong?

Perhaps nothing; but Ed Hearn represented them, and if he did anything wrong, they would have been painted in his colors.

No manager is ever adequately prepared for these things.

I wasn't ready. I arrived for work at Peerless that hot midsummer morning in 1952 soon after the representation election only to be confronted by pickets carrying signs as I turned into the parking lot. I knew these people, and I worked with them, but now they jeered as I crossed their picket line and walked through the employees' entrance. In their eyes, I had just declared war.

They had voted, and the business agent of the union had prevailed over the representative from management. Bigger vacations, better benefits, higher wages—these are the carrots that lead a workforce into strike. It always starts with higher wages.

Senior management huddled. Whatever we thought we were going to do that day had been preempted, and we didn't even have a labor council at Peerless. One of us called the company lawyer, who promptly informed us that he was a general practitioner without specialized knowledge. What we needed was a lawyer with that specialized knowledge and experience of organized labor.

By that time, we had gathered all our first-level managers together: Ed Hearn, Melvin Cunningham, Randall Hughes, and Jim Jones. The situation was immediately critical because the picket line was across our shipping doors, so that we couldn't just load up and ship what stock was already there.

Our attorney directed us to Ice, Miller, Donadio, and Ryan, a firm with an Indianapolis lawyer, Owen Neighbours, who specialized in organized labor law. Owen Neighbours was quick to arrive. He had a fresh client, a fresh strike, and his fee generation was certain. He told us what to do and that's what we did.

First, our legal counsel emphasized the need to negotiate in good faith since the representatives had been certified to negotiate for the hourly employees; otherwise, we would be in violation of the Labor Relations Act. Then we set the dates for negotiation.

Next we turned our attention to the two railcars of sand sitting on our siding. If we were not invoicing anyone, we were not sending out bills for collection. The sand sitting in those railcars was to be used in the molding process to form parts. Most of our parts were made in small quantities, as we rarely manufactured in quantities of a hundred or more. It was clear we would not be producing anything if we didn't get the sand out of the railcars. Tom and I armed our sales force with shovels and we began shoveling sand.

Demurrage is the rent paid to the rail carrier for using its siding access. A picket line prevented us from getting our loads of sand off New York Central's siding. So, on day three of the strike, we began paying demurrage of around five hundred dollars per day to New York Central, money that was being thrown away.

It was a tug of war. By the end of the week, the railcars were empty. Salaried personnel crossed the picket lines and performed whatever manual labor was needed to demonstrate to our hourly workers that they were not going to stop our production. Tom and I were particular targets of rising curiosity amid hostility. We could see the question in their eyes as they watched us: How long can those two keep on shoveling?

The answer that emerged, to their surprise and consternation, was "until they have the job done." How did we break that picket line? We stopped paying demurrage, we shipped out our finished goods to the maximum percentage possible, and we induced our customers to cross the line to pick up their shipments. In those days, pickets were often not maintained in force throughout the night, so we leased a semi and waited until two in the morning to back it into the dock and have it ready for loading the next day. The "scab" of a truck driver was I.

Management must never give up. A strike must be effectively broken or the company will never negotiate convincingly with its workforce. Only when the money is skinny at home will management have any pull at the bargaining table.

That work stoppage at Peerless lasted four to five weeks. Tom and I grew tired of doing two or three jobs at once, but a couple of our sales personnel who played basketball at night and exercised regularly were in quite good physical condition and more than up to manual labor. Together we maintained the flow of goods necessary to break the strike.

The second lesson I learned as a result of the strike at Peerless was the importance of preemptive action by management. An alert, wise manager will be connected to the workforce so that he or she gets wind of organization efforts before they mature. This lesson was soon reinforced when Peerless and Iron Fireman were merged into Electronic Specialty Company and I was sent to Cleveland, Ohio, to facilitate the relocation of their manufacturing center to Harrisonburg, Virginia.

A Recipe for Organization

Iron Fireman had been organized by the AFL-CIO for twenty-five to thirty years before I entered the picture. Its employees had known nothing but organized labor as their bargaining agent.

In fact, the organization of labor was driving the executive decision to move the company to Virginia, a right-to-work state. In Cleveland, labor had the management whipped.

Upon the sale of Peerless to Electronic Specialty Company, I became the vice president and general manager of Iron Fireman in Cleveland in addition to my other tasks. My first two days in the office at Cleveland, I spent time walking around and getting acquainted with the salaried management of the company. I was going to need some of them to move to Virginia with me. By my fourth or fifth day on the job, I let the president of the company know I was extending my forays to the factory floor. He didn't like it. He balked.

"I'd just like to see what is going on there and get a feeling for things," I persisted.

He called in the plant manager (calling him the "foreman") and insisted I go only with him. We appointed a time and place to meet, and I ventured out into the factory, with him as watchdog, at the scheduled time.

The first thing I noticed was a group of workers huddled together in a tight circle talking with each other. One man was gesticulating emphatically. I stopped to listen only to discover he was describing the big fish he had caught on his vacation two weeks previously. I stood there listening for almost five minutes.

There was no indication the story was going to end. Finally I sidled up to the man and interjected, "That's really an interesting story about the walleyed pike you caught. Why don't we meet here on your break and finish it?"

The man was huge. For a moment he stood silent, looking down on me scornfully.

"Who are you?!" he spat out.

"Well, I am your general manager."

The man sneered. "Oh, well, we have one of those about every six months."

"I can assure you," I replied drily, keeping my eyes level and my voice matter-of-fact, "you are going to have this one longer than six months."

"I tell you what, sonny," the huge man bristled threateningly, drawing himself up to his full height and towering over me, "why don't you just go back to your office and do your thing and let us take care of what's going on down here?"

I would never have thought of looking down on a superior and talking to him in that manner, but the situation was too late to recover. That incident was my first real encounter with the consequences of allowing a strong, organized labor presence in your business because the presence of a strong, organized labor force follow close on the heels of a detached, disconnected, uninformed management.

I persevered with my plan to be a presence on the factory floor, and the big guy, a line supervisor named Jerry, eventually came to the point where he'd kind of smile and say "Hi, boss" when he saw me, and I'd say "Hi, Jerry," greeting him in return. As I became more familiar with the history of Iron Fireman, I learned the president had such an attitude that he would never have allowed his hands to be soiled by going into the actual factory and seeing what the union wanted and why they wanted it, thereby not being able to negotiate with them on an equal footing.

Six months later we began the move, relocating from a 250,000 square foot facility in Cleveland to 660,000 square feet in Virginia. We were housing six additional businesses under the same roof as Iron Fireman.

We had been operating at 40 to 50 percent capacity for about a half a year when the boilermakers, an AFL-CIO union, materialized on our doorstep in Virginia, following us from Cleveland. No one had been naive enough to think they would get lost on their way, it being a question of "when," not "if," as they had lost a substantial piece of their membership when Iron Fireman left Cleveland.

Dues paid the salaries of the union hierarchy and provided their extra benefits. If they lost a bunch of elections, their compensation went down; the more elections they won, the higher their compensation. Our new plant in Harrisonburg promised significant returns for the union organizers.

I was not disconnected from my production floor, and I smelled labor organization. Iron Fireman was just the first of five other plants slated to be consolidated under the Electronic Specialty roof in Virginia. Labor had already lost the one in Cleveland, and if they won the battle in Harrisonburg, they would gain far more than they had lost.

I thought back to my experiences with the Peerless strike in Indianapolis. In addition to putting their salaried personnel to work doing manual labor, the management there had used scabs (non-striking hourly employees who opposed unionization) to break the strike. My operating mode was to see what the labor union wanted and convince them why they couldn't have it.

I was pretty sure I knew quite a bit about labor relations when, actually, I was just about to learn.

O'Melveny and Myers were the legal consultants for Electronic Specialty Company, headquartered in Los Angeles. They employed two men in their LA office who did nothing but train managers like me to avoid unionization and to win labor elections, if organizing efforts developed that far. Before the boilermakers showed up on our doorstep, the company had provided me with additional training that was valuable and unconventional.

Three entry gates guarded the two-hundred-plus fenced acres of our Harrisonburg facility, enclosing even the parking lots. We had guardhouses at each entry, positioned so they could be closed quickly and tightly, denying unauthorized parties access to the property. When union organizers finally arrived, we knew within minutes they were there.

Their first objective was to induce and win an election.

Management can't stop organizers from inducing an election. If people are showing up at the gate to listen, it is certain that they have 30 percent of the workers signed up somewhere.

At that juncture, the typical management response is to flood the floor with bulletins. I talked with people on the floor. We could do that at our expense on our time in our building, and we did not have to invite a union representative to be present. It seemed a strategic and wise investment of our time and money to visit with people on the job.

We staged demonstrations of our own, guided by our counsel at O'Melveny and Myers. I was raising horses at Court Manor and just happened to have a very good manure spreader. O'Melveny and Myers suggested I put it to work. We spread manure on the field inside the gates of our property and hung banners on the fences: This is Union Bull.

The governor of Virginia had attended the opening of our plant. The state wanted a factory with fifteen hundred employees in Harrisonburg. They did not want strikes hindering our productivity or frightening off other investors. It was in Virginia's best interests for us to win that election. The presence of state police underscored that commitment.

In short, the moment we knew union organizers had arrived, we implemented an anti-union campaign that we had previously developed in preparation for their visit. The boilermakers weren't used to that, and they had expected us to fold our arms and play dead.

Every morning over the next three or four weeks, when our people arrived at work (and at this point they were still "our" people), we had a selling point, demonstrating that ours was a good place to work. I invested time on the factory floor, actively debating the union's election campaign. I used our turf and our time to address our people: any loss in productivity was more than adequately compensated by our election win.

And we did win.

To seize the initiative and vigorously challenge the claims of organized labor is management's best response. This strategy makes for some easy wins, and easy wins are always to management's credit.

CREATING A LABOR STRATEGY AT COSCO

By the mid-1960s, Columbus, Indiana, had a total population approaching 26,000, and Cosco employed 850 of these people. During the first meeting related to a new contract, I sat across from Clint Frank, preferring to keep silent and look like a dunce rather than to jump in and risk alienating the chief of labor relations; but I made sure he knew I was there after the meeting.

"Clint," I suggested, "I'd really like to catch up a bit more on what's gone on here in labor relations. Could just you and I talk, some evening this week?"

Clint eyed me a bit warily. "Why evening?" he asked. "I have something else going on every night, but I guess I could do it Thursday."

"Could I buy you dinner?" I offered.

Clint had been one of the people interviewing me heavily for the job at Cosco, and he knew I was there to be president of the company. He was obviously not overjoyed to have my spoon in his pot so soon, and I understood he was being territorial but not hostile.

I had just spooked him. We had dinner, and I learned that he had been aggravated for years with his upper management of Johnson and Murphy in Tennessee. In Clint's estimation, they had been over-conciliatory in their labor negotiations and had set a bad precedent for the future.

Over the course of that meal, Clint discovered in me someone at Cosco's head who supported a stronger position vis-a-vis labor. We began coordinating our efforts, strategizing for the next meeting when a contract needed to be ratified.

When the union representatives presented their demands to us, we had prepared our response. "Those things all make sense to us," Clint and I agreed. "We appreciate your coming in with your suggestions. We did the same thing, and here is a copy of our suggestions."

Cosco was on the offensive. We were going to counter everything they wanted economically with our own requirements. Among other things, we reduced the expected dollar increase based on Arvin's and Cummins's rates.

Arvin Industries, headquartered in Columbus and listed on the New York Stock Exchange, manufactured automotive exhaust systems—the second largest manufacturer of automotive exhaust systems in the United States. A portion of the exhaust system market related to each of the original equipment manufacturers (OEMs) in the United States belonged to Arvin, whose employment base was the largest of the Columbus manufacturing group. The labor relations reflected in its union organization was mirrored in the Cosco bargaining unit.

Consequently, we triggered the first strike ever for Cosco. It happened at the Columbus plant and lasted almost seven weeks. The effect on my management position was corrosive. Clarence Hamilton had reason to complain that we were trying to take labor relations out of his hands and that we were going to have a strike for sure. He was right on both counts.

But Clint and I had a plan. Reducing taxes takes a burden off people's backs, but the same end can be attained by reducing union dues. If you reduce their burden, they will follow. When you don't do those things, they want to run the other way.

The strike at Cosco culminated in a huge ratification meeting on the bleachers of the grandstand of the Bartholomew County fairground. The union at Cosco was the only union of its type: the United Brotherhood of Carpenters and Joiners of America out of the AFL. The Teamsters were also involved, negotiating with the Carpenters as one entity. I drove my car behind the bleachers and listened.

The best workforce I ever negotiated with were the people from our Tucker subsidiary. They were marvelous, but their president, Filo Tocci, was a man of his word and set the example. Clarence Hamilton was better at keeping his word than the average businessman, but the average is probably worse than most people suppose.

All three major plants in Columbus were operated by people of much higher integrity than the company I had left behind in Virginia. A business is the life of the people who own it, and if you are going to work for them, you should know them so well you can guess what they have for breakfast. Also, the character of a workforce will reflect the character of its management.

To Clarence's relief, we peaceably negotiated that contract with Cosco. Clint and I now focused on the next time, preparing to dig in our heels. News came that we had a wildcat strike in our factory at Gallatin, Tennessee. No one had any idea it was coming, but at eleven fifteen in the morning, people just started walking out of all the doors of the plant.

Pete Peterson had replaced Owen Neighbours as our labor counsel at Peerless. Cosco had become his client before my appointment as its president. Clint and I were guided by Pete's expertise.

A wildcat strike is a strike that has not been authorized by the union, nor has it involved the business agent of the union or engaged in discussion with company management. The existing contract had not expired but was legally still binding and valid between parties. Under the Taft-Hartley Act, wildcat strikes are illegal.

There had never been any kind of work stoppage at the Cosco plant in Gallatin. It was Cosco's newest factory, completed two or three years before my employment with the company. I was quite certain we could break the strike there the same way we had broken any other strike: we would not let them bind us.

Two days into it, we led a parade of automobiles with strikebreakers into the property. Most of our strikebreakers were existing employees but some were genuine scabs. Someone needed to lead that parade, and I found upper management willing. The president of the Gallatin division, myself, Pete Peterson, and Clint Frank rode in the first car. The strikers built a human wall in front of us.

Bob Wendling, VP of Gallatin operations, was our driver, and he let the car idle and inched forward until we were out of inches. Strikers began rocking the car from side to side, and suddenly the vehicle rolled over. Clint, Pete, Bob, and I were hanging from the ceiling, with things raining down from the floor and the engine roaring.

"Bob," I suggested composedly, "Would you please turn your car off before it catches fire?"

Fortunately, there had been no gun under the front seat. I hated to think what might have happened next had a gun materialized.

Four or five policemen turned our car back over while we still hung from the seat belts.

In the end, by attacking our car, the workforce had lost their fight. They had broken the Taft-Hartley Act when they walked out, and the police arrested a number of people for the destruction of private property. At a hearing in a local court the next morning, the strikers were arraigned. Before the strike was finished—some two and a half or three weeks later— we had identified, through photographs, strikers who had shot the radiators out of automobiles in front of our strikebreakers' homes. The fight will always belong to those who play by the rules.

By the time my association with Cosco ended, my approach to labor relations had solidified, refined in the fires of experience. Managers must lead from strength, from in front and not from behind. I walked the factory floor in every plant I had anything to do with, knowing a substantial percentage of people by name.

Who had taught me that critical lesson? Harold Mutz.

MARCY'S WALKOUT

I had not trained my daughter, Marcy, for this rough-and-tumble world of business negotiations and labor relations. She was certainly capable of mastering it, but she had also inherited her mother's beauty, poise, social graces, and gifts for music and interior design. I not only wanted to see her develop these natural abilities; I wanted to protect her. To be caught in the middle of a confrontation between angry union members and management was something I did not want her to experience.

Marcy's graciousness contributed to her popularity growing up in Columbus. At seventeen, she was chosen to represent the town in the Indiana Junior Miss Pageant. I proudly escorted her and her "court," a group of five or six girls, to dinner at the only gourmet restaurant the town then boasted (its reputation was ensured when J. Irwin Miller supplied its chef). Five dollars was considered a ludicrous amount of money to pay for a meal in those days. The first time I spent that much money on a meal was when I had taken Jean to dinner at the same restaurant only a few months earlier to celebrate our twentieth wedding anniversary. Taking Marcy's court to dinner there was not just a big deal for them; it was a big deal for me!

The state pageant was held in Frankfort, Indiana, some months later, and Marcy was first runner-up for Miss Hospitality. Less than a year later, she pledged the Pi Beta Phi sorority at DePauw University as a first semester college student. As part of their initiation rites, the freshmen pledges had to figure out a way to successfully cross the upperclass Pi Phis. Marcy suggested they stage a "walkout." She organized a strike for the initiates, who were required to work for the upperclassmen on weekends.

She had already figured out how to remove somewhere around fifteen college freshman women from the DePauw campus in Greencastle with her brother's help and hide them at Court Manor West. When I learned of her plans, I called my old friend from Howe High School, Jim Cook, to ask his advice.

Jim also happened to be the executive vice president of DePauw University.

After exchanging pleasantries, I went straight to the point. "Jim," I asked, "if my daughter and her brother load up fifteen freshman Pi Phis in a horse trailer and transport them to my farm in Columbus for a weekend, is it going to cause problems for you on your campus?"

After clarifying the details, Jim seemed rather relieved. "Oz, I can't think of a better plan," he reassured me. "We'll know where they are, and they are safer at your place than anywhere else they could go. They surely can't get into too much trouble on a horse farm!"

I didn't quite share his confidence and was more than a little concerned at the liability I was undertaking for hauling a group of young women from Greencastle to Columbus in my truck and horse trailer. Marcy and Bill, however, successfully completed the walkout, and Jean and I entertained the Pi Phi pledges for the weekend.

I had access to the Cosco plane for personal use as long as I paid the commercial fare. We also had a pilot who had shuttled Eisenhower in and out of Moscow at the end of the war. Now a retired Lieutenant Colonel, I hired him to shuttle my daughter and her friends back to Greencastle. Cosco's twin engine could only hold seven people, so Marcy took a small group with her back to DePauw in the plane, and Bill and I each drove an automobile-load back to campus.

In spite of her father's reservations about involving her in the stressful world of management/labor relations, my daughter pulled off the most successful walkout I have ever witnessed!

By this time, however, Marcy was not entirely inexperienced in contract negotiations. Both my children understood that the primary responsibility for financing their college educations rested with them. Near the end of her senior year, Marcy approached me about working a summer job at Cosco. She found a job in our plastics department, running a 200-ton plastic injection molding machine. To run the machine, she would fasten her hands into a harness since the touch of both hands was needed to make the machine stroke. The job looked dangerous, but I would not have allowed her to do it if any real danger were involved.

She had just made enough money to bankroll the purchase of her college wardrobe when contract negotiations at Cosco soured. Talk of a strike filled the air. Marcy became the target of every disillusioned or unhappy employee in the plastics department. I was quite certain the time had come to remove her from that environment.

Consequently, she became one of the shortest-term workers in Cosco history. Eventually, she graduated magna cum laude from Purdue University and taught for several years in Cleveland, Ohio, and Bartholomew County, Indiana, but if I had thought then that her business days were over, the future would prove me wrong.

TAKE AWAYS

o From the worker's point of view, the first level of management above them is the "company." Frontline employees need to know the names of top management; there must be relationship. How management relates to workers is reflected in worker-level performance: if management does their job well with honesty, integrity, and backbone, workers will tend to follow their example.

o Management must never give up during a strike. Only when money is skinny at home will management have any pull at the bargaining table.

o A detached, disconnected, uninformed management will face the consequences of a strong, organized labor force on the floor.

o An alert, wise manager will be connected to the workforce so that he or she gets wind of issues before they mature.

o A strategic and wise investment of time and money is to visit with people on the job.

o Management's best response to organized labor is to maintain the initiative, aggressively challenging union claims rather than allowing them to be the challenger. This strategy produces some easy wins, and easy wins are always to management's credit.

o Reduce the burden off people's backs and they will follow. When management doesn't do these things, workers will run the other way.

o A business is the life of the people who own it. If you are going to work for them, you should know them so well you can guess what they have for breakfast. The character of a workforce will reflect the character of its management.

o The fight will always belong to those who play by the rules.

o Managers must lead from strength and be in front, not behind.

(Left to Right)
Jacob, Maria, and O. U. Mutz I

Jacob and Maria Mutz and family (Standing Right) O. U. Mutz I (Standing Fourth from Right) Maria Mutz (Standing Fifth from Right) Jacob Mutz (Standing Left) Dick Francis (Oscar's nephew)

O. U. Mutz I and O. U. Mutz II, age 2
Taken at a photographer's studio

Sawin Family celebrating the 50th wedding anniversary of Asa and Anna Sawin (Seated Left to Right) Aunt Nell Johnson, Grandma Anna, Grandpa Asa, Aunt Edith Waterfield (Standing Left to Right) Uncle Bill Sawin, Aunt Mary Ray, Uncle Ransom Sawin, Mom (Laura Belle Sawin Mutz), Uncle Fred Sawin

Three Generations
(Left to Right) Bill Greiling, O. U. Mutz II, Harold Mutz, and baby Bill

Three Generations
(Left to Right) Emma Greiling "Grammie,"
Jean, Laura clutching a ball of scotch tape, Marcy

Laura Belle Sawin Mutz
I remember this picture was taken at L. S. Ayres

Harold Winterberg Mutz, age 75

Evelyn holding Harold,
Marie & Frank Mutz

Florence Winterberg Northart
(aunt of the Mutz children)

Our Wedding Day
August 22, 1948

Freshman college days at Indiana University, 1945, reading
The Date Magazine, an IU publication

O. U. Mutz II Taken at Space Conditioning the day we left Harrisonburg

Marcy at Court Manor

Bill at Court Manor

Hide-A-Way's Laura Belle, age 6 months

Court Manor's Fire Bell weanling champion of 5 futurities

Court Manor's Wild Fire!

Junior Seay riding Miss Marcy

Life is a Cabernet (Rudy) $50,000 winner of All American Cup with Brad Cougill

Top Brass as a yearling

Two Generations (Left to Right, Standing) Marcy, Jean
(Left to Right, Seated) Bill, O. U. Mutz II

Our Columbus, Indiana home 1968

December 17, 1988

The Greiling Family
Bill and Emma Greiling Jean, Bill, and Paul

Chapter 14

COURT MANOR WEST

PLEASE TAKE ME with you, Mr. Oz!"

I looked over at Lee Young across the back of a horse. Laura Belle was my first brood mare, an offspring of Jim Aikman's breeding program at Hide-A-Way Farms. I had bought her after the move to Harrisonburg, Virginia, and I fully intended to take her with her new foal, Whispering Belle, back to Indiana—but I hadn't counted on taking Lee Young. His wife was a strong woman with fixed ideas about where she wanted to be and what she wanted out of life, and I was not about to mess with her, especially on the eve of my new job back in Indiana.

"I'm sorry, Lee," I shook my head, "I'll call you when I need you."

Every other week, after our return to Indiana, Lee would call me. "Do you need me yet, Mr. Oz? Do you need me?"

Lee had turned into a reliable horseman along with his other many duties around Court Manor. He had taught Bill how to hammer a nail and how to build a fence when fixing up the house and barn. Once the horses arrived, he had Bill mastering the princely art of cleaning out stalls.

I was quite sure he was exactly the kind of person I wanted to look after my growing stable of Saddlebreds at Court Manor West once we had finished its construction and were settled. With considerable pleasure, I was finally able to give Lee a different answer to his perpetual question than "Not yet."

"You come two weeks from Saturday, Lee, and you'll even have your own place to stay," I told him, gratified by the exclamations of pleasure that started pouring in from the other end of the line.

A little over two weeks later, I met Lee and his wife, fresh off the bus from Harrisonburg, Virginia, at the station in Columbus. One look at his wife's face told me they had come to stay.

And stay they did. Columbus, Indiana, would be their home for the rest of their lives.

Although they eventually owned their own home in Columbus, Lee always had living quarters in the barn at Court Manor West. He knew the location of every screw, nut, and bolt that the farm owned. I was quite confident that with Lee there, Court Manor West was on its way to producing some of the finest Saddlebreds in the country, even though my time and energies were expended on growing Cosco.

THE RESURRECTION OF A DREAM

Bex Rex was a Saddlebred with very good action. The more his performance improved, the better mine looked. As a boy I had begun to fancy that I was going to be competitive in exhibition. Jim Aikman, by then my best friend, was quite sure he was going to be competitive, and his parents were ready to do whatever it would take to make him so. After they replaced Star, the horse that my parents had almost purchased and which had triggered that first and last hostility between Jim and me, Jim's transition into exhibition accelerated and his personal interest in Saddlebreds crystallized.

"Aren't you just thrilled about Oz's interest in horses?" asked Jim's mother one day while she and my mother watched us putting our mounts through their paces.

"Yes, I'm thrilled," Laura Mutz replied, "but there are other things I think Oz should be thrilled about too." She repeated the conversation to me later, emphasizing the "other things," such as music and sports and my young people's group at church, in such a way that she left no doubt in my mind about how far she was prepared to support my riding dreams.

Jim's parents, however, fed his passion for horses. When his interest expanded into the area of breeding, they bought him his first brood mare, Angel Wings. Not too long afterward, they purchased a young stallion named Mr. Christopher from Orchard Lawn Farms in Muncie, Indiana. Orchard Lawn belonged to the Ball brothers, whose fortune was made through the production of glass canning jars. Although the Balls were known for pro-ducing excellent Saddlebreds, the offspring of Chris were a disappointment to Jim.

But there was no disappointment with Gallant Lady, the mare they had bought Jim to show. She was a beautiful, three-gaited mare who was a handful for any rider. By the time Jim had mastered riding her, his life's passion was assured.

Eventually Jim's parents purchased Hide-A-Way Farms in Marion County, Indiana. They didn't know when they bought the place, which straddles three counties, that in addition to the barn in Marion County, the property housed a still in Johnson County and a small airport in Shelby County. Bootleggers had owned the land during Prohibition, producing considerable quantities of "white lightning." If law enforcement came out to stop them from Marion County, the proprietors would simply walk across the county line where the officers had no jurisdiction. Biplanes could land very short, and they would come in, pick up their illegal cargo, and fly back out.

In the process of remodeling the barn after they had purchased the farm, Jim's father found the old still in the barn's basement. In high school, I helped Jim paint the barn for his father. George Aikman would stand below, looking up at us while we painted, and trot out one of the pithy little sayings he was known for.

"A pint of paint on a barn is kind of like makeup on a woman's face, boys," he would begin. "It sure covers a lot of sin!"

He was lucky we didn't forget ourselves and drop five gallons of paint on him!

When Harold and Frank Mutz began looking for a farm, they settled on a property just two miles from the Aikmans' on Acton Road, and George Aikman probably helped them find it. The original hamlet of Acton had been sold off, as it was never very large. The big brick farmhouse stood next door to the old Acton grade school, and the old Acton cemetery was located directly in back of it. Virgil Russell was the Acton blacksmith and an excellent horseshoer, and Jim and I would take our horses to him to be shod when necessary. A short walk of three or four blocks took me from our farm to the door of Virge's shop. Jim eventually used Virge to haul his horses to Thomas's Stables five to seven miles away.

When Jean decided to let me marry her, Jim's current best brood mare, Grasslands Debutante, had just had her first foal by Indiana Ace. Jim, who had always liked my mother, named the newborn filly Hide-A-Way's Laura Belle, after my mother. He entered her into the American Saddlebred competitions at the Kentucky State Fair as a weanling and won first place for the champion weanling. As Jim made his way out of the exhibition ring, proudly bearing his silver bowl and blue ribbon, Garland Bradshaw, a well-known figure in the Saddlebred world, accosted him.

"Son, will you sell me that horse?" he asked in a soft Southern drawl.

"Yes, sir, I'll sell her," Jim replied.

"What will you take for her?" Bradshaw continued.

"Twenty-five hundred dollars, sir."

"What's your stall number, young man?"

I had just been married on the twenty-second of August, and I had been planning on buying that filly from Jim, but Jim knew I didn't have that kind of money. It was more than either he or I had imagined the horse to be worth.

Jim gave him the stall number, and Garland Bradshaw met him there with a check in hand. He bought Laura Belle and took her to the Indiana State Fair, where he won the weanling championship with her. Bradshaw owned Hide-A-Way's Laura Belle for the next sixteen years, but I knew where she was. She produced several very nice colts, including two or three that consistently won competitions.

After my mother died in 1963, I inherited a modest sum from her estate. During the following year of processing our grief and negotiating the sale of Peerless to Electronic Specialty Company and the move to Court Manor in Virginia, I determined to take that inheritance and go to Danville, Kentucky, and buy Laura Belle back from Garland Bradshaw. Jim Aikman negotiated the sale for me, and Bradshaw sold her to me, in foal, for two thousand five hundred dollars.

I had exited the horse business with the sale of Bex Rex my sophomore or junior year in high school, although I had been showing horses since age twelve. My parents made the actual decision to sell, but I never resented that decision. In fact, I was fully supportive, as I was responsible for his care, which meant spending a day a week going out from Indianapolis to the farm in Acton to clean and exercise him (our tenant farmer took care of his daily feed).

By this time, my dreams of competing in exhibition had become more realistic. I knew that Bex Rex's high back would disqualify him in most five-gaited classes because of his conformation. He was not a show horse and not a breeder, just not a good enough horse. I was too busy with other interests to put in the time necessary to become excellent, and I was the only person who rode Rex regularly.

All things considered, I wanted out of the horse business. With the move to Court Manor in Harrisonburg and the purchase of Hide-A-Way's Laura Belle in 1965, I suddenly found myself back in it.

COURT MANOR FARM

In Virginia, I discovered I enjoyed the breeding side of the Saddlebred business and created Court Manor Farm. Laura Belle was heavy with foal when I purchased her in 1965. Less than a year later, Whispering Bell was foaled at Jim Aikman's Hide-A-Way Farms while Court Manor Farm transitioned from Harrisonburg, Virginia, to its new location at Court Manor West in Columbus, Indiana. I had bred Laura Belle to Jim Aikman's stud, Firefly Supreme (by Valley View Supreme out of Spring Cheer). Firefly Supreme had produced several world champions, including weanlings, yearlings, and three-year-olds. He also won the three-year-old five-gaited stake before Jim retired him.

Fire Bell, Firefly Supreme's colt out of Laura Belle, was the best horse Court Manor Farm ever raised. He won the World Championship Weanling Class in 1967. Wildfire! was the last of Laura Belle's offspring; she was twenty-two when he was foaled. He won Reserve World Champion Two-Year-Old in 1972. Lee Young, his request finally granted, witnessed every one of these events after Court Manor Farm was moved to Columbus.

Easter Storm was the second brood mare added to the stable while in Virginia, purchased from a man named John Hale, back in Indiana. Jim Aikman, whose longevity in the Saddlebred breeding business is unparalleled in the country, guided me in making good purchases. Not long after we had begun our breeding program in Virginia, he called me, and I could sense he was a bit excited. He had received a telephone call from a man in Columbus with a Saddlebred for sale.

"People tell me you would be interested in a good saddle horse," the man had told Jim.

"Well, I would," Jim replied.

"It belongs to a woman I married a few weeks ago," the man continued. "You wanna look at it?"

Jim had gone to see the horse, and now he was on the phone to me. "Oz," he finished, "buy the horse, just buy the horse! She won't cost you much. Six hundred dollars will do it, and I guarantee you'll get your money out of her!"

I was not about to ignore a tip from such a reliable source. Brynfan Prophet's Delight was duly purchased and later moved to Court Manor West with the rest. She was a gorgeous Saddlebred mare with extreme action. Her first colt, Fire Up!, was World Champion Weanling in 1968.

Fire Bell had been World Champion Yearling in 1968.

The stables at Court Manor West had won back-to-back world championships in its first three years of operation!

Our first foal out of Laura Belle, Whispering Belle, was a good-looking horse, but her neck was too short to be a big-time winner. We bred her as a two-year-old, and she produced Miss Marcy, who placed third in the three-year-old world championship in 1973. We had three or four more foals out of Whispering Belle and then sold her. Her offspring were good but not great, and in the competitive world of horse training, we could only afford to train championship-caliber horses.

From its beginning, whatever we added to the stable at Court Manor

West seemed to work. Large-scale breeders such as Garland Bradshaw maintain twenty to thirty brood mares in their stables and two to three stallions. Bradshaw would win a mature horse championship every two to three years throughout the late sixties and early seventies. Such breeders considered themselves fortunate to have 80 percent of their mares to be in foal in any given year.

At Court Manor West, 100 percent of our mares were in foal, and we were winning championships every year with a herd of four brood mares.

THE HORSE BUSINESS

Northern Dancer won the Kentucky Derby in 1964. Almost twenty years later, Sheikh Mohammed bin Rashid Al Maktoum of the ruling family of Dubai (United Arab Emirates), bidding in a pool of buyers at Keeneland Racecourse in Lexington, Kentucky (which included representatives of the Queen of England), paid the record-breaking sum of $10,200,000 for Snaafi Dancer, the yearling offspring of Northern Dancer. As a yearling, Snaafi Dancer had never been broken or raced. At that point he was just a pretty horse with royal parents.

Unfortunately for Sheikh Maktoum, Snaafi Dancer could not race and could not produce progeny. He had paid over ten million dollars for a sterile horse. Within a few years, the market for yearlings at Keeneland broke. It rallied again in the late nineties, but thirty years later it still remains unpredictable.

When the market for thoroughbreds goes down, the market for standardbreds goes down, and so does the market for American Saddlebreds. Foala Firefly was a nice five-gaited mare by Firefly Supreme, the second foal of Brynfan Prophet's Delight. We eventually sold her, and she had thirteen foals during the process of our trying to find our way back to the bloodline that produced those early 1970s winners.

Queen Jean was foaled the same year as Miss Marcy and was unquestionably the prettiest horse we ever raised. We sold her to one of the preeminent horsemen in Kentucky, who was never able to get a training horse out of her. She produced twelve foals, but not one of them was what we would call a "take-it-to-the-bank" horse. Marketing genetics, which is what the horse business is all about, is one of the highest-risk industries to invest in.

Shortly after he had been recognized as the Grand Champion of the weanling class, I bought Life is a Cabernet. While I didn't pay anything remotely near to Sheikh Maktoum's record ten million dollars, I paid what I considered a lot of money for a weanling. After that, I saw that he was taken care of. He was put into training when he was a year and a half old, and when he was three, we won the Grand Championship for Three Year Olds with him.

That was an extra bonus: he won fifty thousand dollars. As a weanling, Rudy (his stable name) had won $37,600. Two years later, he won another $50,000 and seemed like a safe investment.

We continued to keep Rudy in training, and I was quite certain I had another World Championship ahead of me. Then the horse developed a restriction in his throat. After a rather serious operation to gauge his ability to breathe under pressure, it became evident that he would never be able to maintain the kind of performance it would take to be a great horse. Therefore, we donated Rudy to the equestrian program at Stephens College in Columbia, Missouri. A veterinarian from Kentucky, looking over their horse herd one day, saw him being ridden by a novice horsewoman and diagnosed what was wrong with Rudy's breathing. He offered to donate his services to Stephens, who politely referred the decision back to us.

"No, we've given you the horse," we said, "The horse is yours. Whatever you choose to do with him is all right with us."

So the college accepted the vet's offer and had him operate on Rudy. Now he is competitive again in his events.

I was deep enough into the horse breeding business that I generated fairly solid interest in my horses when I tried to sell them. A common truism among horse trainers worked against me: that a beautiful weanling will not turn into a beautiful mature horse. Some horse breeders, of course, operate on the theory that a world champion weanling will also be a world champion three-year-old and a world champion in maturity. Partly to prove the those trainers wrong and dispel what he and I consider a myth, Jim Aikman organized the creation of the All American Cup, the ultimate competition for young American Saddlebreds.

Ironically, of the twenty-six first, second, and third place weanlings that have been crowned at the All American Cup, only one to date has won the three-year-old class. That was Rudy.

The horse that sired that one double champion was his sire, Kalarama Cabernet.

I purchased Court Manor's Top Brass after he was the World Champion Weanling in 2010, certain that he would be the World Champion Three-Year-Old in 2013. He had already netted his previous owner thirty-five thousand dollars; the opportunities for a return on my investment if he won the three-year-old championship were very bright.

I put Top Brass in training in Simpsonville, Kentucky (close to Lexington). A little over three months into the program, his trainer called me: "Mr. Mutz, you'd better come and look at your colt."

I was reluctant to expend my limited mobility on a trip to Kentucky to see a horse, so I asked Jim Aikman to size up the situation for me. Jim's phone call was sobering.

"Ozzie, your horse has wobbles."

"Wobbles?" I was quite certain that in all my years in the Saddlebred business, I had never heard of "wobbles." "Jim," I replied, "I've never had a horse with wobbles before."

Jim was deeply sympathetic. "Neither have I, Oz," he said.

I talked to the horse's vet, who described wobbles disease to me. Typically caused by a neurological malfunction in the horse's vertebrae, the horse will develop instability in its gait. In advanced cases, like that of Top Brass, the horse will simply and suddenly fall down while being ridden.

Top Brass is a beautiful, big horse, standing at seventeen and one half hands. We followed medical recommendations, had surgery, and put him back in training, but stability remains an issue.

For me, the jury is still out. When I was in the hospital business, trying to figure out what caused alcoholism, I came across a British study researching the possibilities of a genetic role. Their research showed that half of the children whose biological parents were alcoholic had significantly higher rates of alcoholism even when raised by "genetically sober" adoptive parents. I continue to consider genetics, not maturity, as the decisive factor in a weanling's potential. Jean and Marcy will roll their eyes and humor me; Bill, who worked with the horses of Court Manor Farm on a regular basis and developed considerable expertise as a trainer in his own right, will say, "I know, I know. Cupped foot on the left front one generation, cupped foot on the left in the next."

DOWNSIZING

After our initial success in the Saddlebred breeding business in the late sixties and early seventies, we plateaued. Laura Belle was in labor with her fifth foal, at the age of twenty-three. It was a Saturday morning and I was at home when Bill came and fetched me to the barn. "Dad, you need to come and look at this mare." The whites of the old mare's eyes had turned to yellow, and I knew there would be no more foals from Laura Belle.

In 1973 I had bought a chestnut mare at an auction, and she was in foal by a chestnut stallion. Once we had her installed at Court Manor West, a black cat took up residence on her back and lived on that mare's back. Lee Young could be a little superstitious at times, and the black cat was on his mind.

"Mr. Oz," he finally asked, "if that mare has a black colt, will you name it after me?"

His interest reminded me of that promise when the mare started to bag. To everyone's surprise but Lee's, her foal was coal black—but there was still one problem: it was a filly.

"Do you still want me to call her Lee Young?" I asked him.

"No, sir, I don't want you to do that," Lee dissented. "I want you to call her *Miss* Lee Young!"

And so I did.

Leaving Lee Young was difficult after so many years in the horse business, but by 1979 the corporate ladder had taken me back to Indianapolis. I was tired of driving a hundred miles round trip to work every day. Marcy and Bill had finished college and were launched into families and careers of their own. We had purchased a second home in Naples, Florida, where Jean could spend the winters away from the biting Midwestern cold that aggravated her arthritis. During winter, I spent every other weekend in Naples with her.

So we embarked on yet another construction project and built a house in Indianapolis. In 1980, we sold Court Manor West, and with its sale came the dissolution of most of the stock of Court Manor Farm.

After we sold Court Manor West, someone had come to the farm and bought a mare, and I arrived home from the office about the time he was winding up the sale. I sold him two more weanlings, clinching the sale by telling him we'd deliver them as we had delivered our horses many times before.

Jean's birthday, August 9, was always during the Illinois State Fair. She was very game about having to share her birthdays with equestrian events, but giving up seeing my father on her birthday to deliver some horses made her reluctant.

"We have already planned to meet my dad and stepmother in Lexington," I suggested. "Why don't we just take the horses to Huntington, West Virginia, ourselves and make an outing of it?"

Jean agreed, and we loaded up the horses and headed for West Virginia. The day began sunny and mild, but the closer we came to Huntington, the more ominous the weather grew. By the time we arrived at Camden Park,

West Virginia, and located its owner, who had bought the horses, it was cold and snowing heavily.

The man asked us to drive to the top of a nearby mountain and deposit the horses in a pasture there.

I objected. "These horses are from flat land," I protested. "I can't do that." I was also rapidly assessing the growing snow cover on the roads and my truck's condition.

The man was adamant, and Jean was upset.

"Ozzie, let's just take them home," she said.

"If the man has bought them," I countered, a bit grimly, "he has the right to tell us where they go."

I refused to drive the truck all the way to the top, and ended up walking two of the horses to the mountaintop; their new owner walked the other one.

By the time I arrived on the top of that mountain, I was pretty sure Jean was right. We should have taken the horses—a mare and two female foals—home.

Jean would have nothing to do with leaving those poor animals there. She had never really liked horses. In fact, they frightened her a little. But she was categorically opposed to dumping our Indiana bred and born live-stock on an Appalachian peak in the middle of a snowstorm. "You can't be serious, leaving those horses in this climate!" she repeated in shocked disbelief.

I didn't feel I had any real options. Our time at Court Manor West was at an end.

Chapter 15

TOUCH-AND-GO

URING THE YEARS of Marcy and Bill's childhood, Jean and I would look for creative ways to carve family time out of my hectic schedule. We had arranged that she and the children would drive to Washington, DC, from Virginia, where they had gone to visit her mother, and they would meet me there when I flew in. After spending a few days absorbing the culture in the Smithsonian and touring national monuments, Jean and her mother and Marcy would drive back to Indianapolis, and Bill would fly home with me.

A fog was keeping us grounded, so Bill and I were in the waiting room of the executive terminal, a small area not much larger than an average living room. I was still in the airplane business, flying a Cessna from Sky Travel. I was standing there, waiting for the weather to change, so Bill and I could begin our journey.

Suddenly a group of people began crowding in from the back door of the terminal. I immediately recognized a very tall figure as the vice president of the United States, Lyndon Baines Johnson. I was aware from the news that he had just been representing the country at talks in Berlin.

"Bill," I asked, "how would you like to meet the vice president of the United States?"

He seemed willing enough. "Fine! Come with me!" I added, immediately steering him toward the vice president's entourage. When Bill registered the crowd of people ahead of him, he began to drag his feet, but I ignored his growing reluctance.

"Mr. Vice President," I hailed him, "I am Mr. Mutz from Indiana. I have a nine-year-old boy here who would like to be able to say he had shaken the hand of the vice president of the United States."

"Why, of course," Lyndon Johnson agreed in his Texan drawl. He reached over and picked Bill up as if he were a lead pencil, held him on his arm, and said, pulling his other hand out of his pocket, "Son, here's a ticket to my box in the United States Senate. I am going to sign it, and anytime you take it to the Senate, your dad can sign it and you can sit in my box."

I felt ashamed of myself for not voting for him because he was so considerate to my son, Bill, who didn't want to wash his hand for a week!

Lyndon Johnson was the first president-to-be I met, but he certainly wasn't the last. During the midseventies, I was appointed president of the Mid American World Trade Association, the brainchild of Indiana Governor Edgar Whitcomb. The mission of the association was to connect Indiana business interests internationally. By then Japan had certainly become a global player, poised to impact the automotive industry. By encouraging closer ties through the Mid American World Trade Association, Ed Whitcomb hoped to create an access to that pot of gold for Indiana manufacturers and businesses.

Ed, who had been a second lieutenant in the Army Air Corps, served as an aerial navigator in the Philippines. He was the only qualified celestial navigator competent in a flight of planes, progressing from North America to South America, across to Africa, and then from Africa to the Philippines. Seventeen minutes after they had landed at Clark Air Base near Manila, the Japanese began bombing. It was December 7, 1941. His book, *Escape from Corregidor*, describes Whitcomb's subsequent capture, torture, and imprisonment by the Japanese. With another prisoner, he successfully swam the shark-infested straits between Corregidor and the Philippine mainland, and eventually made his way back to Allied territory under an assumed identity.

I later served as president of the Mid American Trade Association under Ed's directorship. In that capacity, I went with Ed to the Indianapolis airport to meet with the governor of California, who had come to evaluate how Ed had formed the world trade association and assess its applicability to the state of California.

Governor Ronald Reagan could not have been a more gracious, gentle, decent man. He was dressed immaculately, and I started looking for a copy of his suit immediately afterwards, but never found one.

We had two governors, the state police, plainclothesmen, and airport security at that meeting, but Ronald Reagan had no entourage with him. He was in Indianapolis to assess the situation for himself, an action not uncommon for him.

Two or three years later, when I was in Washington, DC, with a delegation from Indiana, President Ronald Reagan recognized me. He had his budget director present me with a pair of cufflinks that said "Ronald Reagan" on their backs. Perhaps his liaison had run through a list of names and knew who was going to be present that the president had met, but I was convinced that Ronald Reagan had recognized me.

"How is Governor Whitcomb, Mr. Mutz?" he asked me.

His advance team had done their job well.

TOUCH-AND-GO TRAINING

In an ideal landing, an airplane pilot structures his or her glide path in such a way that touchdown is in the first third of the runway, but not in the first part of that first third. The goal is to stop in the cross section where the runways converge. Landing short can make a pilot miss his goal.

Missing the goal can create all kinds of problems for getting the craft back on track. For example, at most airports there is typically a drainage puddle in the corners of the cross section. If you landed short and stopped before the cross section, it was easy to turn too short and miss the taxi line. If a pilot is not following the taxi line, a wheel can slip in this triangle of water, mud and concrete. This situation creates a real problem for a light aircraft whose wheel is not much bigger than the four-to-six-inch-deep ditch in which it is stuck.

Good pilots who do multiple landings may have this happen once or twice a year. When it does happen, the pilot has only one option. He or she must shut the airplane down so the turning prop won't inadvertently kill someone who carelessly gets in its way. Then the pilot must get out of the airplane and manually get it back on the runway.

Bill and I were landing in Indianapolis on our way back from Washington, DC, where he had just shaken the hand of Lyndon Johnson. About twice a month, Bill flew with me. The privileges of owning my own airplane included the privilege of paying to fly it. Relative to other forms of transportation, it was expensive to operate. For this reason, I'd try to have someplace I was going for business before I'd take a family member with me. I didn't have to go to Louisville or Kokomo or Terre Haute or South Bend that often, but when I did, it was good training experience for them. The Purdue airport at Lafayette provided an excellent venue for practicing landings and takeoffs since it was maintained in particularly good shape for training pilots. In my little plane, we could take off from Sky Harbor in Indianapolis and be on the ground in Lafayette in twenty minutes.

I was not an inexperienced pilot the day Bill and I arrived on the runway in Indianapolis from Washington, DC, but I was a rather dense father. I landed short and caught a wheel of my Cessna in the corner ditch of the cross section. Bill at nine years of age was used to being my helping hand.

"Shut it down, Dad," he offered, "and I'll pull it out."

He popped out of the cockpit and reached down to pick up the wheel and set it on the concrete. His fingers brushed the disc brakes, and suddenly I was calling ground control, desperate for help, because my son's fingers were burned terribly. The response seemed long in coming. First I had to tune to the right frequency on the radio; then I had to identify myself, tell them where I was, and explain the need for mechanical help as well as emergency medical aid. They had to shut the airport down while hooks were placed on the front of the airplane and we were tugged to a fixed operation base. They did, however, remember the first aid kit.

If I had had a hundred more hours in the air, the incident would never have happened, as I had gone beyond my level of competence. With a little more experience, I would have foreseen the probability of this happening.

I always pulled the airplane by its propeller. Bill, who is mechanically much more adept than I, had quickly sized up the root of the problem and applied action where it was most needed. I was not experienced enough to anticipate this response from him.

We do recurrent training in business to provide the experience necessary for successful operations. The flying of an airplane does not demand the highest level of competence. It's the landing and take-off that does.

The military developed the touch-and-go training exercise to optimize pilot experience in this delicate, precise, and life-and-death art of landing and taking off. The pilot touches the ground in the first third of the runway. As he rolls over the next 20 to 30 percent of the runway, he checks his alignment and his airspeed and synchronizes his instruments. Then he uses the last third or more of the runway to jam the throttle up to full power and take off without ever coming to a complete stop. To execute a touch-and-go properly, the pilot must be able to shut the engine to idle speed in the air as he (or she) is preparing to land and glide the craft onto the runway.

Touch-and-go serves at least three critical purposes for the US Air Force. First, it produces pilots whose flying expertise optimizes use of runways. Because the training can be done in formation with other aircraft, airplanes can land or take off three abreast, allowing an airfield to get three times as many planes on or off the ground in an hour or two of good weather. Second, because pilots can circle the practice runway and repeat the touch-and-go multiple times, they can accrue significantly more experience in landing per hour of flight time than typical trainees. Finally, being prepared to take off while landing gives the pilot unique experience in what to do if a landing must be aborted at the last minute.

LEARNING TOUCH-AND-GO AT COSCO

The first significant action I had taken on assuming the presidency of Cosco was to sell Cal-Dak. I had visited it in Little Rock, gathering information from other business connections in the area that only locals could provide. One day's inspection had told me all I needed to know, and we sold Cal-Dak as quickly as we could.

Clarence Hamilton wasn't sure about my decision.

"It is inconceivable to me, Mr. Hamilton," I replied, "that I would ever have had anything to do with buying that business."

"I decided to buy that business," Clarence huffed back.

"That doesn't make any difference," I returned evenly. "I would not have been involved in that purchase had I been your employee. If I am serving you the way I should be, I'd be getting rid of it."

Cosco had purchased Cal-Dak, but they never bought Rubbermaid. We danced with Rubbermaid every time they played the waltz, and we had one chance to merge with them. We should have done it. We would have done it, but I was under pressure from Clarence.

Clarence couldn't be chairman.

The chair of Rubbermaid was very clear on this point. "We've got a deal that we can do," he conceded, "but I have to be the chairman."

"No," Clarence insisted. "If we merge, I am going to be the chairman."

Newell finally bought Rubbermaid. We danced with Newell, too, and it broke up for the same reason.

Twenty years later, the chairman of Newell and Fred Risk and I all had homes in Naples, Florida, where our wives would winter. Clarence Hamilton and his wife wintered in Phoenix, Arizona.

George Hamilton was Clarence's son and thirteen years my junior. I knew a significant purpose of my job was to get him ready to run the business. My goal was to be his father's successor; George's goal was to then succeed me. That scenario should have been realized, but Clarence undermined it when he refused to recognize the superiority of Rubbermaid's claim to the board chairmanship.

Rubbermaid had no controlling family at its helm, as Cosco did.

But Clarence couldn't get over the slight.

KOHLBERG KRAVIS ROBERTS & COMPANY

I had been president of Cosco for a year when two young men, Henry Kravis and George R. Roberts, contacted me. Kravis and Roberts were first cousins, in their twenties, and worked for the investment banker Bear Stearns. They were interested in buying Tucker.

"Do you know how to do a leveraged buyout?" they asked me.

My response was glassy-eyed. "I don't know how to do that," I admitted. I wasn't unusual at that time. The first leveraged buyout (LBO) was in 1955. Kohlberg, Kravis, and Roberts, pioneering the process for Bear Stearns, had just engineered their first significant leveraged buyout, by acquiring Orkin Exterminating Company in 1964. In these experimental stages of leveraged buyouts, the three associates were targeting small, private companies headed by retiring owner/operators seeking alternatives to acquisition by a competitor. I needed an injection of cash for Cosco, and Tucker had been on KKR's radar.

I was in my office on a Friday afternoon, gathering papers and preparing for a Sunday flight to New York, where a third or fourth generation contract lay on Henry Kravis's desk, ready for me to sign at eight o'clock Monday morning. Cosco's board of directors had authorized Tucker's sale because they recognized that the company needed cash.

Clarence Hamilton called me into his office at four o'clock.

"Stop the sale," he barked. "I don't want to sell Tucker!"

I debated, but in the end I had no choice. We pulled the plug.

I couldn't understand his actions. Clarence had the authority to block the sale, but it didn't make sense that he would. It was an obviously unwise thing to do.

I informed Henry Kravis and George Roberts that the deal was off, but I couldn't elaborate further.

On Sunday, we went to the country club for lunch after church as usual. Clarence and his wife were there as well, which, too, was typical.

I knew he was ticked, since we had butted heads on Friday afternoon over the sale of Tucker. I wasn't concerned by my conflict with Clarence over Tucker because I knew I was supported by Cosco's board. They had no inkling of his change of plans.

My wife and children are sensitive, perceptive people, and Jean seemed to sense something more than strain in Clarence Hamilton's behavior.

"What's wrong with Clarence?" she asked me.

I shrugged. "We butted heads over Tucker."

"Ozzie, he's acting strange." Jean's eyes were wide and expressive but her voice soft. "I think he's thinking about firing you."

Monday morning, Clarence called me into his office at eight-thirty. By nine I was fired.

Clarence considered himself gracious. "Oz," he said, "instead of saying 'Pack your gear and get out of here,' I'm giving you three months to relocate."

He had it all worked out.

The situation was hardly comfortable for me or my family. I stayed at Cosco a couple of weeks, longer than most would have done. It was the way I would have wanted to be treated had the roles been reversed. I downloaded all the essential private information to subordinates and stayed long enough to get that done.

In a company with two thousand five hundred employees, people don't go into mourning because the boss has been fired. Some are always happy. In the final analysis, Clarence Hamilton kept Tucker but lost money. Cosco was a fine manufacturing business with high technology using steel tubing, and its manufacturing capabilities were excellent, although not as exceptional as Tucker's. However, selling Tucker would have provided the capital to sharpen Cosco's competitive edge, a concern one would have thought had priority from Clarence Hamilton's point of view.

Selling a business is never a question of "if" but "when." I did a present value calculation of Cosco when it later sold. What KKR had offered us for Tucker was a greater present value than the nineteen million Clarence Hamilton received for all of Cosco, including Tucker, five years later. Clarence didn't want to sell Tucker, but his failure to make timely, hard choices and address the financial need behind our negotiations with KKR meant that he and his family were eventually forced to sell.

By that time, Fred Risk and I were more successful than either of us had dreamed of being, developing the business model that we most enjoyed: mergers and acquisitions.

Chapter 16

JENN-AIR

CLARENCE LONG GRADUATED from the Indiana University School of Business in 1939 and went straight to work as an accountant in the Indianapolis branch of Ernst and Ernst (now Ernst and Young). I met him over the fence in our backyard.

Jean and I, still relatively newlyweds in spirit even though we had celebrated two wedding anniversaries, had just settled into our new home located at 3913 Devon Drive, the house we built with our first savings. Clarence and Millie's house fronted Forty-Second Street, but our backyards met somewhere near the halfway mark between Devon and Forty-Second. When Clarence Long was first hired by Alwin Ernst in 1939, he worked as one of three employees staffing the accounting firm's base in Indianapolis. Alwin Ernst maintained his company headquarters in Cleveland, Ohio, where he was born, but by the time Clarence Long had completed his long tenure with them, the Indianapolis branch had become their second largest office, moving from a payroll of three to a payroll of about two hundred fifty people.

In the 1960s world of Ernst and Ernst, no one dared rock Clarence Long's boat. He had landed the Eli Lilly and Company account for Ernst and Ernst in the early fifties, and he was considered untouchable after that.

Indeed, he went on to become a managing partner in the firm, at that time one of the Big Eight, then one of the Big Six, and now one of the Big Four firms who mediate the crossroads of the world's fortunes.

When Cosco jettisoned me, Clarence Long was of indispensable help in mediating the crossroads of my career—Clarence *and* Kohlberg, Kravis, and Roberts.

INDEPENDENCE

Recognizing that they had contributed to my termination, Henry Kravis and George Roberts felt badly and contacted me.

"If there's anything we can do to make up for this, don't hesitate to ask us, Oz," I was told. I was an established corporate executive in my thirties; they were young entrepreneurs in their twenties.

At the time, I was still suffering from shock and had nothing in mind. Once someone on the company board gets unhappy with the company president, it is only a matter of time. They will begin hanging every mistake, every unfavorable turn of fortune, on him or her. A generation was turned out of their senior positions in American business by company boards and chairs during this time period. I was just one of them.

Fred Risk was soon to be another.

Fred was having trouble at Indiana National. He was running the bank aggressively as per his Board of Directors' wishes, but problems had surfaced with particular board members. If the writing was not on the wall for Fred by that time, he could feel the hand poised in the air preparing to put something there.

"Don't worry, Oz," he reassured me when I called and broke the news of my firing to him. "We'll find something to do."

"We" was the operative word in that telephone conversation. Since Peerless days, when Fred was our company banker, we had worked together, doing acquisitions and mergers for our employers—Fred for Indiana National, and I for Peerless or Space Conditioning or Cosco. Our individual expertise had grown. When I left Cosco, the foundation of my business philosophy was reasonably well developed: buy, build, and sell.

All companies are sold. I know how to acquire a company, correct its obvious deficiencies, and resell it. I did not know who would buy it from me when I was acquiring it, but someone would, I was sure of that. The reselling may not happen in the classic sense of the word—the acquiring of this "new and improved" version I created for someone else may be through the merger of companies.

The thought that "bigger is better" (*better* being understood as more powerful or more useful) drives the thirst for consolidation. I can always make a little money from the person thinking this way. Too big, however, undermines profitability. That is why all businesses are eventually bought or sold.

When the driver of the bus changes, the philosophy determining the bus's direction changes. I'd had enough experience with bus drivers and buses by 1971. I now sought to figure out how to be both the consolidator and the one who does the breakup. In fact, if you are one, you need to develop the skills to be both.

Consolidate or break up. Buy or sell. My structural philosophy for growing businesses was clearly in place.

Fred had arrived at the same conclusions, and our partnership was a match made in heaven. But it was Clarence Long who launched us.

ENTER LOU JENN

Working for Ernst and Ernst, Clarence always had leads. I didn't want to move again, and I didn't want to leave the Midwest. "Clarence," I asked, "help me find something to buy or sell. You're in an accounting firm. Accounting firms always run across someone who should be selling."

"Lou Jenn." The first two words out of Clarence's mouth were to become something of a blessing and a curse. "You know Lou Jenn, don't you, Oz? He needs you, but you will have to be careful how you approach him. Make yourself available as a consultant because that is all he thinks he needs. But what he really needs is you, full-time."

By May of 1971 I was back at work as an independent consultant to the Jenn-Air Corporation. By that fall, two things had surfaced.

The president of Jenn-Air had fallen into increasingly tense relations with the company's owner. Lou Jenn owned 100 percent of his company. He had begun to make overtures to me about becoming his executive vice president.

I was flattered and told Lou so. "But I would have to be the chief operating officer, bottom line, and I would have to have a contract and the ownership of a substantial part of the stock. If we can't do that, Mr. Jenn," I finished, "I'm not available."

We negotiated and negotiated and negotiated. I was not about to give up my newfound and rather hard-won independence.

By December of 1971, we had agreed on a deal. I bought 12.5 percent of the business with an option to purchase enough more per year that in five to six years I would own a third of the company, paying for the stock as I went. My salary fundamentally replaced the income he had provided me as an independent consultant with a bonus based on the company's performance. Those two elements were sufficient to finance the 6 percent of company stock I was qualified to buy per annum. My bonus would be going back into the company as buyout funding.

Cash is the essential resource needed to buy a business, and I gave Lou Jenn cash on the day we closed. I borrowed from Lou Jenn the balance of money needed to make up the difference and paid it back to him as my quarterly bonuses accrued. In addition, my contract specified at least two days a week away from Jenn-Air, so I could hunt other deals. I had no intention of losing my independence again and having my family's fortunes at the mercy of another man's whims.

As an independent consultant, certain elements of my compensation had been unique. I had had a pension, an automobile, and the other trappings of being an employee of Jenn-Air. However, I had continued to operate as an independent merchandiser of businesses. Lou Jenn had already seen me do this because I had acquired a few businesses for him.

Certainly that is why Jenn was trying to hire me. By 1973 I had become president of Jenn-Air.

Although I was provided two days per week to develop my acquisitions and merger business on the side, Jenn had insisted on caveats. I was independent only in the sense that I could continue working on the deals that we had already begun and that were specifically listed in my contract. Fred was still chairman of Indiana National, and I was doing most of the work connected with our fledgling partnership. I could continue in my independent capacity only until I had successfully closed the purchases then in negotiation or had removed them from our pool. We had an unwritten agreement that Jenn himself had first crack at buying those from us. I had to give him the right of first refusal.

I was working on the acquisition of Mid-Con and Masterfit corporations at the time, among others. I was never working on less than six acquisitions or mergers at any given time, so there were others on that list as well. It certainly included Lou Jenn's personal brainchild: Atrium Housing, Incorporated.

ATRIUM

In 1937, not long after our family had moved from Edinburgh to Indianapolis, Harold Mutz had loaded us into the car and taken us to see an example of a historic initiative by the national government: one of the first federal public housing projects. Under FDR's New Deal, the Public Works Administration had launched fifty low-cost public housing projects across the United States. Lockefield Gardens in Indianapolis was one of those original fifty and unique in its spacious, parklike, community-friendly construction. It was often touted as the flagship of federal low-cost housing, it sprawled over twenty-two acres along Indiana Avenue, replacing a slum notorious for its one "habitable" residence out of 363 "homes."

"That will be our next slum," Dad commented drily. I couldn't have been more than nine or ten. As I peered alertly out the car window, I was having a hard time seeing those bright, modern new apartments as a slum. My parents discussed how it takes more than buildings to change attitudes or mind-sets. I associated their comments with our neighbor next door, a

World War I veteran who had used his government bonus to buy a brand-new grey DeSoto that depreciated the moment he drove it off the auto lot.

I hadn't really understood the importance of Dad's words or our neighbor's example at that time. Not long after involving myself with Lou Jenn's Atrium Project, both came back to haunt me.

If Clarence Hamilton had lacked taste and decision, Lou Jenn overdosed on both. Jenn had a lot of vision, and following his vision could take another person somewhere he really didn't want to go.

By the midseventies, my father's prediction had come to pass. Rather than replacing a slum, Lockefield Gardens simply perpetuated it, becoming the new slum. It has since been leveled and rebuilt again, and considered one of the most dangerous areas of the city. A trio of billionaires are currently pushing a third generation of renovation in the area. It remains to be seen if they can break the cycle of new construction to slum to new construction to slum.

Lou Jenn thought he could do this in 1973. Through Atrium Housing Incorporated, Jenn proposed to replace slums and project housing with manufactured housing. He had developed and patented a model based on four mobile homes formed into an atrium or quadrangle, providing insular communities in a garden setting. Lou saw the cost savings of replacing stick-built structures erected on site with manufactured housing, but he failed to consider the availability of land. If we didn't have the ability to level an old slum, and the financing opportunity that accompanied that, where would we find the land for Atrium?

Under Lou's oversight, we incorporated Atrium Housing. Lou owned 50 percent of Atrium and I owned a third, and we began to market the 16.66 percent balance to a select group of Indianapolis businesspeople and lawyers. Lou was convinced his brainchild was going to be a barn burner and involving these people could only accelerate its growth.

F. C. Tucker, better known around Indiana as "Bud" Tucker, was the state's leading realtor. Anyone interested in land in Indiana knew he would eventually have to "Talk to Tucker." Bernie Landman was a brilliant FHA lawyer who had a great practice and was already wired into Washington, DC. Joe Boleman, who would eventually succeed Bud Tucker as a president of the Indiana Association of Realtors, also owned a piece of Atrium. We knew we needed these men on our board and actively involved to take Atrium public.

By late 1973 my forward vision had cleared and I knew we needed to get out of Atrium, but convincing Lou Jenn of that conclusion was the real struggle. Two facts were staring me in the face when I closed my eyes at night, two facts that could chase away sleep. First, I could not simultaneously be president of Jenn-Air and president of Atrium; and second, we were not going to acquire the dirt on which to build Atrium's model community.

My name wasn't on the patent; Lou Jenn's was. In the end, that convinced him. We couldn't get the land, and a clear conflict of interest stood in our path. It was time to cut our losses and run.

Jenn's solution was something that I had never seen done prior to my connection with him, and that I would never be involved in again. We refunded our investors' money. I wrote a check for a third of their investment and Lou wrote a check for the other two-thirds.

I had never before seen anyone do that. I probably wouldn't have done it myself, but Lou insisted, and I had no choice but to follow suit. At the time I thought it was his pride that forced him to this action, but since then, and after knowing him better, I am quite convinced it was entirely selfishness.

Ten years later, when I was well out of the picture, Jenn resurrected Atrium and succeeded in realizing its potential with himself as sole proprietor and his children as his investors. Atrium benefited Lou Jenn and only Lou Jenn. Everything plowed into it came back full circle to the Jenn family. He knew in 1973, he wanted to go ahead on his own. Their exhibition model proved to be unsuccessful. It was built on the original Atrium site.

My preferred operating model is a partnership. I consider the sharing of profit more than compensated for by the multiplied gains in opportunity, insight, and management strengths. Lou Jenn was perhaps a true entrepreneur. He didn't want to share anything.

The truth emerged slowly but clearly. Clarence Long, functioning as Jenn-Air's accountant with Ernst and Ernst, had seen this and strategically positioned me to counter Lou Jenn's weaknesses and help to keep Jenn-Air propelled forward. Jenn was a man of substantial creativity and genius. If I could define a need for him, he could figure out a product to fulfill that need. He had that kind of skill and that kind of vision. He's the kind of man who will succeed in spite of himself.

But Jenn abused his business about as badly as a business could be abused. He worked long hours, he worked creatively, and he produced products with a Unique Marginal Difference (UMD). Any money invested in Jenn-Air after its fifth year of existence was safe as long as Jenn had a halfway decent manager working for him. I don't know what he could have done to mess it up, but it is easy to get off on a tangent. Lou simply didn't know how to get his head down and gain three yards in a cloud of dust, to paraphrase Woody Hayes.

During the three years I was president of his company, we doubled the gross volume of Lou Jenn's sales and made as much money for him in 1975 as he'd had in gross sales in 1973, simply by getting a new customer for Jenn-Air products in San Francisco. R & K Distributors purchased more Jenn-Air products in one year than the entire sales the company had generated the year prior.

Jack Riggs was the "R" in R & K Distributors. Clarence Hamilton had hired him at Cosco to run our housewares division. Later Jack discovered that he preferred being in business for himself. Instead of becoming retaliatory or angry, I affirmed his talents.

"Jack," I told him, "if people want to do something badly enough, they will do it. I'd just like to keep working with you and see if we can't make lemonade out of our lemons."

Good hires now make good connections later. Hiring decisions are always the keys to the future in business.

Consequently, Jack Riggs and I became good friends. When I assumed the presidency of Jenn-Air, I knew he was to become the KitchenAid distributor in California, so I contacted him.

"Jack," I began, "I need your advice." I proceeded to explain to him our marketing issues. "If you were in my situation," I concluded, "what would you do? I need someone with your experience to give me some direction on this."

"Oz, the first thing I'd do," Jack replied, "is to get connected with a bunch of KitchenAid distributors who know how to market what you're selling." I listened while he explained how I could sell him on Jenn-Air.

Then I sold him on Jenn-Air. From that point on, we had a railcar sitting on the tracks every day, being loaded or unloaded for R & K Distributors in California.

Jack was an excellent merchant, and R & K had secured a supplier in Jenn-Air that never forgot them when they needed them.

Perhaps I was making Lou Jenn a little too successful. Given his performance with Atrium, I rather think he never intended me to realize my buyout of one-third of Jenn-Air stock.

Les Howell, my instructor in freshman accounting at Indiana University, had left academia to become a full-time practitioner in accounting and law. I knew Les well when he had been executive vice president for Jenn-Air.

Later, he became a mentor to me. On occasion, we would discuss how things were going for him with Lou Jenn. Les considered Jenn a difficult boss. He recognized Jenn's creativity and other virtues, but emphasized that working for Lou was no cakewalk. Eventually, he was fired and replaced by a man with a big company title. Les's replacement was the man I had replaced.

Forewarned is forearmed. Had I not been fired from Cosco and had I not had backroom knowledge about Jenn-Air, I could not have defended myself from Lou Jenn on my way in. Both companies were reputed "people eaters" by the local cadre. But I had a good contract, and Clarence Long was really the person who had seen to that.

When Lou Jenn called me in to his office to fire me in 1975, I warned him.

"Mr. Jenn, I think you are making a very serious mistake, and it will be a very expensive one."

"Are you threatening me?" he barked back.

"No, I am not threatening you," I returned evenly, "but we have a contract, and I expect you to live up to your share of it. I am sure I have."

Our contract had given Lou the right to terminate me with notice. One of the causes for termination with notice was his determination that my involvement in another business negatively impacted my performance for him.

"Before you start talking about that contract," he snarled (and I noticed "the" contract had become "that" contract to him), "you need to know that we have some real differences there! You'd better figure out what you did for this place, how you made us a lot of money."

"Because," I vocalized his implication, "I suppose I really didn't do anything?"

"Yes!" he snapped. "I agree with you there! You didn't do a thing! You've never even fired one important person here!"

"Was that in my job description?" I asked, innocently enough. "That I had to fire an important person?"

"Most good managers have to do that at some time or other," he insisted.

"You and I must have a different idea of what a good manager is." I was quiet now.

"All those people making money for me..."—he had picked up the ball and was running with it—"they were all here when you started. You didn't hire and you didn't fire!"

"I think I helped you get a customer or two."

"If you mean Kenna and Riggs, Mr. Mutz, I guarantee you I'll keep them long after you are gone."

"Well, if I did my job—and I assure you, Mr. Jenn, that I did do my job—you *will* have them long after I am gone." I paused, gathering my thoughts. Lou Jenn was not going to run over me. "Let me clarify something, sir. You are saying that I didn't hire or fire anyone important, except for a few customers, if you want to call that something."

"Yes!" Lou Jenn fired back at me. "You used my people!"

"Well, sir," I agreed, "you are exactly right. I took a group of individuals and I made a team out of them. And I expect to be compensated for that."

I walked out of his office and into a lawsuit. In the end, Lou Jenn was forced to pay three-quarters of a million dollars to terminate my contract.

The world is a real place, like it or not. I didn't like it the day I left Lou Jenn's office for the last time, but I had been "Cosco-ized" before, and I knew the future is never as uncertain as it can seem.

After all, Fred Risk and I had already successfully launched our partnership with the purchase of Mid-Con, and Henry Kravis and George Roberts had been there when we needed them.

TAKE AWAYS

- The ability to make wise hiring decisions has far-reaching consequences beyond the boundaries of business.

- Missing a goal can create all kinds of problems for getting back on track. Recurrent training in business provides the experience for successful operations.

- Once someone on the company board is unhappy with the company president, it is only a matter of time. They will hang every mistake and every unfavorable turn of fortune on him or her.

- The thought that "bigger is better" (*better* being understood as more powerful or useful) drives the thirst for consolidation. It is possible to make money from someone thinking this way. Too big, however, undermines profitability. This is why all businesses are eventually bought or sold.

○ When the driver of the bus changes, the philosophy determining the bus's direction changes. Figure out how to consolidate and how to break up. Develop the skills to do both.

○ It takes more than building to change attitudes or mind-sets.

○ My preferred operating model is a partnership. I consider the sharing of profit more than compensated for by the multiplied gains in opportunity, insight, and management strengths.

○ Good hires now make good connections later. Hiring decisions are always the keys to the future in business.

○ The first step in any acquisition is the technical analysis of the business you are buying. The second step is to know how you are going to operate the business after you own it.

○ The foundation of my business philosophy was reasonably well developed: buy, build, sell.

Chapter 17

MID-CON AND THE LEVERAGED BUYOUT

D o YOU KNOW how to do a leveraged buyout?"

"No," I answered, but I made a date to meet the man on the other end of the phone, at Maremont's headquarters in Chicago. He was the vice president of acquisitions and mergers for Maremont Corporation, the third-largest manufacturer of automotive exhaust systems in the United States.

Arvin Industries, Inc., was the number two company in automotive exhaust systems in the United States. Corporate headquarters were in Columbus, Indiana.

When I moved from Space Conditioning to Cosco, I was not thinking of becoming a sizable entrepreneur in my own right. I really had no choice but to become independent. When drafting a contract with Lou Jenn, I knew my independence was nonnegotiable.

I had also concluded that I wanted to be involved in businesses that perform well in adverse economic climates, and that pointed me in the direction of Maremont.

It helped that I was also a shareholder in Arvin.

Maremont, Inc., was one of Arvin's two principle competitors. At Cosco, I had been the only manager with experience in corporate shareholder relations. As a result, I had developed relationships with Lee Balter and Dr. F. Palmer Weber of Troster Singer, a large over-the-counter investment banking firm, and learned Maremont was under a consent decree with the Federal Trade Commission to divest their parts distribution business. Maremont had no choice. Whether they wanted it or not, they were for sale.

STRATEGIZING AN ACQUISITION

The first step in any acquisition is the technical analysis of the business you are buying. The second is to know how you are going to operate it after you own it.

The course of our first acquisition did not run quite so smoothly for Fred and me, simply because we found ourselves in the middle of negotiations before we realized we were the buyers. We would never have aimed so high had we thought we were acquiring Maremont's distribution business for ourselves.

Fred was with Indiana National, but his board relationships were increasingly rocky. I had not yet moved from my capacity as an independent consultant to president of Jenn-Air. We knew we each had a flair for acquisitions and mergers and we worked well together. Fred would start a sentence and I could finish it for him, and he could do the same for me. By combining talents, we were quite sure we could do better for ourselves than by working for anyone else.

I had already begun sorting through the facts and developing a strategy for the future before contacting Maremont. The customer base of Arvin and Maremont were distributors who sold exhaust systems to jobbers or dealers such as Advance Automotive. Wholesalers were back another step in the chain of distribution.

The retail market in automotive parts was highly fragmented, characterized by small businesses without any threads of continuity between them. NAPA had begun networking them and had become the dominant retailer, emerging from the consolidation of lots and lots of little entities—one man and two men stores.

Googling for this kind of information to come up quickly with the necessary figures was not an option then. It took me a while to get it all put together in my head, but when I did, I knew I wanted to talk to someone from Maremont about buying their parts distribution interests.

Henry Kravis and George Roberts had offered to help me after our fiasco with Tucker. I phoned Henry and asked him if he knew how to do a leveraged buyout.

"Of course, Oz," Henry replied. He could have added, "You dummy!," and I would have deserved the epithet; I soon realized that was exactly what we had been doing with Tucker. Instead he said, "Let me noodle it out on a piece of paper and call you back."

I went to Chicago and met with Maremot. Not only were they under a consent decree, I discovered, but they were under deadlines. If they did not divest by a certain date, the court was going to do it for them.

We had about three weeks and not much more than that to put together a deal. With the support of Henry Kravis and George Roberts at Bear Stearns, I had gotten hold of the tail of a tiger.

It was time to meet with Fred Risk.

"Fred," I began, "this is big. We could spend tons of time and money to get this into condition—"

"And we're going to be short on—" Fred knew exactly where I was going.

"Money!" I finished.

"How are we going to procure that?" Fred asked.

"Let's sell this to Ben Domont, and finance the future!" Fred said.

Ben Domont, the Pepsi Cola bottler in Indianapolis, was also on Fred Risk's board at Indiana National and had recently sold his business.

"You may not want to do this, Fred," I cautioned.

Fred wasn't concerned. "It's just a question of time, Oz," he shrugged. A lot of people our age who had moved up the corporate ladder so far and were still reasonably young were getting relieved of their responsibilities at that time, as board chairs were looking for someone to blame for their own misdirection, I believed. Fred was in the line of fire at Indiana National, as I had been at Cosco.

I put the figures into presentation shape and we pitched the sale of Maremont's distribution business to Ben Domont.

Ben didn't know the automotive aftermarket from a pogo stick. "We could drag this out and talk about it a long time, but I've already made up my mind." Ben jumped in as soon as I had finished my first pitch. "I don't want it."

"But Ben," Fred persisted, "you've been talking to me and to Oz and to two or three of our friends about trying to get a bigger business stake in a big leap instead of going forward in small steps. This will do that. You are not going to find something as neat and packaged as this is right now. It's gone through the Federal Trade Commission. It's cleaned up its business."

"I'm not interested," Ben repeated. "I want finished goods, not automotive exhaust systems and components."

Fred was a bit nonplussed. "Ben, you've just saved me a lot of time," he retorted drily. "You've been after me to find something for you to buy, and now I've laid one in your lap that is practically finished for nothing."

After Ben had left, Fred and I just sat in the office in silence.

"Fred," I began, "Do you know you just quit a big job?"

Fred didn't seem too upset. After a period of time Fred said, "Oz, let's you and I buy it."

"You can't do that," I protested. "You have a conflict of interest."

"Oh, yes I can!" Fred countered. "Cleveland Trust Company has a very bright young man I've been mentoring. I can arrange for you to borrow your half from him, and I will borrow mine from Chase."

KKR AND THE LEVERAGED BUYOUT

Instead of obtaining Maremont's distribution enterprise for Ben Domont, Fred and I bought it for ourselves. I could stay at Jenn-Air, and I had one acquisition to put in my pocket.

To be effective, a leveraged buyout allows the management of the entity being purchased to acquire a chunk of its assets, thus ensuring that the buyer has good management in place to help guarantee the company's future success. Maremont's management was perfectly capable of running their business, so we were happy to have them as operating investment partners.

The leveraged buyout was the springboard that launched Fred's and my partnership. It was the deal maker, the piece we needed. Between us we didn't have adequate capital to make the purchase. We had to be able to write a check for five million dollars. I was worth one hundred fifty to two hundred thousand dollars, and Fred slightly less.

The leveraged buyout allowed us to offer Maremont five million dollars for the distribution businesses it was being forced to divest. We requested that Maremont finance two and a half million dollars at a very friendly rate of interest while we borrowed the other half. Chase Manhattan had agreed to guarantee the loan Maremont extended to us.

In addition, we planned on selling the businesses we had just purchased to the people running them. Under these conditions, Maremont would get their five million, and we would have money to complete the sale with operating capital left over.

Because of the deadlines attached to the Federal Trade Commission court order, Maremont had very little time to shop for a buyer; consequently, they agreed to these arrangements. The distribution arm Maremont divested was a twelve to fifteen million dollar business, far beyond anything Fred and I had dreamed of when we first made our plans to go independent. We owned a thriving business, we had operating capital, and we made money our first year of ownership.

Leveraged buyouts were an evolving methodology during those years. The merger and acquisition (or M and A) transaction had dominated corporate buying and selling up until that time. Now leveraged buyouts have become an industry in their own right. Henry Kravis and George Roberts left Bear Stearns in 1976, three years after they penned out the plan that bought Maremont for Fred and me. They founded the private equity investment firm KKR. Since then they have leveraged the two largest buyouts in corporate history: the 1989 buyout of RJR Nabisco, and the 2007 buyout of TXU. They pioneered the way for a talented manager to buy a business that's making money, even if he or she doesn't have the capital for the initial purchase.

By the end of 1973, Fred and I had money, management, and work. I had a continuing job at Jenn-Air, and Fred continued at Indiana National.

We christened our new baby Mid-Con, Inc. As the former distribution arm of Maremont, we sold from factory to wholesaler and from wholesaler to retailer. In short, we were Maremont's primary wholesaler/retailer.

Fred and I now found ourselves in the merger and acquisition business, which means the buyer must be a seller at all times and vice versa. In M and A, the buyer/seller is willing to accept what previously would have been considered too small an amount of money in terms of either profit or ownership by an owner/seller. An owner/seller is too invested in his or her business, both in terms of money and time, to settle for the smaller margin that can make the deal for a merchant banker.

For example, we had just created this entity called Mid-Con that provided distribution services to jobber customers of Maremont products. We wanted to grow a manufacturing business, so we found an exhaust system manufacturer named Gabriel and explored the possibilities of acquiring it. When Gabriel was not interested in selling its business to us, we immediately switched roles.

"Perhaps you might be interested in buying Mid-Con from us?" I asked.

As it turned out, Gabriel was *not* interested in Mid-Con. Seven years later we sold Mid-Con to Alco Standard instead. Alco was an M and A concern like us but much larger, as they had started with one business and built it up. They had entered the automotive industry by becoming the US distributors for Jaguar but wanted an aftermarket presence in addition to Jaguar since the aftermarket generates more profit than the onetime new car sale.

It was, of course, Clarence Long who put us in touch with Alco Standard, Ernst and Ernst being the auditor for both Mid-Con and Alco. The offer to Gabriel was a casual one. By the time we sold to Alco seven years later, we were seeking a buyer in earnest, although there was no organic reason to sell Mid-Con. The business was healthy, but we needed to procure additional capital to bankroll our expansion into the health care industry.

Ultimately, under Mid-Con, we owned and operated thirty Autopro stores across the Midwest with distribution centers in Indianapolis, South Bend, Fort Wayne, and Evansville, Indiana; and in Lima and Cleveland, Ohio. Mid-Con sold to small towns throughout Indiana, Illinois, Ohio, and Iowa. We had three jobber stores in and around Lima, five stores in the Cleveland area, and at least that many again in Indiana, among them Speedway Autopro and Indy Autopro in Indianapolis, Rockville Autopro, Richmond Autopro, Newcastle Autopro, and Kokomo Autopro.

TRUCKPRO

More lucrative than the auto parts side of Mid-Con was its truck parts division. We backed into the heavy-duty spring and alignment business. While negotiating the purchase of its automotive parts stores and distribution centers, I flipped a match in the fire and told Maremont they would have to include the two truck spring businesses they owned as well. I had discovered these from our operating partners, who were partnering with us in the LBO, and I believed these concerns were very profitable.

"The only way we'll close this deal is if you sell the heavy-duty truck parts business," I told Maremont's officer during our meeting in Chicago.

"Mr. Mutz," he replied, "we are not prepared to do that."

"Sir," I returned, "I am not prepared to do anything else."

Maremont's man was silent for a moment. "I will have to talk to my boss," he finally conceded.

With Maremont under a Federal Trade Commission decree and working against a deadline, his boss reluctantly included Edgar A. Brown Company (a heavy-duty truck suspension provider) and Cleveland Spring at inventory value.

To verify the reports and make certain we were getting what we were paying for, I went to Cleveland to check them out. My concern centered on the viable existence of the inventory we were buying. If the inventory were present, EAB and Cleveland Spring were a good buy, but if not, we were not interested in acquiring them as a gift.

I had never been exposed to a heavy-duty spring and alignment business. EAB's manager reported to Reed Lear, the manager of Cleveland Spring, so I met with him first.

"Mr. Mutz," he asked as soon as we had shaken hands and greeted each other, "why is Maremont selling my business?"

"I don't know that. We wanted to buy it and they said they'd sell it to us."

The man had tears in his eyes, and I was a bit dumbfounded. "I don't understand why they'd sell me," he lamented. "I've been sending them money for years, and I hardly ever see anyone from the home office."

"Why don't you tell me about your inventory?" I interjected, abruptly changing the subject.

"What about my inventory, Mr. Mutz?" Reed seemed a bit bewildered.
"Is it here?"

"Absolutely!"

"No possibility you'd be short of inventory?" I persisted.

"Absolutely not! See all those kegs of bolts and parts and pieces?" I looked along the walls where he pointed. Kegs of bolts and nuts and common parts, twenty-four inches tall, lined the walls, stacked three high.

"Yes." I wasn't sure where we were going in the conversation.

"Well, they're not even on the inventory."

"What do you mean, they're not even on the inventory?" I wasn't sure whether I should feel alarmed or reassured.

"I had an inventory shortage several years ago," Reed explained, "and it was very embarrassing for me. The auditors came in and counted my stuff up, and I didn't have enough. So for years, I've kept setting them over on the side, stocking it up."

Now I was intrigued.

"Say," I asked, "what year was it when you had this inventory shortage?"

"1939."

I was discomposed. "What?"

"1939." He paused and thought a moment and then continued. "Yeah, it was 1939." I was shocked and amused to receive this information in 1975!

I had come to Cleveland anxious to make certain we had the inventory in stock that we would be purchasing. My offer had been made and accepted based on such-and-such an amount, and I had just discovered a huge overage of inventory. To some employee, sitting in an office on the thirty-second story at Maremont on the Outer Drive of Chicago, it would not have meant much. But we were just starting this little business.

Maremont hadn't visited Cleveland Spring more than once a year. We had a pile of inventory of common parts we knew we could liquidate, and that meant that money would be no problem. That inventory was very material to us because of our small size, and immaterial to Maremont because of their much larger size.

Ernst and Ernst would not sign off on our deal unless we had sufficient inventory to do business. We set a date to have them take the inventory, and when that was all over, the Ernst and Ernst audit team came to us and said, "You have a big inventory overage. We can write it up or leave it alone. It looks to us like there may be some fraud going on here, and we suggest you leave it alone. Don't disclose that you know there is an overage. We'll monitor it on spot-check and see how it goes."

They spot-checked our common parts at Cleveland Spring/EAB inventory two years in a row, but the overage was not of a significant nature. Further investigation, however, revealed we were being defrauded on a consistent basis. For years, Cleveland Spring's manager and his CFO (a clerk who had "Accountant" on his door) were skimming: taking checks payable to Maremont Corporation and depositing them in bank accounts on which they shared signature rights. We estimated they had stolen two or three hundred thousand dollars. We proved they had stolen at least sixty-three thousand dollars because they thought we were going to waive charges if they cooperated. We settled the issue with Maremont and replaced the management.

The incident had another silver lining. We had discovered that the truck parts business was a profitable segment that we could increase. The industry was small and fragmented, but the margins were excellent. We began expanding Mid-Con by buying truck parts stores in a variety of locations.

TEX JOHNSON SPRING AND ALIGNMENT

Tex Johnson was a person who owned a Tennessee-based truck parts business in Murfreesboro that Fred and I were quite sure we wanted for Mid-Con. It took us several trips to Tennessee to finalize the purchase, and even then, as we sat at the closing in a lawyer's office in downtown Murfreesboro, the sale almost didn't happen.

Tex was almost bald, but I don't think that was the reason he lived in a ten-gallon hat. If he graduated from high school (a fact we could never confirm), we doubted he had gone to college except to attend a Tennessee Volunteers game. Tex was a rabid fan of the University of Tennessee. Wherever the Volunteers went, especially for a bowl game, Tex was sure to follow.

Tex's wife, Geraldine (Geri), was active in the company's business too and had accompanied her husband to the closing. In the middle of exchanging papers and signing forms, Tex suddenly sprang from his chair.

"I jist can't do it!" he cried.

Geri jumped up beside him. "Me neither!" she agreed.

Fred and I looked at each other across the table, eyebrows raised.

"What is it you can't do, Tex?" I asked.

"I can't sell it. I'm not gonna sell it!"

We had spent a lot of time and money negotiating this purchase, but all we could do was sit and stare while Geri walked out of the room. Her husband was right behind her.

"Is this the normal deal with him?" I asked the lawyer.

He looked uncertain. "I don't know," he replied. "I've never had him for a client before."

A few minutes later Tex and Geri returned to the room and sat down. "Well...," Tex began, "we'll listen to what you boys have to say."

It was as if we were beginning again.

Fred and I were on the same page.

"We have to catch a plane," I said.

Tex was offended. "You don't have to be huffy about it!" he retorted.

"I'm not being huffy," I replied, "I'm just telling you how it is."

Tex got up and left again. Geri followed.

Once again, they returned a few minutes later.

Normally, when Fred and I bought a business, we would hand it over to a group leader to take care of closing it for us. It was plain Tex and Geri were unsure of this arrangement.

"Who are we going to report to?" Tex asked as soon as he and Geri were at the table again.

"To us," he shot back.

"Y'all will be the ones we talk to?"

"That's right." Neither Fred nor I blinked an eyelash, and the contract was completed.

But that was only the beginning with Tex. For the first eighteen months of our ownership, either Fred or I had to go to Murfreesboro and do the quarterly review with Tex and Geri.

Every time one of us was there, Tex and Geri were both in the room.

One or the other or both of them would shake their heads and remonstrate mournfully, "We jist made a terrible mistake!"

An attitude adjustment process would take place before any business could be discussed.

By the end of eighteen months, we'd had enough. We had just arrived in Murfreesboro, and Geri and Tex had just commenced their head wagging and mourning, when we made the surprise announcement.

"Tex, Geri," I interrupted, checking their grief, "Fred and I are going to sell you your business back. You give us the stock we gave you for the business, and we will give you back the cash. Then it will be all yours again. You can do whatever you want with it, but we're not going to mess with Johnson Spring anymore."

They were stunned.

"You ain't serious," Tex faltered.

"We couldn't be more serious." My patience, never my strong point, was at its end.

Tex let out a sigh of relief so large it deflated his ten-gallon hat. "Mister Mutz," he replied, brightening visibly, "you have jist taken a load of worry off us. All this time we thought we didn't git enough money for Johnson Spring, but now that y'all want your money back, I guess we did git enough." He paused, looking at his wife. She looked at him. They were clearly on the same page.

"I guess maybe we don't want it back right now," Tex stated.

Fred and I never again had trouble with Tex and Geri.

DENT TRUCK-PRO

By expanding Mid-Con, our strategy was to gather a collection of acquisitions in a very small but very profitable industry to the point that we could exercise influence over that niche market. To that purpose, we maintained a list of potential acquisitions. If we happened to be in Syracuse, New York, and knew of a potential acquisition in the area, we'd call on its owner. If he told us he wasn't interested, we'd wait. Then the next time we were in the Syracuse area, we'd go to see him again. Sooner or later, every business is for sale. One just has to keep trawling the waters.

One day while we were in our office, Fred received a phone call from Cecil Dent, a nice guy who owned Dent Spring and Alignment Service in Cincinnati, Ohio. He'd always take the time to visit with either of us when we were in the area, and he'd certainly let us buy him lunch, but Cecil had no interest in selling to us, so we had reduced our calling frequency. There were other fish in the sea.

Cecil didn't waste time on civilities.

"You fellows still wanting to buy my business?" he asked Fred.

Fred figured he'd play along. "Sure, Cecil."

"I'm ready to sell it to you for a song."

"What do we have to learn to harmonize with you, Cecil?"

The man on the other end of the phone was in no mood for games. "That's not funny, Fred," he retorted. "If you're serious, you need to get your rear end over here by noon tomorrow and I'll make you a deal you can't forget!" Cecil's employees had voted to unionize him and he was hurt. What hurt most was the fact that they had voted unanimously to unionize.

We bought Cecil lunch the next day and asked him what he had in mind for a sale. He literally penciled out the deal on the back of a napkin. We took one look and knew we weren't going to argue with him about anything.

It was an excellent offer. We bought Dent Spring and Alignment for less than we would have paid for it, but Cecil was so angry at his employees, he just wanted a piece of paper saying he didn't own the business anymore. We had very good labor relations counsel and we weren't worried about buying a newly unionized business.

When Alco Standard bought Mid-Con from us, they purchased only the auto parts side of the business. We tried to sell Truck Pro to them, but they were not interested. By that time, any association with Lou Jenn was long over. Mid-Con had been the beginning of a long and lucrative partnership with Fred Risk. Forum Group would represent its pinnacle.

TAKE AWAYS

o   To be effective, a leveraged buyout allows the management of the entity being purchased to acquire a chunk of its assets, thus ensuring that the buyer has good management in place to help guarantee the company's future success.

o   In the merger and acquisition business, the buyer should be a seller at all times and vice versa.

o   Sooner or later, every business is for sale; one just has to keep trawling the waters.

o   In any LBO, you have to reserve your right to negotiate any labor relations contract that has not been previously executed.

PART FOUR

FORUM GROUP

Chapter 18

EXCEPTICON INC. AND SARGENT & GREENLEAF

ROWING MID-CON HAD given Fred and me key insights into the consolidation aspect of mergers and acquisitions. We had gained entrance into a fragmented market in both the auto parts and the truck parts industries. Through the process of acquisitions, we had consolidated those businesses into one entity under the Mid-Con umbrella. Consequently, we now had a sizable company attractive to someone else in mergers and acquisitions—businesses like Alco, but who had more money and could consolidate bigger entities.

Originally we had considered it a possibility, especially in the truck parts business, to consolidate to the point that we dominated a substantial percentage of the truck parts suspension business. We sold Mid-Con because we no longer believed this goal was feasible. We had operating people and acquirers who understood the business well. We had worked hard at consolidating truck parts businesses, but it had not been an effective investment of our time. There were not many Cecil Dents in the industry. Our assessment was that the truck parts suspension industry couldn't be nationalized within a reasonable time.

Perhaps Alco had come to the same conclusion and that is why they had declined to buy Truck Pro.

We had just negotiated the purchase of Haygood, Inc., in Memphis, Tennessee, to add to our Truck Pro businesses, when the Stephens brothers from Little Rock, Arkansas, began making overtures to buy it. A young man with an MA from the University of Arkansas, an investment counselor, had told Stephens they could nationalize Haygood and dominate the truck parts market. We believed they couldn't, but we saw our opportunity for a sale. We negotiated with them to take over the Haygood deal and buy Truck Pro with it. That sale was one of our last. Fred and I were done with hard goods. We had decided to enter the health care market.

A LAST HURRAH IN HARD GOODS

Sargent & Greenleaf already held 80 percent of the market for specific segments of high-security locking devices when we purchased it. Eighty percent of a market represents challenging critical mass: someone who owns 80 percent of a live market can increase prices. Eighty percent of the market was the goal we couldn't reach for Auto Pro and/or Truck Pro. When Sargent & Greenleaf first fell into our hands, we intended to sell it within a year. Instead, we owned it for twenty-five years. Sargent & Greenleaf became everything we had hoped for from Mid-Con.

It takes an unusual kind of man to run a security business. People in the industry at that time didn't think in big numbers or beyond a localized area but concentrated on local locksmiths. The automotive relock side of the business doesn't make much money, but those who have contracts to relock a twenty-story building make substantial money.

Not only did Sargent & Greenleaf have 80 percent of the segments of the high-security market, they had a subsidiary, SafeMasters, which conducted localized government padlock business from a storefront on Martin Luther King Avenue in Washington, DC. They didn't just have a contract to relock a twenty-story building; they serviced the government of the United States of America. This service area included every federal embassy or consulate on foreign soil.

We bought Sargent & Greenleaf from Harry Miller and his two sons. The sons served as presidents of the businesses, but they needed reorganization beyond their scope. We put a manager in the company and suddenly found we were in the security business in earnest.

We were in a fragmented industry and were building our segment of the market through acquisitions, following the Mid-Con model. There was a significant difference with Sargent & Greenleaf, however, as we had the market share and the money to consolidate.

People would come to us and ask, "Would you be interested in an alarm service business?" Our first response to such approaches was a flat "no." Then we noticed growth in that side of the security industry and became interested.

A short time later, we received a lead on a business that belonged to a man and his wife in Florham Park, New Jersey, just outside of Morristown. They had started with a single store that sold alarm systems, connected to a central monitoring service for residential homes. Like most of the localized concerns in security, they probably did not ever have a "big picture" in mind, but grew their business to a string of five to twelve stores in the natural progression of owning and operating a successful store. Then the man died and his widow was no longer interested in owning the business. Oddly enough, it was a dentist in Miami who gave us the lead. He had been the owner's best friend and was seeking offers on behalf of his friend's wife.

We investigated, and in a very low-key transaction, bought it, closing the deal in a picturesque little inn in Lancaster, Pennsylvania. We paid cash for Dictograph, borrowing part of the purchase price from the seller in a leveraged buyout. As with Sargent & Greenleaf, we purchased Dictograph expecting to flip it quickly.

The company needed a new president. We handed its management over to Terry Hershberger, who owned 20 percent of it (which we had sold him on a book value per share basis), and let him know it was his to run and make bigger. He hired a man to work under him to function as president. Within the year we had made a million and a half dollars in the alarm service business. Dictograph ultimately became the largest residential alarm service provider in the United States.

It was apparent to us that Dictograph had become a keeper. We should have kept it, but we didn't. Within three years, we sold it with the proviso that they would not enter the commercial alarm market under a no-compete clause. John Risk, Fred's son, leveraged the sale to optimize the start-up of his own alarm service business with Bill Nelson. Nelson Alarms continues to be very successful.

Meanwhile, Fred and I were dancing with a new partner, the health-care industry.

HAAG DRUG

In 1980 we bought Haag Drug Company.

We were approached by a big eight accounting firm which had served as an advisor to Haag's current owner, and was not satisfied with their performance. They knew we would aggressively develop Haag, and influenced a major insurance leader to help finance our purchase.

Haag owned a hundred and one drugstores, and we owned Haag—at least for a short time. Very soon after the sale was completed, I had a phone call from a man who promptly introduced himself as Bud Fantle, CEO of Peoples Drug company.

"Mr. Mutz," Bud began, "you have bought something that I have to own."

My seller instinct sprang to attention, but not without reservations. We had purchased Haag as a framework for a public company to build the Indiana/Illinois/Ohio company base for the development of a mini-conglomerate.

During that period, acquirers were concentrated on two coasts: California and New York. There were a few in Chicago, but in general, acquirers came to the Midwest from California and New York to pick the ripe cherries off our business industry tree.

With the purchase of Haag, we saw an opportunity to change those dynamics. Now someone had called me, saying we owned what he needed and wanted to buy. This was not what we had in mind, but the way the wagons were circling, we sensed a couple of million dollars profit in the offing. Fantle was persistent, and we agreed to talk. We met for a couple of hours at the Indianapolis Airport Hilton Hotel.

"I know you don't know much about the drugstore business." Fantle cut to the chase quickly. "Peoples is a crescent that surrounds Haag, open on the west end in Iowa, and I am prepared to make you a very good offer."

We lost no time structuring the sale of Haag to him with the following caveats: First, we gave him the opportunity to buy an option to purchase Haag if we were unable to market it to our fellow industrialists in Indiana and Ohio within two weeks. Second, it had to be structured as a long-term capital gain sale for tax purposes. The holding period to qualify for a long-term gain at that time was six months.

At that time, I was the chair of the Indiana Manufacturers Association. We proposed we sell Peoples an option for two million dollars to buy Haag, exercisable six months and five days after the day we closed our purchase at a pre-agreed price. If they failed to exercise the option, we would have a two-million-dollar profit and never make a payment on the funds borrowed to buy Haag. Our first payment was due one year from the closing date of our purchase.

I took this plan to the board of directors of the Indiana Manufacturers Association (IMA) and explained how Haag would become Indiana Industries, Inc. I also warned them of the results it could have if we were to lose banking centrality in the Midwest. It would go to both coasts.

Of the manufacturers present at my meeting, only two realized the impact of what we were trying to do, and they committed to a reasonable level of participation in the enterprise. No one at the Indiana Chamber of Commerce indicated interest. Our plan didn't get off the ground; however, the decision to sell to Bud Fantle was made for us.

The banking capitals of the United States are now entrenched on two coasts. The Midwest may have missed its moment in history to become something more than a manufacturing center. The fallout of those missed opportunities is painfully evident in Cleveland, Detroit, and Indianapolis.

For us, the sale of Haag taught a unique and valuable lesson. We weren't foolish enough to think we had the IMA or the Chamber of Commerce in our pocket walking into those meetings, but vision is always worth acting upon. Take hold of the opportunity to sell it because maybe you can. If you can't, walk; "shake the dust off your feet." We tried with Indiana Industries, Inc., and it didn't work, but we walked away and made two million dollars for our little company in a matter of a few months.

The future is never as uncertain as it seems. Neither is it always as predictable.

EXCEPTICON INC. AND THE EMERGENCE OF FORUM GROUP

In 1967 Harold Mutz had formed Mutz Corporation to buy Peerless assets connected to the manufacturing of HVAC air distribution systems. Frank, Tom, and I were also founders, as were Jim Jones and Paul Shively.

Tom and I had tried to keep Dad from pursuing this opportunity. He was sixty-five years old. We had helped to achieve the liquidation of his manufacturing assets so he could retire gracefully, but Harold was not interested in retiring.

Dad was less than flattered by our concern. "While I appreciate your advice," he replied shortly at the end of one family council, "I've made up my mind what to do, and I am *not* going to retire. I am going to get back to work, and I need your money to do that, so just get your checkbooks out and give me some money!"

We had operated as Mutz Corporation for a year or two. I had invited Fred to our board when we became a public company in 1973, offering our stock for eleven dollars per share. We had purchased Mid-Con for cash, but when Mutz Corporation bought Mid-Con from Fred and me in 1973, with each of us holding 50 percent of its shares, we became the largest share-holders in Mutz Corporation and changed the name to Forum Group, Inc.

Forum was an acronym for Fred and me. "F" stood for "Fred" and "O" for "Oz." The "R" was for Fred's last name, "Risk." The "UM" stood for "Ulysses Mutz."

As long as I worked for Lou Jenn and Fred was at Indiana National, Forum Group remained a secondary focus of our professional careers.

I first heard of Excepticon Inc. from my brother-in-law, Bill Cheek, my sister Marion's second husband. His job took him to Lexington, Kentucky, where he became acquainted with Hugh Sturgell, a budding young invest-ment banker. He was so impressed with one of Sturgell's clients, Excepticon, that he had bought stock.

When he described Excepticon to me, I was impressed too. Bill arranged a visit for me.

The company was in the process of building a residential facility for the treatment and care of developmentally disabled people. John Swan, a young man in his mid-to-late thirties, was the founder and president. He met us at the construction site of Excepticon's new facility. They were in the process of taking the company public under an s-311a exemption for small public offerings. Of the companies in Kentucky and other states that went public via the s-311a exemption in 1973, Excepticon was one of the few still flourishing in 1980.

John Swan was impressive from the start. He owned Cygnet Farm, and he and the others associated with Excepticon had all been employees of the health department of the State of Kentucky at one time or another, rendering care services to the disabled. The State had been housing 660 people in a facility in Frankfort, a facility built during the Civil War to house prisoners, albeit not that many. Standards had been so far below acceptable conditions for human beings that a federal court had ordered it closed. The State was under duress to find a viable alternative, and Swan, seeing an opportunity to dramatically improve the care of its residents and make money doing so, provided them with an attractive and viable option.

Swan's new facility under construction in Lexington would house 186 people. A similar but larger facility, built by the State of Kentucky and State owned, was scheduled for erection in Somerset, Kentucky, depending on the input of capital from the legislature.

I received a quick education and enough understanding to know I wanted to buy stock in the company. I revisited them two or three times after that.

If I had been smitten with Swan on a personal basis during my first visit to Excepticon, by my second visit I had become intensely interested in what he and the company were doing. I also noticed things they were overlooking that my business and industry background told me could be valuable to their success. By the time of my next visit, I was on their payroll as a consultant.

The facility was well thought out and built with money loaned by local banks, which sold packages of five hundred shares of stock here and there to scattered buyers, which kept the bills paid. The pressing need was for long-term planning and financing, and I became their long-range planning consultant for the construction of buildings and related matters.

Fred was still executive vice president of Indiana National Bank. He had broken his leg in a skiing accident the week before, but I persuaded him to fly down to Lexington on a charter plane to look at Excepticon's facility. As a result, Indiana National became the lender and banker of record, and I became a member of Excepticon's board to ensure no one ran away with INB's money. My position there both protected Indiana National and generated some consulting income.

Excepticon's residential facility opened in 1974, and when Fred and I consolidated Mutz Corporation and Mid-Con to form Forum Group, Inc., John Swan joined our board of directors. In addition, Fred was added to Excepticon's board of directors. We had another vote without too much trouble, and became a nucleus of people who worked well together, jointly looking at the health-care industry as our newest avenue for expansion.

If Excepticon were our entry into the health-care industry, it was equally responsible for our purchase of Sargent & Greenleaf. A banker on the board of Excepticon had stuck his neck out and made a substantial loan to a company that had just been moved to Lexington from Rochester, New York, and needed to get the business divested and off his bank's lending books as a criticized loan. Excepticon did not have the money to do this, and wouldn't have known how to do it if it had.

John Swan called me on the phone. "Oz, could you and Fred take a look at this business for us? I have to do something right away to get this banker out of trouble. Could you come tomorrow?"

Fred and I went. We looked the business over, but we knew nothing about locks. We talked to Harry Miller and his two sons and tried to find out as much as we could in one day to make an informed recommendation.

We concluded that the business could probably make money, if it were managed correctly, but they were running it like a lending library. The urgent need was to change management, but Miller and his sons owned it. We had been looking for a niche market that we could dominate, and Sargent & Greenleaf had an 80 percent share of its niche. The price elasticity was irresistible.

"If you're going to buy it," urged Swan, "you should buy it quickly and at a low price."

We went back to Excepticon's board, knowing those board members well. Dr. Willis McKee would not be opposed, and Bert Combs was just a real nice guy. Combs was also the former governor of Kentucky and had a keen interest in mental retardation (his daughter was developmentally disabled). In the end, he couldn't see where locking devices had any relevance to a facility for the mentally disabled, and such was the weight of his influence, the deal died on the board table.

We went back to Harold Mutz.

"What do you think of Mutz Corporation being interested in Sargent & Greenleaf?" we asked him.

"Not much." Our board chair shook his head. "We don't know anything about locks and locking devices."

"You don't need to know anything about it," I argued. "What you need to know is that you can raise the price because you have 80 percent of a specifically defined market."

"I don't think we want to buy it." Dad remained unmoved.

"Do you care if Fred and I buy it?" I persisted.

In a sense, it was a moot point. Fred and I controlled Mutz Corporation after it had been consolidated with Mid-Con, but Dad's consent was still important.

Finally he agreed. "Go ahead and buy it."

We bought Sargent & Greenleaf for a five hundred thousand dollar equity investment and sold it twenty-five years later for fifty-five million dollars after receiving dividends, salaries, wages, and benefits worth thirty-five to forty million dollars. It made us about a hundred million dollars.

Five years later, Harold Mutz would remind us, "Now, you boys know I wanted to buy that business from the start!"

We had intended to flip it quickly. We wanted to sell it the week after we bought it, but everytime someone muscled up to the buyer's bar, the federal government stopped the sale by insisting that they couldn't provide a security clearance on them.

I had a top secret security clearance for years. Sargent & Greenleaf was the premier developer/manufacturer of high-security locking devices in the free world.

We kept the Millers, the former owners of Sargent & Greenleaf, for a year, but we had their replacement on deck. Tom Bossort, my former professor at Indiana University, had found Terry Hershberger for us, one of Tom's former students in the MBA program at IU.

"I think Terry's anxious to make a change, and if he is, hire him, Oz, before someone else does," Tom told me.

Sending IU a little money from time to time proved a sound investment!

Terry joined Sargent & Greenleaf as the executive vice president under Harry Miller and had a contract with us. If Harry told Terry that he was the boss, Terry was smart enough to play dumb. When they disagreed, Terry would walk away. He had that kind of diplomatic flair. After a few weeks, we let Harry know that his service to Sargent & Greenleaf would be over at the end of the year.

The Millers had a line of credit at Chase Manhattan Bank that was badly stretched, and they were going to go broke in a matter of weeks if something wasn't done about their cash position. We personally guaranteed a line of credit at Chase for three million dollars in exchange for a ninety-day option to buy Sargent & Greenleaf. In the kind of position Harry Miller was in, you sell the option.

KNOWING WHAT YOU DON'T KNOW

When we decided to put Mutz Corporation and Excepticon together by a Type A shared merger, Excepticon was in the process of buying a business started by a young man in his thirties, which had three branches of residential care for the developmentally disabled. This company was in the process of acquiring another company, Emergency Medical Services (EMS), to enhance its attractiveness to a buyer.

EMS was an automotive converter company with a health-care spin. They bought vans and converted them into ambulances. We had some experience in the automotive industry and decided to check out EMS on the ground in Dallas. Reliable people were sent to check out the residential-care businesses while Fred and I went to Texas.

As we approached the EMS site, almost a quarter of a block away, we began to smell paint fumes. Immediately the possibility of an explosion concerned us.

On arrival, we were shown the painting system, especially the overspray. We knew immediately we wouldn't have opened the door of the place on day one. Once back in Lexington, Fred and I were blunt with John Swan. "We won't take title of that residential-care business until you get rid of EMS," we warned, "It's an explosion waiting to happen."

To divest EMS, Excepticon had to build out almost two hundred Ford-conversion ambulances and sell them to the city of New York. We couldn't immediately shut the door on EMS; we had to milk it until it was dry.

We built the ambulances and shipped them to New York, and the city put them to use. Then we shut the business down completely and put the buildings up for sale. It was our one notable "non-venture" into the emergency medical services industry. We walked away from it as quickly as we walked toward merging Mutz Corporation and Excepticon into Forum Group.

Good managerial and financial decisions involve knowing when to walk away as well as when and how to buy. We wouldn't have wanted to spend four hours on the premises of EMS; three hours and thirty minutes were too much. We knew a little about painting from the association with Ransburg, enough to recognize a bad risk when we saw it. But if we had not checked the business out on the ground, we would never have known what we didn't know, sitting in Indianapolis.

The same principle is equally pertinent in hiring decisions. My first training hire was in his early thirties, had three or four children, was a very sharp dresser, and appeared to be the prototypical marketing type. I was the sales manager at Peerless and on the lookout to hire sales personnel who had the potential to become high-performance sales managers, and one man looked very good, so I hired him.

I invested a lot of time in this man because I believed he was good material and had excellent potential. Then, suddenly, somewhere down the line, he didn't show up for work.

When I got reconnected, I found out where he was and what he was doing. He was not doing what I hired him to do. As well as being an alcoholic, he worked as a male stripper. I dismissed him immediately, and his wife appeared in my office the next day.

During the initial interview process, I had taken them both out to dinner, but I had showed up at their house unannounced during the week to see what kind of show she had on her own. It was a form of extreme interviewing, but when you are looking for an employee who is really top-end work, you do some extreme interviewing. Where our trainee was concerned, my extreme interviewing had sprung a leak. His wife had made him appear to be what he wasn't. She was the reason he looked so good. I didn't know what I didn't know.

That disappointment was the trigger that put me in touch with the University of Chicago to find a better way of screening people. The consensus today would be that you can't go to that much trouble to hire somebody. Whether it's worth the trouble or not depends on one's objectives. If your objective is to create a business that will generate decent wealth, you cannot afford *not* to find out what you don't know before making a hiring decision.

There is no magic formula to growing a business, but sweat will be on every page of its corporate records. Fully investing our time and resources in the hiring process and in the purchasing process was critical to finding out those things we couldn't know any other way, and knowing what we didn't know was critical to our success with Mutz Corporation, Mid-Con, and Excepticon.

In 1980 we consolidated Excepticon, Mutz Corporation, and Mid-Con with our nursing home company, Somerset Corporation, and Forum Group was officially born.

TAKE AWAYS

- Eighty percent of a market represents challenging critical mass. Someone who owns 80 percent of a live market can increase prices.

- Vision is always worth acting upon. Take hold of the opportunity to sell because maybe you can. If you can't, walk and "shake the dust off your feet."

- The future is never as uncertain as it seems; neither is it always as predictable.

- Good managerial and financial decisions involve knowing when to walk away as well as when and how to buy.

- Find the best way of screening people. The consensus today would be that you can't go to that much trouble to hire somebody. Whether it's worth the trouble or not depends on one's objectives. If the objective is to create a business that will generate decent wealth, you cannot afford not to find out what you don't know before making a hiring decision.

- There is no magic formula to growing a business, but sweat will be on every page of its corporate records. Fully investing time and resources in the hiring process and in the purchasing process is critical to finding out those things you couldn't know any other way. Knowing what you didn't know is critical to success.

Chapter 19

RETIREMENT LIVING, INC., AND THE DALLAS COWBOYS

UCH WAS THE impact of the Great Depression on the pundits of my generation, almost every business professor in the country in 1949, the year I graduated from Indiana University, prophesied imminent recession. Had we acted upon what they taught, Fred and I would have hocked everything we owned and worked picking up garbage, preparing for economic disaster.

As it was, we acted upon the optimism and confidence of youth and the better judgment of the hour and rose to positions of managerial leadership. We were the generation of middle management in the early seventies, and as such, when the economy did turn sour in 1971 and 1972, we were the generation upper management held responsible for their woes.

One of my friends was fired from his position as chairman of a Dallas-based public company. Another was relieved of his responsibilities in the oxygen acetylene business. Like many of their contemporaries, both had worked tirelessly to deliver superior performance, moving from one professional management job to another. It was a phenomenon that largely went unnoticed unless you were affected.

I noticed.

I was affected.

I was fired from Cosco in 1971. Instantly, I formed my consulting company, Court Manor Corporation. Over the next ten years, I too worked very hard, compensating for the loss of opportunities and misplaced confidence in working for someone else. That hard work had paid off: Mid-Con, Excepticon, and Sargent & Greenleaf were all very profitable ventures. With the advent of Forum Group, Fred and I were advantageously positioned for robust growth.

Excepticon accelerated our growth in the health-care industry. We considered Mid-Con and our auto parts businesses to be defensive positions in a negative economic climate. Once Mutz Corporation and Mid-Con had been merged into Forum Group, we accelerated our drive into health care, wanting Forum centered on the health-care industry.

In 1981 the newly consolidated Forum Group acquired a small public company, Retirement Living, Inc., headquartered in Wilmington, Delaware. After my experience with Jenn-Air, I had begun intensely hunting products with industry targets for replacing parts. Fred and I were looking for countercyclical investments, businesses that would succeed in spite of the economy and in spite of poor management because of their products. Perhaps it was a legacy of the Mutz family's Depression-era success with Peerless, which sustained its profitability because it produced replacement parts for parlor stoves when few people could afford to buy the new stoves, which were not readily available.

One thing was apparent to me: the nursing home industry offered replacement residences to people who needed them. The health-care industry is entirely centered on replacement products. Put any permutation of the industry under scrutiny, and the bottom line is always concerned with some form of replacing bad health or the effects of aging with an attractive, viable alternative. It is an industry in which one can safely invest almost blindly, providing there is reasonably competent management in position. Those entities that have failed did so because they lacked good management. Most would probably be profitable even with that lack.

Add good management to a business that can succeed in spite of itself, and you should have a very profitable investment. If that industry sector is fragmented in terms of business units and ownership, you have the opportunity of a lifetime. An investor with vision can put together those pieces to influence an entire market. Adding the value of price elasticity to these kinds of products is a most rewarding objective to achieve.

HEALTH-CARE MODEL

With the acquisition of Retirement Living, Inc. came the possession of several nursing home businesses. Beverly Enterprises, headquartered in Little Rock, Arkansas, owned one hundred twenty thousand nursing home beds. Somerset Nursing Homes was considerably smaller. In the health-care industry, we usually don't invest in facilities; we invest in licensed beds. Somerset owned seven homes when we bought it; by the time we sold it several years later, it had expanded to twenty-seven homes, including twenty forty-bed homes, commonly referred to as 20/40 bedders (totaling eight hundred beds plus Somerset). Increasing the number of facilities, however, was not our goal. Profitability is linked to the number of beds (i.e., people being served).

Retirement Living, Inc., began defining our model for growth. New facilities needed to include a minimum of sixty or more nursing home beds, fifteen or more assisted living suites, and a hundred or more independent living apartments. All of these were housed under one roof, providing full service in the form of food, maintenance, and cleaning. In addition, as Forum's expansion model progressed, mental health sections, housing for victims of stroke (transient ischemic attack or TIA), and separate residences for Alzheimer's and Parkinson's patients were developed.

GENDER BIASES IN HIRING DECISIONS

In 1977, my daughter, Marcy, had been teaching school for four or five years. She already owned an interest in our auto leasing company, Forum Financial, which had given birth to Forum Group. She had graduated magna cum laude with a bachelor's degree in education from Purdue and had earned a master's degree from Indiana University.

Jean and I followed the pattern we inherited from our parents in raising our children, and preparing a daughter to follow in her father's footsteps had not been part of that pattern. My sister Marion and I were sixteen months apart, so we had always been close, even when as youngsters we sometimes found each other's company inconvenient. Maturity, however, brought a different quality of closeness. We received the same grades in high school, but she seemed to do the most studying. She still studies things intently. If a matter develops that requires liaison between family members, Marion will do that better than I.

Because my mother suffered significant illness when we were young, I was taught how to do chores that we thought of as "feminine" work, but Laura Mutz was most concerned that her daughter knew how to sew, cook, and clean the house. The possibility of her going to the office with Harold and learning stenographic work or manual labor never entered any-one's thoughts. Those kinds of chores weren't something Marion was to be taught. I was taught to do them and taught how to manage others doing that line of work, but Marion was being equipped for a different role.

Throughout the early years of our marriage, Jean and I never sat down and discussed a division of labor. The patterns we grew up with seemed to have worked well, and we were satisfied with them. I never thought that Marcy would be interested in or should know how to build a house, although I considered that knowledge and experience essential to my son's training.

I, who prided myself on my ability to hire wisely and maximize the potential of my employees, and who prioritized the development of my human resources (knowing nothing would increase my profit margin more), had completely overlooked that element of mentoring my own daughter. As I pondered the personnel needs of our burgeoning retirement living business, the thought suddenly struck me. I have no excuse for why that thought had not entered my brain years before, except that the pattern I had inherited from the past had blinded me to the possibilities of the future.

Marcy was better educated than most of the salespeople on our payroll. She was aware of that too, as became increasingly evident from the questions she was asking. She also made considerably less money than they did.

"What's wrong with you, dummy?" Oz the father upbraided Oz the businessman. "She can make more money and be happier doing it if you would get her into the sales and marketing side of your retirement business, or you could give her the choice of being in the service side of the business."

"She'll have to be certified," Oz the businessman replied.

"We can do that on the job," the other Oz countered, unconcerned. "Now…what does she want to be? What does my daughter want to do?"

We lived two blocks apart in Indianapolis. Jean and I had built a house there after shutting down the farm and selling it. Marcy and her husband had built a house on my father's farm, and there they began their family. Harold Mutz was seventy-six years old when they made their home on his farm. He had zealously promoted the plan because he not only liked Marcy but also appreciated the security of having someone living less than a half mile away. Now, Marcy had relocated back to Indianapolis.

I was developing an appreciation of the talent pool represented by my own children and our advanced management training cadre. We began engaging Marcy in the sales of retirement living units, although we started as a rental retirement business. Marcy first worked for Retirement Living, recruiting new lessees for us through our marketing department. She worked first as a marketing person, and then as a manager of the department. Finally, she served as the manager of a retirement community on a broad basis. I had not specifically educated her for this work, and the lost potential that this oversight cost was apparent. Before long, Marcy had earned advanced certification as a licensed health-care administrator and contributed significantly to our economic productivity.

If I were to live this part of my life over again in today's world, I would incorporate two principles into my people management model. First, I would be gender blind. Second, I would be much more intentional about developing and practicing family-based, formalized training. I had developed and managed training for my sales force at Peerless, but I should have assigned books to read and assignments to be completed by my children and my grandchildren. Despite my training shortfall, Marcy developed a strong business-skill mentality that I greatly respect.

Following up on removing gender as a consideration with Marcy, I also did the same with Bill. Following the example of my own father, I planned a development program for Bill that could have been labeled "adult show-and-tell." Most people agree that shelter (a home) and transportation (a car) represent the largest concentrations of capital investment to be made in most people's lifetimes. With this in mind, I considered training in these two areas the wisest investment of Bill's training time and money.

How better to develop the industry knowledge to market cars than to become an automobile dealer? Why not build a reasonably sized home to acquire the knowledge and skills necessary to be a successful building con-tractor? Both of these ideas seemed reasonable to me. So it was that, during the summer between his freshman and sophomore years in college, Bill worked with Jim Belding, vice president of Dunlap & Company, to build a house.

Bill and Jim constructed a two thousand five hundred square foot brick veneer home on a lot at Court Manor West. He and his lumber company partner, Dunlap & Company, sold this home for two hundred fifty thou-sand dollars in the "market time of 1973." This home has been re-sold profitably on at least two occasions since, underscoring the viability of his management and labor training.

We launched our automotive initiative later. Together, Bill and Marcy purchased an automobile dealership in Lakeland, Florida. In better years they exceeded one hundred million dollars in volume; even when they did not set operating sales volume records or break profit objectives, they operated profitably. If I were committed to a construction/re-development program regarding either an auto dealership or residential construction, I would not hesitate to support a comparable endeavor to the two of them.

THE RILEY WILCOXEN PRECEDENT

This combination of education and on-the-job training was always exercised within a focused, intentional Christianity. Marcy continues to be an active leader in Bible Study Fellowship and serves her community through Junior League. Her earlier involvement in Junior League's social support programs provided additional "on-the-job" training opportunities. Bill too volunteers his talents and expertise in support of Christian endeavors. From the time they were young, Jean and I told them we hoped they would go to college.

"But," I would always add, "you should be prepared to pay your own way. If you don't want to go badly enough to pay for it, you probably shouldn't be there."

"Did you pay for yours?" they were quick to ask.

"Every dime!"

"And Mom?"

Jean was equally quick in her response. "No, but...," she responded, interjecting the "but" before they could stop her, "I did what my parents asked me to do. They wanted me to practice the piano, so I practiced four to five hours a day."

Our children took us seriously. They worked to earn and save money for school. They grew up on a farm and always had productive opportunities. By the time Marcy began her college education at DePauw (she transferred later to Purdue), she had saved a fair sum of money. She had finished her first year and a half and her resources were holding up fairly well.

"If you were in the 'real' world," I coached her, "what would you do?"

"I'd borrow money," she said.

"Where?" I asked.

If you don't want to work, there are few ways to make money. Inculcating that thought process into one's children means they should usually do pretty well. I had apparently succeeded in doing that.

But to say I was proud of my children's persistence and consistency would be an understatement. They had raw talent, obviously, but I had learned long before that persistence and steadfastness are more important ingredients in success than talent.

Riley Wilcoxen had taught me that lesson at Peerless. Duane "Bus" Williams had been the director of engineering at Peerless. Bus had been an excellent hire, a sound investment in terms of employee development: smart, hard-working, and reliable in judgment and performance. His advice on product development and his input into other managerial decisions had been right enough times that I knew I needed to listen to Bus. However, when he kept recommending a young draftsman by the name of Riley Wilcoxen for training as a salesperson, I questioned his reasoning.

We had screened Riley Wilcoxen on the way in, and his IQ measured just north of 100. I did not think we needed to invest time and money and energy in him. Six months later, Bus was knocking on my door again.

"Oz, this man is a superior employee," he insisted. "He does things right and he does them right the first time."

I just didn't see the potential. Bus persisted. Three or four conversations later, he gave me a program for Riley's development and what its goals would be. I gave in. I turned Riley Wilcoxen over to Bus Williams, who promptly put him through a rigorous training program with the purpose of turning Riley into a salesman.

Riley not only completed the program successfully, but he did it with honors. He did the things he was told to do, the way he was told to do them and in a timely fashion. His performance stood in stark contrast to that of some of the more "talented" members of our sales force, whose gaps were largely self-imposed, the result of lapses in personal discipline or dedication.

If Riley were told to paint a wall blue, his first response would be "What shade of blue?" as compared to the others in his cohort who might first ask, "But what about painting them green?"

Eventually Riley wound up in a task force of sales personnel I was directly training, and everyone was paid on the basis of salary and incentives. The salary kept them from starving, and the incentives created an opportunity for them to make considerably more money. I could not begin to add up the money I paid Riley Wilcoxen over the years he worked with me, but I know I gave him one bonus check for fifteen thousand dollars. When I left to join Electronic Specialty Company in Virginia, he offered to resign because he wanted to be sales manager of Space Conditioning in my stead. I wouldn't have left without giving honest write-ups of all my personnel, and I gave Riley what I considered an honest write-up.

Riley ultimately became sales manager of Space Conditioning, Inc. Had he been just a salesman, he would have outperformed all my predictions. Persistency and consistency had taken Riley Wilcoxen far beyond any place raw talent would have generated.

I was looking for just such an employee for Retirement Living, Inc. Sales, and I had found her very close to home.

THE TEXAS CONNECTION

Over the lifetime of Forum Group, Fred and I developed twenty-two retirement centers in thirteen states. The largest concentration of facilities was located in Texas.

Perhaps it was this Texas connection that drew the bank's attention to us in 1984. The executive vice president of Manufacturers Hanover Bank in its Senior Loan Office in New York contacted me. When I answered his phone call, I could not have anticipated his question.

"Oz, you guys ever think of buying a sporting team?" he asked.

Well, yes, Fred and I had considered that option.

"What do you think about it?" he wanted to know.

"We aren't interested," I replied.

"Are you sure?"

I thought back to Fred's and my conversations on the subject. "Pretty sure. We have talked about it quite a bit. It destroys an investor's anonymity. Your life is never your own when you are in the sporting business. I don't think either Fred or I want to live that way."

I noticed a funny note in his voice, and I considered the possibilities before proceeding further because I had a hunch I might be missing something important.

"Of course," I lightened up, "if the Dallas Cowboys were for sale, we might be interested in buying them!"

The banker was silent a minute.

"Oz, that's who I'm calling you about," he said. "The Dallas Cowboys are for sale."

I was speechless. The banker capitalized on my silence.

"Clint Murchison is dying. The team has to be sold to fund the settlement of his estate."

I had finally recovered my voice. "Well," I replied thoughtfully, "that puts a different hue on it for me. But there's still a big problem. We don't have the money."

"You don't need the money, Oz. If you and Fred will sign personally, you can borrow all the money you need to buy that team—forty-four million dollars. But you have to stand behind it personally."

"We wouldn't like the personal endorsement, as you know." I was processing the ramifications of this opportunity rapidly. "Does Tom Landry go with this deal?"

"Tom Landry knows that we are calling you," he answered, "and whether he goes or not depends on you and how you handle it."

I had served on the national board of the Fellowship of Christian Athletes (FCA) for several years with Tom Landry, and we had become well acquainted. My personal regard for the man was huge, and I was quite aware of the strength of his Christian commitments.

COUNTING THE COSTS

After getting off the phone, I broke the news to Fred. We talked it over and decided to take a closer look. We talked with Tom Landry on the phone and went to Dallas to talk to Tex Schramm and Gil Brandt. We spent a day with them, and by the time the day was a half to three-quarters over, we had learned some pretty important things about sports franchises.

For instance, whoever owns a franchise in the NFL must commit to being present at all owner meetings, and we couldn't take turns doing this. The same person had to be present at all meetings.

Neither of us was interested in moving from Indianapolis to Dallas. We both already had second homes in Naples, Florida, where our wives could winter away from the Midwest cold and snow.

Moving the Cowboys to Indianapolis didn't make sense. It would have been disastrous to the integrity of the franchise. And while horses might be a familiar staple of the Midwest, Indiana is a state of farmers, not cowboys. If the team stayed in Dallas, we would be flying two thousand miles in a private jet for every home game. Transportation alone would be no small cost.

In the early eighties, the Cowboys weren't making money. In fact, they were losing money—a lot of money. The line across their profit-and-loss graph was a sawtooth: one year they made three million, the next they lost three million. Whatever they made one year, the renewal of players' contracts took away from them the next.

We were now asking the hard questions. We were only three questions deep into the initial discussion with Tex Schramm when it became obvious to me there was an issue, with him at least.

"Tell us what next year's budget is," Fred inquired of Tex.

"We don't have no budget!" he replied defiantly. "We tried budgeting a couple years and it didn't work. I run the team, and when I need money, I call Mr. Clint and get it!"

Schramm wanted us to understand that he didn't like us. He sent us to the airport with four people crushed into the front seat of a vehicle that had only three seatbelts.

We went home undaunted and did our arithmetic.

The only thing that made money for the Cowboys was the Cowgirls. The Cowgirls also had a substantial piece of property in Arlington that went with the deal. The rest seemed to us like a pile of negatives and the loss of our anonymity.

I'd had a front row seat at what the loss of that anonymity could look like. Earlier, I had been in Tom Cousins's office in downtown Atlanta. Tom owned the Atlanta Hawks. We had just decided to get a bite to eat at the Capitol City Club. A car radio was playing softly. I hadn't even noticed it until Tom suddenly drew himself up rigid and stopped.

"Oh, no!" he exclaimed.

I halted beside him. "Oh no, what?" I asked.

"Did you hear that announcement, Oz?"

I shook my head in bewilderment. "What announcement?"

"It sounds like they fired the coach of the Hawks today. They've been talking about it for weeks, but I didn't know they were going to do it today." Tom was obviously upset. "We won't have a minute to talk, Oz. People are going to need to tell me how to run a ball team."

We had barely sat down and started to eat when the deluge began. A woman walked defiantly over to our table. She looked down at Tom with as much disgust in her face as she could possibly muster.

"I hate your guts!" she said to him. "You just fired Cotton!"

"Pardon me, ma'am." Tom turned toward her with his knife and fork poised halfway between his mouth and the table. "I just heard it on the radio on my way down here. I don't know anything about it."

The woman sniffed as if she didn't believe him and, turning her back on us, stalked away.

Similar incidents happened two or three times after that, punctuating our day. Their memory was vivid. I was quite certain Fred and I didn't want to get in a business where we belonged to the public, exposed to anyone on the street who felt it was her right to walk up to us and confront us by saying, "I'm so-and-so and I hate your guts!"

Three days later I called Tex Schramm, knowing he disliked us but knowing it was the proper thing to do as well. "I thought I should do you the courtesy, Mr. Schramm," I began, "to let you know we are not going to buy your team. However, we know a man in Dallas who might be a good candidate to purchase the Cowboys. His name is "Bum" Bright—Harvey Bright."

Schramm was truculent. "Mr. Clint doesn't like Bum," he objected.

"Well, sir," I replied, "I think I am obligated to give his name to the bank. I know Harvey personally, and I think he might be interested."

I gave Harvey's name to Manufacturers Hanover Trust, and Bum ended up buying the Dallas Cowboys for forty-four and a half million dollars. His estate sold it to Jerry Jones for around one hundred and five million dollars. The team may be worth around two billion dollars today.

Jones has drawn a lot of bad press over his management of the Cowboys' football team, but he has done a brilliant job of managing facilities, stadium concessions, and those other items that must be managed well if the team is going to make money. We were not up to being that kind of active owners.

But Fred and I should have bought the Dallas Cowboys. We made a mistake when we didn't. The sale involved substantial risk—and it was uncomfortable risk, both financially and personally—but it was risk I believe we should have taken. Money is good for only one thing, to be invested. You can invest by spending it or by giving it away, but if you can't do both of these things, your money is not doing you any good.

The great irony of my business career is that at the very moment I shrank from spending money on the Dallas Cowboys—which would have been a very lucrative investment—we committed to huge inputs of capital into retirement living facilities, constructed from a flawed financial plan. If the Cowboys represented our greatest failure to invest, Retirement Living, Inc., would become our greatest failure by overinvesting. We just didn't know that yet.

My son, Bill, had been walking this tightrope between knowing when to invest and when to avoid overinvesting with our horse business. Bill managed the labor side of Court Manor West, annually recruiting a work crew to paint fences, maintain barn upkeep and check the pregnancy status of our small mare herd. Each year a newly appointed assistant manager had helped him "break" and train our show colts. Without question, the quality of this training was directly related to potential selling price. We knew that it was more profitable to sell younger animals than it was to continue their training through two, three, and four. Only if you hit a "home run" in the advanced development of these youngsters was it profitable to extend their training.

Jim Aikman had mentored Bill in the breaking and training of show colts at Hide-A-Way Farm when Bill was in his early teens. With Jim's most effective assistant, Tom Mohler, Bill scored well in the exhibition of these show colts. The result of walking the tightrope between investing and overinvesting resulted in increased net profits.

TAKE AWAYS

- In 1949, many business professors in the country prophesied imminent recession. Had we acted upon what they taught, we would have hocked everything we owned and worked picking up garbage, preparing for economic disaster. Instead, we acted upon the optimism and confidence of youth and the better judgment of the hour and rose to positions of managerial leadership.

o Search for products with industry targets for replacing parts, businesses that would succeed in spite of a sluggish economy and poor management because of their products. Add good management to a business that can succeed in spite of itself, and you should have a very profitable investment. If that industry sector is fragmented in terms of business units and ownership, you have the opportunity of a lifetime. An investor with vision can put together those pieces to influence an entire market. Adding the value of price elasticity to these kinds of products is a most rewarding objective to achieve.

o Consider hiring potential associates outside the past pattern to maximize the potential of employees and the company.

o Be gender blind. Be more intentional about developing and practicing family-based, formalized training.

o Money is good for only one thing: to be invested. You can invest by spending it or by giving it away, but if you can't do both of these things, your money is not doing you any good.

Chapter 20

AMERICAN MEDICAL CENTERS

DR. M. A. Tarumianz had been fighting overcrowded hospital conditions for the mentally ill during most of his forty-plus-year tenure as Delaware's state psychiatrist and superintendent of mental health institutions. Tarumianz, who immigrated to the United States from Russia, had been a medical officer in the Russian army and assumed his position with the State of Delaware in 1918. Over the course of his professional career, he became respected for his advocacy not only for the mentally ill but also for the intellectually disabled. Tarumianz's vigorous campaign to replace outmoded, inefficient, and overcrowded large state facilities with networks of patient-responsive, patient-sensitive smaller centers had provided the model for new initiatives like John Swan's Excepticon. In the latter years of his career, Tarumianz's concerns had expanded to include retirees and the elderly.

Consequently, when we purchased Retirement Living, Inc., in early 1981 from Tarumianz's son, Alex, we found ourselves not only the owners of more luxury retirement centers than any other company in the United States but the owners of a well-appointed psychiatric hospital as well. Alex Tarumianz had created and developed that hospital in conjunction with his father. Excepticon was as close as we had come to investing in the medical service sector until then. Within two years of buying Retirement Living, however, we had concluded the purchase of American Medical Centers in Nashville, Tennessee, and were launched full steam ahead into the health-care industry. Health care was the industry of growth in the 1980s, and Forum Group was to be synonymous with health care.

FROM RETIREMENT LIVING TO DOC-IN-A-BOX

With the purchase of American Medical Centers, we began the process of acquiring and/or building hospitals of all sizes and shapes, from general hospitals to psychiatric facilities like Tarumianz's hospital in Wilmington, Delaware. By the time Forum Group sold its interest in hospitals five years later, we had expanded our acquisitions from one to fifteen medical centers scattered across six states. Among these were four hospitals in Texas (Lockhart, Midland, Bryan, and Waco), three in Georgia (Hahira, Ridgecrest, and Clayton), three in Virginia (Portsmouth, Norfolk, and Salem), three in Florida (Tampa, Ocala, and Homestead), and two in Missouri.

Both St. Joseph Medical Center and Martin Luther King, Jr. Hospital were located in Kansas City, Missouri. After King's assassination in 1968, governmental authorities rushed to rename public fixtures after him, from streets to schools to hospitals. Kansas City, Missouri, had been particularly affected when, in the aftermath of King's murder, city school officials had refused to cancel classes the day of King's funeral. When police used teargas to disperse a student protest at City Hall, citywide riots ensued, leaving in their wake at least five dead and twenty injured.

A decade later, authorities connected with Martin Luther King, Jr. Hospital still weren't "getting it." Government initiatives continued to operate on the rationale that "fair and equal" meant a state-of-the-art hospital servicing only or *primarily* the African American community. The MLK, Jr. Hospital was designed to be the alpha and omega of African American health care. Its implementers seemed oblivious of their underlying segregationist mind-set. African Americans weren't interested in having their own "all black" hospital; they were centered on achieving fair and equal access to *all* hospitals. In the wake of the civil rights movement, the opening of the Martin Luther King, Jr. Hospital had added insult to injury.

We bought MLK in the early eighties because it was losing money and the government owned the buildings. Perhaps more germane to the sale, it was managed by the same people who managed St. Joseph Medical Center for us.

Along with MLK and St. Joseph's, we bought a business in what I called the "doctors service industry." The business had contracts with physicians from all over the United States and Canada, and one or two from Europe, a total staff of sixty-three or sixty-four emergency-qualified MDs. Emergency medicine had just been recognized by the American Board of Medical Specialties as a medical specialty in 1979. We had caught the crest of a new wave.

DOC-IN-THE BOX

At the time of the collapse of the Hyatt Regency's Sky Bridges, our latest health-care venture supplied physicians to the emergency rooms of all of the greater Kansas City hospitals. The Kansas City branch of the business also rented a storefront retail outlet, staffed with one of our doctors—the precursor to the walk-in clinic of today.

The Hyatt Regency Hotel had been open for business a little over a year. Part of the Crown Center development near downtown Kansas City, the newly constructed Hyatt, at over forty stories, was then the tallest building in the state of Missouri. Its lobby, an open-ceilinged atrium stretching four stories high, framed by glass, and crisscrossed by walkways across the second, third, and fourth floors, was considered an architectural marvel. The soaring concrete and steel walkways were dubbed "sky bridges" by hotel employees for obvious reasons. They were the principal architectural features of the new Hyatt, more like balconies suspended in air than walkways.

On the night of the Tea Dance competition, July 17, 1981, those balconies were full of merrymakers watching the dance on the lobby floor below and cheering on the competitors. The lobby itself was packed. At least fifteen hundred people, in various stages of exuberance and/or inebriation, filled the atrium. Suddenly all of the gaiety came to a halt. Some sound rendered the entire conglomerate of human beings speechless. They all seemed to be inhaling air simultaneously before exhaling in a gathering tidal wave of screams and oaths. Nebulas of dust rose from the lobby floor.

Two of the sky bridges had collapsed. Along with their loads of packed human beings, they had also taken significant portions of the lobby's interior walls with them. Human limbs and water mains alike had been severed in the sky bridges' fall. Water began flooding into the area. While voices from unseen bodies trapped beneath the wreckage cried and pleaded for help, the onlookers still safe on the remaining sky bridge could only watch in dumb horror.

Over a hundred people died that night. Over two hundred were seriously injured and rushed to emergency care. Doc-in-the-Box had been responsible for supplying almost every one of those emergency room physicians.

Emergency physicians were sent directly to the Hyatt. One man's leg was pinned under the concrete. The only hope of saving his life was to amputate his leg, and the only instrument available for the amputation was a chainsaw. One of the Docs-in-a-Box did the amputation, but the man did not survive.

And, of course, Doc-in-a-Box was sued for that. No doubt the legal suits resulting from the emergency treatment of the Hyatt victims had motivated its sale to us in the first place. We weren't experienced enough in the health-care business then to realize we had just purchased an albatross.

In the aftermath of the Hyatt Regency catastrophe, a man appeared in one of our emergency rooms on New Year's Eve. He had been dancing on a glass coffee table—all two hundred and fifty pounds of him—and the table had broken. His back looked like that of a porcupine; glass shards bristled out of his skin like porcupine needles. Our physicians worked on him all night, picking the glass splinter by splinter out of his back. They missed one small piece.

That piece worked its way between the man's vertebrae and severed his spine. He was paraplegic after that. For him, the bottom line was simple.

His spine was cut.

A piece of glass cut it.

Our guys had missed that piece of glass.

After the Hyatt Regency experience, we knew "if" was not the question. It was only a matter of "how much."

Over my protest, and Fred's protest, and the protest of the doctor who was president of Doc-in-a-Box, our insurance company refused to settle for the two million dollar compensation we had negotiated with the man's attorneys. They were certain they could win, so they pursued the suit.

In the end, we paid over four or five million dollars to that man.

We withdrew from the doctor business.

LESSONS LEARNED

In terms of a development model for growing Forum's investments in the health-care industry, the physician business did not pay off, at least as we were doing it with Doc-in-a-Box in 1982. Our physicians, not the hospitals they worked in, carried the liability. The doctors were on our payroll, and that shielded the hospitals from liability.

They also worked by the hour, literally. They were paid on an hourly basis and not on contract. At that time, Canada was embedded in socialized medicine, and we found we could cherry-pick highly qualified doctors out of Canada to work for us. They would leave sixty thousand dollar and seventy thousand dollar positions to become our "hourly" employees, so eager were they to get out of the Canadian medical system. But typically that was not the whole story. I discovered the dark side of Doc-in-a-Box quite by accident.

I was in Kansas City to meet with the president of Doc-in-a-Box. After picking me up at the airport on a Friday afternoon, he took me to our company headquarters. To my surprise, when we walked into the waiting room, it was full of people sitting patiently in a long queue.

"What's going on here?" I asked the president.

"They're waiting for their checks," he shrugged. "Their wives pick up the checks."

"They are inclined to let their wives pick up their checks?" I was a bit taken aback. "Board-certified emergency room physicians?"

My incredulity was lost on him. It was obviously nothing out of the ordinary to him. Images of O. K. Davis flitted through my mind, and the office at Peerless, crowded with the wives of our molders. The wives would appear at four o'clock every Friday afternoon, anxious to pick up the paycheck before it could be spent on booze instead of groceries.

Did the wives of our doctors not trust their husbands?

I had to think back to our first negotiations with Doc-in-a-Box. It was a stockholder-owned company, and the stockholders were the physicians and their wives. Shareholder meetings were scheduled from seven p.m. on Wednesday to two a.m. Thursday so that emergency rooms weren't stripped of their staff. That first introductory meeting was the longest shareholder meeting I have ever attended in my rather long life. Each one of these women had married a doctor who was going to be rich, and each intended to make sure that wealth was going to be realized. Every wife had to have her say on whether or not (philosophically!) it was right to have separate ownership. I thought I would die before that meeting was over.

But we bought Doc-in-a-Box anyway. We owned it for almost two years and sold it as quickly as we could. Even after we sold it, however, we kept the company's president on our corporate payroll several more years. He was very sharp, although he had one bad habit: he was a stunt flyer, and a good one at that. Every Monday I was always a little anxious until I heard that he had made it through another weekend.

The lesson learned from Doc-in-a-Box has to do with having human beings as your company product. Perhaps it's no coincidence that we were looking for a way to unload Doc-in-a-Box at the same time we turned down the offer of the Dallas Cowboys. Human performance is usually subject to the whims and frailties of human nature, and if people are your product, the market is always volatile.

Bob Houck was a man I trusted implicitly. I had known him from high school, and I had sought him out for Peerless. He went with me to Electronic Specialty and came back to work with me in Indiana. He served as chief operating officer of six businesses during our thirty-five-year association. The last fifteen years of his employment with me were characterized by my moving him *down* the corporate ladder.

One eventful morning when Bob was effectively the COO of Harper J. Ransburg Company, a subordinate called to tell me there was a problem. "Oz," he said, "I have to talk to you about something serious. Bob has disappeared."

We had no idea where he'd gone. Five or six days later, Bob called to let me know he was in Louisville, Kentucky, and he was O.K. He came back to work, took care of his business, took care of our business, and seemed himself again. A psychiatric evaluation proved futile.

Then he disappeared again.

When he resurfaced, I gave him a different role, and when he maintained that, I moved him to a management job in another business. He leveled out, then he disappeared again. I moved him to another position, this time of considerably less responsibility. And so it continued for an additional twelve to fifteen years.

Bob's developing mental instability represented a challenge to the successful management of our business, but not to the success of our products. Had he been our product—had we been in the business of supplying other corporations with managers and it was a customer who had to deal firsthand with Bob's problems and not I—the impact of his inconsistent performance would have directly affected our profit line. So it was with Doc-in-a-Box.

Doctors were not a product of the hospital business, however. We left the hospital business for a very different reason. That was yet another lesson.

DRGs and Hospital Corporation of America

Not all of the hospitals acquired through American Medical Centers were desirable investments. As with a retirement center, the profitability of a hospital is measured in terms of beds. The hospital at Clayton, Georgia, for example, was certified for only seventy-five beds. Its small size made it economically unfeasible, but we wanted to acquire Hahira, which was one hundred beds, and Midland Hospital, which was one hundred twenty-five beds.

The man who started the Clayton hospital and held its certification was a recovering alcoholic. His hospital serviced more alcoholics and airline pilots, drying them out, than any other hospital we knew of in the state of Georgia. An alcoholic recovery specialty hospital is still run at Clayton, although pilots now account for less than 50 percent of their census.

In the course of buying the facility at Clayton, we looked at a facility focused solely on the recovery of airline pilots. We evaluated it simply as a matter of due diligence. Once was all it took to decide on a course of action: we got rid of it very quickly. I had a bit of an uncomfortable feeling in the pit of my stomach thinking about all those pilots. The more-responsible managers employed by the institution admitted that some of their pilots would have large drinks of vodka on their way to work.

In the end, we bought and sold two hospitals in Florida, both children's psychiatric hospitals: the Grant Centers, one in Homestead and one in Ocala. We acquired Homestead in 1981 and built Ocala in 1983. By the end of 1983, however, our enthusiasm for expanding our investment in hospitals had cooled, and we had started looking for a buyer for American Medical Centers.

In 1983, the federal government mandated all Medicare payments be regulated by Diagnostic-Related Groups, or DRGs. In other words, the products hospitals provided were classified under possible diagnoses, and the costs of interventions used to treat each diagnosis were standardized. The intent of the initiative was to control abuse of the Medicare system by forcing hospitals and doctors to assume some share of the financial risk when ordering and charging for patient care. We shared grave reservations about the ability of hospitals to remain profitable when prices were effectively fixed by the federal government. The fact that the largest group of people serviced by hospitals were the over-eighties, on Medicare, seemed compelling evidence that Forum Group needed to find a buyer for its hospitals posthaste!

We found such a buyer in Hospital Corporation of America. Dr. Thomas Frist Sr., now considered the father of the modern for-profit hospital industry; his son, Dr. Tom Frist Jr.; and Jack Massey, a Nashville businessman, incorporated Hospital Corporation of America in 1968. While the gentle Tom Frist Sr., a respected, almost revered, figure in the upper echelons of Nashville society, was always the public face of Hospital Corporation of America, Jack Massey appeared to be the ultimate decision maker.

Massey had started a surgical supply business in the fifties with the money he made selling a chain of pharmacies that he had founded at age twenty-five (he had graduated from the University of Florida with a degree in pharmacy). In the early sixties, Jack sold his medical supply company for two million dollars in 8 percent preferred stock in Outboard Marine Corporation. He was approaching sixty and figured that the one hundred sixty thousand dollar annual income the stock brought in would be all he and his wife would need to live well.

But a friend from Nashville called him with a lead, and Jack couldn't resist following up on his information: Some man in Simpsonville, Kentucky, had taken out a patent in fried chicken and was trying to franchise the concept to create the next McDonald's.

"I think he could use your help, Jack," Massey's friend had told him, "and you could probably make a little money on the side with consulting at the same time."

So Massey contacted the man, a Colonel Sanders, and arranged a two-week consulting assignment to evaluate the Colonel's business. Then, he made a second appointment with the Colonel to download what he believed was problematic.

The Colonel was sitting at his partner's desk, a popular arrangement in the finance field. Jack sat on the partner's side and, after a momentary pause, began easing into the bad news.

"Colonel," he said, "sometimes there's just not a real nice way of telling people what they need to know."

Sanders didn't react. He seemed to be considering his response.

"Well, Jack," he agreed, "You might be right. What do you have in mind?"

"What I think," Massey suggested, "is that you and I need to see if we are on the same wavelength. You write a figure on some paper and I'll write a figure on some paper, and then we'll throw it in the middle of the desk to see how close we are."

Jack scribbled down "two million dollars" and threw it in the middle of the desk. The Colonel threw his down too. They had both written two million. The Colonel looked down, pulled out a drawer, looked in it, looked back up, and said, "I'll take it!"

At that moment, Jack's lightbulb went on and he realized Colonel Sanders had mistaken his appraisal of a fried chicken franchise for an offer to buy it. Immediately, Jack seized the opportunity.

"Let's shake hands on it, then," Jack agreed.

As I remember Jack relating it to me, Massey sold half of his two million dollar investment in Kentucky Fried Chicken to John Y. Brown, the future governor of Kentucky. Jack retained the other half. Eighteen months later, the partners sold their entire business for $786,000,000 to Heublein. It appeared to me that Heublein was happy to convert substantial fragrance earnings into fried chicken! The excess cash on Jack's hands needed to be invested in something, and Tom Frist Sr. was his personal friend. With Jack Massey's proceeds from the sale of Kentucky Fried Chicken, he and the Frist family funded the start-up of Hospital Corporation of America.

The official transaction of Kentucky Fried Chicken sales contracts provided for a minimum of layers of management. Colonel Sanders reported directly to Massey and to no one else. "I'd not hear from him for a week or two," Jack later told me, "and then he'd call and tell me how things were going. Sometimes he'd be nice and pleasant, and sometimes he was a real rascal. I couldn't figure out the dual personality."

Six to eight months later, Massey decided to have a tête-à-tête with the Colonel's secretary.

"Well, you know, Mr. Massey," she willingly enlightened him, "Colonel Sanders believes in astrology. If I were you, I'd get the astrological calendar and track his mood swings. I started doing that years ago. I check the calendar and I know when it's a good time to talk to him and when it's a bad time to talk."

Jack Massey obtained an astrological calendar and checked the day of his first appointment with Sanders. On the day he purchased Kentucky Fried Chicken for two million dollars, the calendar read, "Something good will happen to you today."

From that moment on, Massey arranged his meetings with the Colonel around the astrological calendar and made hundreds of millions of dollars from his new business enterprise.

CHARLIE MARTIN'S BIRTHDAY DEAL

I didn't actually meet Jack Massey until the late eighties. We sold American Medical Centers to Hospital Corporation of America without my ever meeting either Massey or Thomas Frist Sr. Charlie Martin was Hospital Corporation of America's senior vice president of mergers and acquisitions. I had been playing push and shove with his subordinate minions, and we had come to a standstill, when Charlie invited me to Nashville to meet with him personally.

I met Charlie and a couple of his senior officers at their company headquarters. We were fifty million dollars apart; fifty million in a two hundred million dollar deal represented a significant percentage. I had just told Charlie we weren't interested in a transaction at that level.

"What are you interested in?" he asked.

"Something considerably higher," I replied.

Charlie eyed me from across his desk and then pushed back his chair. "I think we'd better eat lunch," he said, starting to stand.

Suddenly the door to his office flew open and Tom Frist Jr. slipped into the conference room. I could just catch the whiff of something rather pungent in the air behind him. The interior wall of Martin's suite of offices was made of glass, and through the glass we could see something in a crate being rolled down the corridor. It was a live pig.

"Happy Birthday, Charlie!" Tom exclaimed as the pig was rolled into the office. Tom, laughing his head off, began to sing "Happy Birthday" to Charlie, and I, considering myself a decent baritone, joined in.

Charlie Martin turned as red as a beet. "Tom," he sputtered, "Why are you doing this to me? You're embarrassing me. You brought me a pig! Why would I want a pig like that?"

"I don't know," Tom laughed. "It's a lot better looking than some of the girls I've seen you take out!"

It was Tom Frist Jr. who ended up taking me to lunch. And it was Tom who suddenly looked up from the meal and asked me if I'd take two hundred and ten million for American Medical Centers.

"Maybe," I replied. "It depends on what goes along with the two hundred million—the fringe benefits. Straight-up cash deal, we won't take two ten but we'll take two twelve."

"You've got yourself a deal but with conditions," Tom shot back. "Today is Monday. I will send my first-level managers out to look at your fifteen properties starting tomorrow. They will be done looking a week from tomorrow. They will do a preliminary inspection and evaluation, and by this day next week, I will be able to tell you whether or not we will accept your properties on that basis. If the answer is no, I am not going to fuss and bother with you. I'm just going to tell you 'no.' If our answer is yes, I will tell you 'yes' at this price with no fuss and with no bother."

We had acquired our first hospital in 1981, constructed our first hospital in 1983, and by the end of that week in 1983, not a day later, we were out of the hospital business. The sale of American Medical Centers to Hospital Corporation of America for two hundred twelve million dollars was the biggest consolidated piece of business Fred and I ever completed.

MAKING THE MOST OF YOUR OPPORTUNITIES

The not-for-profits (our so-called charitable institutions) made money from DRGs. Our hospitals were located in just-small-enough cities that we would have been all right with any construction of DRGs. We were wrong to fear them.

Learning how to be sensitive to changes that can impact an industry—without being reactionary—is a difficult lesson. Laws can change between the buying and selling of a company, and an industry can substantially alter while a businessman is in the middle of consolidating his investments in it.

Royce Harrell understood opportunity. He mined for gold when he went looking for acquisitions for Forum Group, and every third time he dug, he hit at least enough pay dirt to keep all the rest going. What we had to sell to HCA was substantially more than what we had purchased in the American Medical Centers package because of Royce. He was one of those fellows who didn't understand the word "no." If you told him he couldn't do something, he took it as an assignment to find a way of making it happen.

HCA included ten men on its staff doing the kind of acquisitions work Royce Harrell did for us, but ten such men couldn't get done what Royce did, although he always claimed to need more help.

"Boss, I need your help," he'd always begin over the phone.

"Well, what's the matter, Royce," I'd always answer.

"You need to get the man I'm working for now to loosen up on me so we can get something done."

It was always a question of how to say yes to Royce without getting another of my managers bent out of shape. But Royce was always clever at filing for and procuring certificates of need for nonexisting facilities. He acquired our certificate of need in Waco, Texas, where we built and completed and operated a hospital where no hospital had ever existed before.

He managed to get a certificate of need in Tampa, Florida, for a hospital that was not there before. The facility in Tampa was actually built by HCA, but we sold them the certificate of need to do it with the American Medical Centers package. Royce had figured out how to procure the certificate by negotiating a joint venture with the University of South Florida, the city of Tampa, and private industrial revenue bonds. He had forged the almost-perfect public and private partnership to bring something into existence that otherwise could never have happened.

The Jack Masseys and Royce Harrells of the business world find something to extract that the rest of us don't see in situations we consider futile. It isn't just the judgment, but it's the courage to make the call when the opportunity suddenly emerges that sets such men apart.

I am not wholly without this quality myself. When I closed the sale of American Medical Centers with Charlie Martin and HCA, I made sure they got Doc-in-a-Box too. If they wanted our hospitals, they had to take our doctors.

It was an opportunity I wasn't going to miss.

TAKE AWAYS

- Human performance is usually subject to the whims and frailties of human nature, and if people are your product, the market is always volatile.

- Learning how to be sensitive to changes that can impact an industry, without being reactionary, is a difficult lesson.

- Laws can change between the buying and selling of a company; an industry can substantially alter while a businessperson is in the middle of consolidating his or her investments in it.

- Find something to extract that the rest of the business world doesn't see in situations often considered futile. Find the courage to make the call when the opportunity suddenly emerges; that is what sets men apart.

Chapter 21

A RISKY BUSINESS

Longines-Wittnauer watches were the Rolex watches of my youth. Sargent & Greenleaf was one of the largest customers of a manufacturing company, Rehlor, which also supplied the Swiss watchmakers who composed the Longines-Wittnauer group. Because of the extreme size and type of the time locks that Sargent & Greenleaf required for the doors to vaults, the manufacture of one vault door could be the equivalent to the manufacture of thousands of watches. We purchased the works for our vault doors and Longines-Wittnauer purchased the works for their watches from Rehlor.

Our supplier was located in the little Swiss town of La Chaux-de-Fonds. My first visit was in conjunction with my thirty-fifth wedding anniversary, and Jean had long been keen to visit the home of the Christian thinker Francis Schaeffer, at L'Abri, so we planned a trip to Switzerland that would encompass both business and pleasure. L'Abri was almost impossible to find. It was not marked on any of our maps, and Schaeffer, who was battling cancer at the time, was unavailable once we did reach his home. However, the entire complex of L'Abri was available for exploring, including the charming chapel. This is thought by many scholars to be a birthplace of contemporary Christian writings, which, together with the writings of C. S. Lewis, influenced the world's evangelical believers. It was a mountain-top experience.

We did, however, find La Chaux-de-Fonds nestled at the top of a ridge of mountains that rose above Neuchatel. The Longines factory was at Saint-Imier, a little less than twenty kilometers on the other side of the Jura mountains. I quickly concluded my business at La Chaux-de-Fonds, and we finished our first European vacation enjoying Lake Geneva.

I did not expect to go back, but the nature of our connection through Sargent & Greenleaf required increasingly frequent trips. We constantly required innovations from the manufacturer in La Chaux-de-Fonds. Perhaps because of the developing association with the region's manufacturing base or perhaps through the International Chamber of Commerce (or perhaps because of both), I had been invited to speak at a luncheon in Geneva. The audience was small because it was of necessity limited to English speakers.

However, the luncheon and the speech went well, and after its conclusion, I was ready to venture out in quest of a present for my wife.

I asked the hotel doorman how to get to Saint-Imier. I wanted to go to the Longines factory and pick out a watch for Jean and a watch for Fred Risk. I was confident that I was going to save considerable money on two very nice gifts.

The possibility I had not entertained was that a watch that cost me two or three thousand dollars in the States might nearly cost me my life at that time of year in Switzerland!

AN UNFORTUNATE CHOICE

The hotel doorman was especially helpful. He explained the usual route to Saint-Imier and then suggested an alternative route, a shortcut from La Chaux-de-Fonds. I marked my map and leaned on the hood of my rental car, pondering my choices. The difference in distance and time eventually made my decision, and I headed for La Chaux-de-Fonds.

It was well over a hundred kilometers from Geneva to Neufchatel, and after Neufchatel I wasn't sure which turn I was supposed to take. I saw a man on the street and said in my best Swiss French, "La Chaux-de-Fonds?"

He stared back at me like glass.

"Verstehen Sie Deutsch?" I asked in German. "La Chaux-de-Fonds?"

He nodded, but I wasn't sure to which question. I took the turn and started up the mountain's hairpin turns. The road consisted of two very narrow lanes, almost completely snowpacked. About halfway up, it slowly dawned on me that I was not seeing many other people on it.

It was now growing later in the afternoon. I was by myself and becoming a little uncomfortable at having embarked on this adventure so late in the day. The car parks at the chateaux along the way became increasingly sparse. I calculated that I was about a fourth of the way from the top when, distracted with thoughts about the hairpin turns going down the other side, I turned a corner too sharply and buried the nose of my rented Mercedes in a snow bank.

The car would not go backward or forward, and no human was in sight.

It was September thirtieth, and snow was still in the distant future back in Indiana. I had failed to appreciate the difference in climate.

I hadn't passed anyone coming down. I was stuck. I cast about in my thoughts for a plan and remembered passing a substantial residence with a large car parked in front about a half mile behind me. The house had been inviting enough that I had noticed it.

I turned the engine off and began to walk down, instead of up, the mountain. About a half mile farther, I heard the sound of an engine around the curve in the road ahead. I scanned the mountainside and saw some kind of motorized device coming down it, crossing over the hairpin turns.

The closer I drew, the clearer I could see the thing, so I started to run a little, slipping and sliding with my all-too-lightweight topcoat askew. I reached the point where they were crossing the road, and from there, saw a shelter holding lots of cars. I had missed it going past on the other side of the road.

My relief was immense. The possibility of dying on that cold, remote mountain had seemed very real. The chateau with the big car parked outside had been welcoming, but empty, a closer inspection revealing that its windows were boarded up with huge wooden shutters. It would have been difficult for a man younger and stronger than I to break them!

It made no difference to me that no one could speak English. I was simply glad that I was not alone. They argued in French, and I gathered it was over how to get me down the mountain. I tried my own style of communication, anxious that they knew I had a car stuck in a snow bank above.

"Oui, oui," one of them kept insisting, trying to reassure me about the car.

After fifteen or twenty minutes of negotiations (which seemed like hours), we arrived back at the Mercedes and, with the assistance of nine or ten other men, I turned the car around and headed it down the mountain. Then one of the men motioned for me to get in the car.

I opened my wallet and drew out several hundred francs. I wanted to impress them. I wanted to motivate them to get me and my car down the mountain.

When we finally reached the last place with any life that I had seen on my way up, I ushered them all inside and bought a round of drinks. I had given them enough money to drink for a long time.

The hotel doorman had been right. The shortcut would have saved me lots of kilometers.

But he'd forgotten that it was closed for the winter.

Once at the bottom of the mountain, I wound my way along the lake to Zurich. I reached my hotel in Zurich just before everything began shutting down for the week. I had thought I was going to save thousands of dollars by doing this on a weekend. I wound up talking my way through the purchase of two excellent watches and leaving instructions to have them Fed-Exed to Indiana.

Then I called Jean. While I had been out on that snowcapped Swiss mountain, watching the sun gradually lower as I stewed about being stranded in the snow overnight, Bill and Pam's son, my namesake Ozzie, had made his first appearance back in Indiana.

Oz III

My grandson Ozzie and I were destined to share another auspicious Mutz family event. By the mid-1990s Bill and Pam had moved their family to Lakeland, Florida. Jean and I maintained homes in Naples, Florida, and in Indianapolis. There was always a place for them to park their RV in front of our house. Their oldest daughter, Cari, fondly dubbed "Kiki Mama" by her numerous younger siblings, was at Purdue. Pam was pregnant with their tenth child but wanted to visit her friends and daughter back in Indiana. Bill had driven them up in their recreational vehicle, deposited them safely in our care, and returned to Florida to work at Lakeland Automall.

The recreational vehicle was fastened to the house via a long electrical cord curled around the leg of a cast iron bench on our front porch. This was to keep the cord from inadvertently being pulled out. Jean and I were sound asleep in our first-floor bedroom. The grandchildren were scattered between our house and the houses of various friends around Indianapolis. A light rain was falling gently from the sky.

Suddenly I felt someone shaking my shoulder.

"Papa?" came Pam's soft voice through the grogginess of my sleep, "I think it's time. I think we need to go to the hospital."

This was a woman who had birthed nine babies. I didn't ask if she were sure.

"Let's get in the car and I can tell you what to do about the kids on our way."

This, however, was a statement I could question. "What do you mean 'do about the kids?'" I asked, a bit bewildered. "Why can't we just leave them where they are?"

"No, Papa. I want them to be at the hospital when the baby is born!"

By the time we arrived at St. Vincent's Hospital on 86th Street, I thought I had been fully briefed. Once Pam had been duly admitted, I drove the car back home, loaded a portion of the children into the RV, and set off to collect the rest.

I had driven about a mile, going west across 86th Street, when someone in the car next to me started pumping his horn. The driver passed and then another car came up beside me, honking. It was now somewhere between three-thirty and four in the morning. I pulled the RV over, puzzled, and still a third driver went past, his horn blaring.

I looked behind and spotted the trouble. I had been dragging the iron bench behind me, the electrical cord secured firmly around the legs!

"Jake, can you do something about that bench?" I asked, directing my question to Bill's oldest son.

"I don't know anything about this, Papa," Jake objected.

"You know enough to get this thing unhooked back there, don't you?" I insisted.

I didn't know anything about RVs. I could put it in the right gear to go, but now I knew why all those cars were honking at me.

Somehow, in spite of the rain, we managed. I collected all of Bill and Pam's children, and together, we went to check on their mother.

Pam was a veteran, but I had not even seen my own children delivered. When it became obvious that she was getting close to delivery, I turned to my grandson Ozzie, who was hanging on my trousers.

"Ozzie," I said, "I think it's time for us to leave."

"Yes, Papa," he replied, wide-eyed.

Pam looked at us. "No, Ozzie, you can't leave," she protested. "You have to come and kiss me good-bye first."

Ozzie looked at her, looked at me, and then looked back at her.

"No, Mom," he said decisively, "I don't want to do that. I don't want to get what you have!"

The irony both for Ozzie and for me was that we were insecure about the wrong things. Life may appear to be risky, especially when you are stuck on a frozen Swiss mountaintop or in a hospital delivery room, but the greatest risk in business is usually spawned by the complacency of success.

MICHAEL MILKEN AND DREXEL BURNHAM

"Oz, if I could get you to come to California with me," the voice on the other end said confidently, "we *would* be your investment banker."

Stanley Trotman had been calling on Forum Group so regularly, we'd gotten on a first name basis. His words sounded less like a promise and more like a prediction. I didn't understand the man's tenacity. He wasn't cocky, just persistent.

"We're not looking for an investment banker, Stanley," I replied for the umpteenth time. "You're the only one who wants me in California. It doesn't make any sense to me."

But Stanley continued his periodic calls to Forum Group undaunted until, finally, I agreed to meet him in Los Angeles. I wasn't sure why I'd done so. Perhaps he had piqued my curiosity, or maybe he had just worn me down.

Stanley wanted me to meet a man named Michael Milken.

"What's so great about him?" I asked.

My companion wasn't saying much. "You'll find out."

An Offer I Couldn't Refuse

At six o'clock the next morning (Los Angeles time), I met Mike for the first time at his Beverly Hills office.

"Tell me about your business and your business background, and about this partner who's a former banker, as Stanley tells me, and you have thirty minutes to do it," he said, noting that the market would open at 6:30.

It was not a very attractive invitation, but when the market opened, he said, "I really do have to go, but you come back at four-thirty this afternoon, and I'll have some ideas for you."

The reason I was there, and the reason Stanley was there, was now obvious. Stanley Trotman was offering Michael Milken's services.

As soon as we were outside the door and walking down the street to the hotel, I started asking questions. "What is this business?" I demanded. "I meet the guy at the crack of dawn, and now he wants us back at four-thirty in the afternoon."

"I don't know, Oz, but we'll find out." Was Stanley playing dumb?

We spent the day shopping for our wives, went back to Milken's office on schedule, and proceeded to wait outside his door for over an hour.

When Milken finally appeared, he took us into his conference room.

"Mr. Mutz, I think we want to bank you, and I think it will take some unique capabilities to do it that others do not have," he announced.

So far, I knew he was just bragging. It was my turn to take the offensive.

"Why don't you tell me about these unique capabilities, Mr. Milken?" I asked.

"Well, I think we can raise fifty million dollars for you quickly and avoid all the road show stuff you normally have to do to raise money for a new client," he began. "We will put you on our agenda for our annual Client Conference. By having you appear at our Client Conference, we will avoid the road show."

I was not batting an eyelash while he talked. I was listening.

"We'll raise fifty million dollars and it's going to look like debentures," he continued. "But if you later want to avoid having to make interest payments, you can always lower the price for the holders to convert debt to equity as a way of encouraging them to do so."

Now, I know what Milken meant. Then, I didn't understand the concept.

"If you choose this way of avoiding having to make an interest payment, then it will be like equity," he finished.

In 1969, Mike Milken joined Drexel, Harriman, Ripley—the firm that later became Drexel Burnham Lambert. With a history going back to the 1830s, it was among the bluest of the blue-blood American financial institutions. Mike expanded its franchise beginning in the 1970s by providing previously unavailable access to capital for thousands of entrepreneurs and smaller enterprises.

In 1974, Mike started a series of annual institutional research conferences, and Drexel grew to become the largest financial resource in the health-care and homebuilding industries. By the time we attended (in 1986) they had seen some 30,000 participants from more than 1,000 institutions in 50 countries. And, in the early 1980s, Mike began to deploy his capital theories to companies like Chrysler and other "fallen angels."

The several year decline in the dominance of insurance companies as capital sources was now complete, coinciding with an acceleration of job creation by non-investment-grade companies, resulting in millions of new jobs in the United States between 1970 and the end of the century. The compounding of these results moved Drexel to the top tier of the investment banking industry.

People like Fred and me would help put them there.

"I can't really afford to invest any more time today than I've already invested, Mr. Mutz, so maybe you can see me later."

He abruptly showed me the door.

And that concluded our interview.

It was easy for a potential Drexel client to confuse Mike's overscheduling for a lack of sensitivity.

But, notwithstanding, I believe his was the most brilliant financial mind of the last century.

The minute we were out of Milken's earshot, I turned to the man beside me.

"Stanley," I began, "I didn't want to admit I didn't know what he was talking about, but I don't. Can you explain it to me?"

A MILKEN CLIENT CONFERENCE

The term debenture was not new to me; I had heard of debentures in Accounting 101A at Indiana University. But when Milken explained that there was a way to make a debt-to-equity conversion more attractive to the debenture holders—and thus avoid our having to make an interest payment—that was new!

Milken proposed that we would sell fifty million dollars of subordinated convertible debentures. I considered subordinated convertible debentures to be the least liquid form of equity. A debenture is a piece of paper that says it is convertible into a specified number of shares of stock. If a debenture stated that it was convertible into one hundred shares of stock, and the stock is convertible into cash at ten dollars per share, the debenture would be nominally valued at one thousand dollars.

I didn't know how Milken planned on selling the debentures, but by selling them he could raise fifty million in cash. After selling them, Milken planned to promote their conversion into stock by "calling" them at a higher-than-stated conversion rate. If the debentures were convertible into ten shares of stock, Milken would offer them at twelve and one half shares as an incentive to convert early to a totally cash instrument. Converting now produced a bigger "kick" from the investment, a 25 percent increase.

Stanley should have talked to me about Milken's procedure for selling the debentures, but he didn't. No one did. Client Conferences were annual events that gathered potential investors in droves and showcased selected companies for their consideration. The next one was only a couple of months away, and Milken had already added Forum Group to the agenda as a featured investment possibility.

When Fred and I were finally brought into the loop, I was told that we would have 1,200 to 1,500 registered guests. For three days (so I was prepped), we would do two things:

1. Drexel Burnham corporate investment clients would present
   data about their companies and sell bonds or stocks as a result.

2. Michael Milken would wax eloquently for an hour or so.

Of course, Milken would not explain how he was going to sell bonds and, two or three months later, call them ("flush them out") so most investors would convert to stock, given a 25 percent conversion premium as an incentive.

Milken's "flush out" was a new concept to do a quick equity financing job.

In the course of explaining this process to his attendees, he would inevitably extol his company's virtues as the most creative financial organization in the world, and perhaps they were. Mike was every bit as smart and creative as he claimed to be and *very* perceptive. In the time it had taken for me to explain Forum Group to him during that first meeting, he had grasped the entirety of our vision. He saw how it could become a very large company quickly, and he saw it eating capital because it would be constructing a lot of buildings. Few better ways exist for chewing through capital in a hurry than buying large tracts of real estate and building on them.

If I'm an investment banker and you are eating up my capital, I am going to want to sell your assets in ever-increasing quantities.

In April 1986, Fred and I attended our first Institutional Research Conference. It began with a fantastic meal served by the Beverly Hilton Hotel. We paid our own hotel bills, so Fred and I stayed at the less expensive Century Plaza, but the conference took place at the Beverly Hilton Hotel. In Midwestern lingo, we called it "living high on the hog." Frank Sinatra was the featured entertainment. In due course, I learned that every time Milken held a Client Conference, it was exponentially larger in attendees than the last one. The entertainment became more elaborate. Indeed, names of people I met at my first Milken Client Conference still appear in the daily papers.

Fred and I gave our first presentation to that conference. Neither of us had done anything quite like that before, and we would never have participated had not both of us been involved. We discovered we did these kinds of presentations well together. We had known each other so well for so long, we could finish each other's sentences.

We needed to be good at these presentations to secure the attention and the confidence of our audience quickly. We were at the conference to sell a hundred million dollars in investor capital (an increased amount) from a relatively unknown company.

We sold them. On returning to Indianapolis with a hundred million dollars in debentures sold, we were the only ones, outside of Milken's inner circle, who knew the long-term game plan. We would soon have the option of converting the hundred million debentures to cash by offering an attractive conversion price.

LEGAL ISSUES

We had done our homework before selling those debentures. Fred and I had explained Milken's plan to Clarence Long, managing partner of Ernst and Ernst, our outside auditor. He was thoughtful.

"Well, guys," he finally said, stroking his chin a bit, "I don't know about this. I'll have to put it in front of our FASB reps."

The FASB was the Financial Accounting Standards Board. Representatives from each of the eight premier accounting firms of that day served on it, meeting periodically to discuss accounting standards and principles to decide which practices were acceptable and which were not. When Clarence presented Milken's plan to the FASB, the concept of a "flush out" was something entirely new.

The FASB concluded that the "flush out" was an acceptable vehicle for selling equity securities for accounting purposes, and that, when Forum Group did the "flush out," we would indeed be converting debt to equity.

That's what Milken had told us. We could make it unlikely we would have to make an interest payment.

The "flush out" allowed us to convert our assets of a hundred million dollars. We simultaneously increased our asset base by a hundred million dollars and decreased our liabilities by a hundred million dollars.

Forum Group was the first entity to do this during modern times, and the FASB had preapproved it. Milken had found a way to raise huge amounts of capital. Later, the chairman of TIAA-CREF approached us with the offer of half a billion investment dollars a year. A major part of the ramp that got us that kind of investor attention was the sudden growth in shareholder equity produced by the "flush out."

Human Relations 101 teaches us that every time we make a lot of new friends, we make a lot of new enemies. Historically, when an entity sold a hundred million debentures, it was in the context of a consortium of investment bankers who have each agreed to sell a piece of it. For example, Drexel Burnham could have served as the lead underwriter and could sell 14 to 20 percent; Merrill Lynch and Manufacturers Hanover Trust could each sell 5 to 10 percent, and so on, enabling a group of firms to participate in the underwriting. When Milken came to the party, he used very creative applications of convertible debt that enabled him to look Merrill Lynch in the eye and say, "I don't need you. I am going to have a Client Conference and sell all of these debentures before noon in one day, and you are not getting any kind of commission."

Drexel Burnham and Michael Milken had grown a small investment firm, in terms of corporate underwriting, to the "big time" on the backs of the investment banking giants. Over a period of four to five years in the 1980s, Drexel Burnham metamorphosed to a first-tier underwriter, simultaneously moving from joint investment ventures with many partners to an exclusionist position.

Small wonder they became unpopular with their competitors. Consequently, the investment banking industry decided to punish Drexel and its clients. Michael Milken was indicted for breaking the law and eventually served a year and ten months in prison for securities and reporting violations (although some prominent legal scholars believe no laws were broken).

And Forum Group began crumbling like the Tower of Babel.

THE MILLS OF GOD

The failure of Forum Group was a financial failure. Two guys named Oz and Fred who ought to have understood financing pretty well were known to say to their operating managers in various businesses, "You run the business and make it work, and don't worry about the financing. We will worry about the financing. If you have the need for financing, we'll finance it."

That statement was prideful. We should have known better. We were proud of being able to do the kind of financing we had achieved through our relationship with Drexel Burnham. Michael Milken had created a smooth-running financial machine. Stanley Trotman had been supported by Bruce Newberg, who understood Milken's system thoroughly. Bruce would ask, "Oz, just tell me what you need."

Small wonder I would tell my guys, "Don't worry about the financing; just run the business. We will get the financing."

One of the "Big Four" (Mike, Gary Winnick, Bruce Newberg, and Alan Rosenthal) seemed always to be in the office. If any one of them told us he could raise substantial amounts of capital, by April, we considered it done.

Within two years, Milken was indicted on ninety-eight counts, not one of which led to a conviction. The violations of securities and reporting regulations to which he pleaded guilty were not in the indictment. Perhaps he thought he could make a deal with the prosecutor, the US attorney for the Southern District of New York, Rudy Giuliani? If he pled guilty to parking stock, I shared hope that Giuliani would let that be the alpha and omega of the whole deal.

In the criminal case, the judge carefully examined all the numbers involved and determined that the total economic effect of the violations was a mere $318,082—a pittance considering the hundreds of billions in transactions that he had handled since the late 1960s. As for the civil cases, Mike made a personal and business decision to dispose of these suits with a monetary settlement. He could afford the settlements, and was concerned about the stress on his family, preferring to focus on other issues, than to spend years in court.

It seemed that every investment banker I knew well in the 1980s parked stock at some time or another. It probably wasn't what Milken was doing that put him in jail but the scale on which he was doing it. Merrill Lynch and Bear Stearns disliked Drexel Burnham because Milken would not "share the wealth" with them. On the contrary, he not only denied their participation in deals, but he had made a way for others to bypass them too. It was not enough to stop Michael Milken. The loopholes he had used to channel investments away from the major banks were a thorn in their sides as well.

Merrill Lynch knew who had raised our money for us. In the wake of Milken's conviction, the FASB suddenly discovered that the principles of accounting involved in the "flush out" were invalid. They had erred. Contrary to their previous written position, FASB should not have authorized conversion to equity facilitated by application of the "flush out." Therefore, we were required to restate our financial records for the preceding two years.

Ernst and Ernst had said our record keeping was absolutely correct. Now our bankers had new records to consider. After the "flush out," the money in the bank had been spent on real estate. Forum Group hadn't even paid interest.

It takes several years to develop a retirement center. Once the developer starts to get behind, particularly if he gets behind on the financing, catching up is difficult.

Forum Group's retirement centers were the right product at the right place at the right time, but we simply didn't have them financed properly. It was not just Milken's fall; we were also dealt a lethal blow by the Tax Reform Act of 1986.

The two events alone could have bankrupted us. As it was, we still came within a hair's breadth of avoiding Chapter 11.

THE TAX REFORM ACT OF 1986

Because Forum Group was in the construction business, its buildings incurred depreciation during the year that could be deducted from taxable income. We had managed our tax program so that the taxes for our new retirement centers were offset by the depreciation value of our properties. Our end-of-year taxes were typically at zero or less. Then December 26, 1986, came along. Congress ratified, or empowered, a new law that no longer recognized depreciation as deductible for taxpayers whose application would generate a passive loss deduction. Instead, it was defined as a pass-through expense that was redeemable by passing on costs to tenants. Four days from the end of the year, suddenly we learned that what had been intended to offset taxes was now something we must pay on top of taxes.

The consequences of the Tax Reform Act of 1986 alone could have killed Forum, and almost did. Manufacturers Hanover Bank really couldn't afford to let us become bankrupt, at least without advance planning. At that time, Michael Milken and Drexel Burnham were fully operational. Manufacturers Hanover knew we could cash out and pay the bank because of our connection with Milken. They gave us time. Five years later, Milken had been imprisoned and our time had run out.

TAKE AWAYS

- We are often insecure about the wrong things. Life may appear to be risky, but the greatest risk in business is usually spawned by the complacency of success.

- A debenture is a piece of paper that says it is convertible into a specified number of shares of stock. A subordinated convertible debenture is the least liquid form of equity. If a debenture stated that it was convertible into one hundred shares of stock, and the stock is convertible into cash at ten dollars per share, the debenture would be nominally valued at one thousand dollars.

- No better way exists of chewing through capital in a hurry than buying large tracts of real estate.

- Human Relations 101 teaches us that every time we make a lot of new friends, we make a lot of new enemies.

Chapter 22

THE FALL OF FORUM

N 1992 I was staring at the writing on Forum Group's wall when my father's voice floated into my consciousness: "It seems to me, son, that every hotel has to go through bankruptcy to be successful."

"What's bankrupt, Dad?" I heard my innocent question from far away and watched the light-blue De Soto car in my memory as it wound along the outer drive in Chicago. Harold Mutz sat behind the wheel with his young son beside him. He was on a business trip to see "Bud the Furnace Man." Bud had five kids—three girls and two boys—and the two boys straddled my age, one older and one younger. Dad often took me with him when he visited Bud, so I could play with Bud's sons.

Dad had just pointed out a huge building sprawling a distance of two blocks north and south along the outer drive, and at least half a block wide and tall. "The world's largest hotel," he had called it.

"What's 'bankrupt'?" I asked again. Dad's thoughts had seemed to stray.

"I'll explain that another day," my father told me.

I didn't forget my question. The mammoth size of that hotel had made an enduring impression on my young mind. "The developers had a hard time generating enough cash to keep it open," Dad finally explained later. "That's what bankrupt means."

The Stevens Hotel had been the brainchild of Illinois entrepreneur J.W. Stevens and his eldest son, Raymond, who jointly owned Illinois Life Insurance Company. It had been built on prime downtown Chicago real estate, overlooking Grant Park, The Field Museum of Natural History, and Lake Michigan. Its first registered guest had been the vice president of the United States of America, its second the president of Cuba. Two days after the hotel opened in May 1927, the Motion Picture Association held its annual gala ball there, graced by such international celebrities as the legendary movie director, Cecil B. DeMille. It contained three thousand rooms, each with a private bath (unheard of in those days), a ballroom, a bowling alley, a movie theater, a hospital, a pharmacy, a miniature golf course on the roof, multiple restaurants and shops, and a room just for pets.

It lost the Stevens Hotel a million dollars its first year of operation and a half million its second year. By 1932 the hotel's celebrated view across

Grant Park was marred by a huge shantytown of homeless men. In January 1933 J. W. Stevens and his son were indicted for embezzlement. In March of that year, J. W. suffered a massive, incapacitating stroke, and Raymond took his own life.

A few months later, shortly after going into receivership in 1933, the Stevens Hotel started making money.

When Fred and I first started in the retirement business, we were very aware that we were embarking on a venture that was capital intensive and people intensive simultaneously. Such an endeavor went against the grain of everything we had been taught in school. By that time, however, we were used to going against the grain. We weren't supposed to be able to finance the purchase of a business with industrial revenue bonds, but we had. We read the legislation carefully and found a hole, and we bought a business with tax-exempt industrial revenue bonds.

We financed the purchase of Sargent & Greenleaf that way. We bought buildings that way. We could see no reason why we could not finance and develop the construction of a retirement community that way. We could not see, but it didn't take long for our eyes to be opened.

THE LITTLE FOXES THAT SPOIL THE VINES

By 1992, Retirement Living, Inc., had to go into Chapter 11 because it was eating money faster than it was generating it.

A full-service retirement community services the independent as well as those needing assisted living, nursing or mental care. It represents a twenty to thirty million dollar investment. For example, a center located in Newport Beach, California, will cost significantly more per acre than its counterpart in Lakeland, Florida. To realize a profit, a twenty-five million dollar structure must be developed, constructed, and marketed for two years before its doors open.

That scenario we had understood. What caught us off guard was opening day. Four elevators had to be installed in the building. Nine residents were the most we ever moved in on a first day, and that was our best result. Typically, we would move in only two or three residents at a time. How could we collect rent on empty apartments, and vacant nursing home and assisted living beds? A kitchen staff, health-care staff, and maintenance staff whose minimal size is mandated by law had to be in place and on payroll and ready to take care of a maximum of fifty residents, but only nine people were generating revenue. The building couldn't be filled fast enough after it was opened because of restrictions on elevators and people.

Expenses were far outstripping revenues. The entire enterprise was eating capital long before it was possible to generate income.

We had just not thought everything through, as our vision was limited. Somehow we hadn't realized that we were going to keep needing lots of capital forever. The centers we had purchased from Alex Tarumianz had been flooding us with income. Had Tarumianz not been dying, he would never have sold Retirement Living, Inc., to us. Tarumianz had been building it very slowly, which is the only way to develop such rental apartment communities and have it be cash flow positive at the outset.

Once a retirement center is filled (or even at 80 percent) and running, it's a great business, rewarding and fulfilling. But our elevator systems were too small and slow, typically handling two or three resident move-ins a day. Now our financing was critically behind our construction. We were in trouble, and we knew it.

We had intended to be the leader in the retirement living business. We wanted to be number one because we thought we could be. We had faced the hard realities that over a reasonable lifetime we would never be number one in auto parts or hospitals, but after careful consideration, we thought it possible to be first in retirement centers. Our goal was to get positioned so that we could dominate some sector of business, even if it were a small one. We wanted money so we could continue our climb to the top of the retirement living business. Selling our hospitals had been a positive cash-flow generator that had allowed us to do that, but now we suddenly needed much more working capital. Tax reform had catapulted us into the red in 1986.

When an investment banker—in our case, Michael Milken—gets in trouble, many of his clients may be in jeopardy too. Our financial woes suddenly multiplied exponentially.

SEEKING THE WAY OUT

In the scramble to save what we could from Drexel's debacle and impending bankruptcy, we focused on getting our centers built and up and running as quickly as possible to maintain a positive cash flow. TIAA-CREF approached us with a question: "If we fund you to the extent of half a billion dollars a year, what will you do with it?"

We were honest. "We can't deploy that much, that rapidly," we responded.

We had changed our approach to financing new centers. Life Care with Equity (a cooperative legal structure) put the cash burden up front on the user. For a set amount, a resident was able to buy into a Life Care community. If the resident were independent and capable of living on his or her own, one hundred sixty thousand dollars bought a two bedroom apartment with a den, living room, two baths, and kitchenette, including a minimum of seven meals per week. It could also include housekeeping, laundry, and chauffeur service.

The payment amortizes at a rate of 10 to 20 percent per year. After five years the resident no longer pays for the apartment or an assisted living room or the nursing facility, although they continue to pay for meals and health-care, but he or she owns equity in the community. Should the value of the property increase or decrease during the resident's period of occupancy, the difference would be split between the resident and the community.

With Life Care with Equity, we salvaged ourselves. We built a one hundred twenty million dollar center in Cupertino, California, and a seventy million dollar center in Naples, Florida. They almost saved us. If we'd had another one hundred million dollars on the books, we could have met the deductible owed under the new tax law.

The Life Care with Equity centers were extremely successful, but we had figured out how to manage the bottleneck of elevators and move-ins too late. When construction began on the Naples and Cupertino centers, we knew there was a risk that Forum Group could not avoid bankruptcy.

The Huizenga family had made a garbage-hauling business, Waste Management, Inc., into the first of three Fortune 500 companies (Blockbuster Video was the second). In business circles, their entrepreneurial expertise was widely admired. Ernst and Young (the latest permutation of Ernst and Ernst) dubbed them "2005 World Entrepreneurs of the Year." In Florida, however, the name was primarily linked to the Miami Dolphins, which they owned. We sold the Naples Life Care with Equity to the Huizenga family. The mechanism for separating our Life Care centers from Forum Retirement, Inc., was so complex, we had difficulty finding an attorney in Naples who could understand the cooperative ownership structure. Eventually, the sale to the Huizengas went through, and we made a substantial amount of money on it. We raised three million dollars in cash when we needed three million in cash, and the Huizengas finished the construction of the buildings and project development. We made a little on the Naples facility; the Huizengas made a significant profit.

Had we been building Life Care centers instead of rental care centers, we would have slowly spent all the money they would have made us, because their financing had been done in advance. If you don't have the capital before you start a building project, no matter how financially successful the entities may become later, you are unlikely to catch up. As with the Stevens Hotel, you will simply have built someone else's future success.

JACK MASSEY TAKES ANOTHER LOOK

Although we sold American Medical Centers to Hospital Corporation of America in the early eighties, I never personally met Jack Massey or Tom Frist Sr. when negotiating that deal. Now we had retirement centers for sale. We were getting into financial trouble and we knew who could open the spigot and flood us with money. Hospital Corporation of America had been interested in acquiring Retirement Living, Inc., during their negotiations to buy our hospitals. Apparently, Tom Frist was still interested in them.

Frist was looking for a way into the retirement living business by buying something of quality from someone he could trust. In his effort to interest his partner, Jack Massey, he mentioned us. "We know where that kind of quality business is," he told Jack, "and it's Mutz and Risk and company in Indianapolis."

Tom had apparently hooked Massey's attention. "Wait a minute," he replied without hesitation, "I want to meet those people. I want to see them."

Tom Sr. shared my concern about the effect of Diagnostic-Related Groups on Hospital Corporation of America's hospital business and how their revenues and earnings might be affected. When they bought our hospitals, they had formed a new corporation to buy them. Whatever HCA didn't want was offered to Bill Fickling's Charter Medical Corporation in Macon, Georgia, and whatever Charter didn't want, Charlie Martin's entity was required to buy. In other words, Charlie bought the least desirable hospitals.

Jack Massey wanted to meet us himself so he could make sure we hadn't created some substandard properties in retirement communities that they might not want.

In the course of that first meeting, Massey regaled us with the story of how he first met Colonel Sanders and bought Kentucky Fried Chicken with a bit of astrological luck. We could sense the purpose behind his apparent lightheartedness. Jack was unloading major points of his life story to see how we'd react. We were specimens being examined against the backdrop of the way he did business.

It wasn't long into our conversation before it was apparent to me that Massey had decided against our retirement centers. Unlike Fred and me, he quickly grasped the critical implications of a gap between opening a facility and filling it. Shortly after our meeting with him, we heard that Jack

Massey was going into the prison business. I wasn't surprised. Obviously, when you build a new prison, inmates are moved from the old to the new prison in a group. The moment you open your doors, you are operating at full capacity.

Yes, Jack Massey had figured it all out, and we were left holding ten retirement centers we wanted to sell.

CHAPTER 11

Michael Milken's approach to relieving the cash flow crisis in Forum Group had been to create a new entity conceived as a limited partnership that provided a pass-through for tax deduction purposes. In other words, the depreciation generated by that entity applied to partners in a limited partnership when it wouldn't have applied to the shareholders of a corporation. We could offset our taxes with the depreciation generated by the retirement centers we were building.

Creating Forum Retirement Partners, L.P., allowed us to sell these limited partnerships as pass-through vehicles for tax purposes. It also provided the necessary means for divesting Forum Group of its expensive real estate, they were purchased by Forum Retirement Partners, L.P.

However, Reagan's Tax Reform Act of 1986 had made Forum Retirement Partners, Inc., almost worthless by negating its functionality as a tax shelter. At the stroke of a pen, the ability for one partner to pass through a tax depreciation shelter to another partner was gone. The tax law was catastrophic for the economy and triggered hundreds of real estate based bankruptcies.

As a way to restructure, the partnership was useless. Time had run out on us. On February 17, 1991, Forum Group filed bankruptcy.

FORUM RETIREMENT, INC.

We had secured our Life Care with Equity centers apart from our other retirement centers. The Forum Retirement Partners, L.P., was under the umbrella of Forum Retirement, Inc. This arrangement provided us the necessary springboard for selling the Naples facility to the Huizenga family. While everything else was being washed away, Forum Retirement, Inc., became the dry path through our Red Sea of failure.

When Forum became a Chapter 11 company, the bondholders who held whatever bonds had not been converted owned the company. Bondholders would have enough common stock in hand to control the company and could, and eventually did, get rid of the management. The immediate task was to stall long enough to keep the people with new keys from showing up on our doorstep when they did not even know how to operate the lock.

We knew we had a quality product in our retirement centers. I wanted to make sure they were well maintained after Fred and I were gone.

A bondholders' committee was formed with the purpose of controlling the business. Technically, they did control the business, but practically, they needed our management, even though none of them could resist the temptation to tell us how we should be managing it. We had more things to do to keep the business operating, and they were increasingly difficult to do with the bondholders at our helm. The head of the committee was greedy. He wanted to run the committee himself, and he wanted us to run Forum for him.

By that time, we had initiated negotiations for the sale of Forum retirement centers with Hyatt and Marriott. Both had entered the retirement living business, and both wanted something from us before taking negotiations a step further. Were they to accept the liabilities of the company and assure creditors that they were going to pay Forum's debts, they wanted to make sure they would have the management of the business and the full cooperation of its employees in return. Our bondholders were making this difficult to guarantee.

By this time, Forum Group was a health-care entity narrowed down to retirement communities, narrowed down to independent living, assisted living, and nursing home care on two care levels consisting of rental units and Life Care with equity units. It also included care for the developmentally disabled, including stroke victims. We had no patent on the model we profiled, but they were solid plans and specifications that attracted both Hyatt and Marriott.

I wanted Hyatt and Marriott to buy our centers because I knew they would manage them well. Both were family-run businesses whose family members were tighter than ticks. They stuck together like glue: if you started negotiating a deal with one, you were likely to be negotiating business with all before you crafted a final deal.

PENNY PRITZKER MAKES A DEAL

Hyatt had publically announced their entrance into the retirement center business when the population bulge became evident in the late seventies. It didn't take a dreamer to see the trends or what opportunities the future held. The Pritzker family controlled many public and private companies including Hyatt Hotels and Resorts. I had shown Penny Pritzker, a young girl of nineteen or twenty, around our retirement centers, helping her to learn the business. She had called and asked if she could make some business trips with me and study our sites.

Orphaned in her early teens, Penny Pritzker had assumed the parental care of her two younger brothers while simultaneously completing degrees in economics and law. Her father had suffered a heart attack while swimming, and her mother had died within six months of her father. Her grandfather, A. N. Pritzker, treated Penny like a daughter. At the time of our association, she reported to him and to her oldest uncle, Jay, within the family hierarchy.

If the Pritzkers were interested in your business, you didn't need a contact to get an appointment with them. If they didn't want to see you, you were not going to see them no matter what contacts you had. We called Penny, and they were interested. A date was set for visiting them in Chicago, and we spent the day discussing the opportunities and the problems associated with the acquisition of Forum Group properties. At that time, the Pritzkers were not public. It was quite possible for them to hold an entire board meeting in the relatively narrow confines of my office. Penny, at twenty-eight or thirty years of age, had a checkbook in her hand and, I believe, was trusted to sign for her uncle.

By the time the bankruptcy proceedings of Forum Group had progressed to court hearings, we had a deal with the Pritzkers.

Marriott had been a little more distant. They had always had a higher respect for their properties than those of others, and I think justifiably so.

Jim Durbin was the chief operating officer of Marriott. He grew up in Rushville, Indiana, where his family owned an inn and popular restaurant. His first wife, Mary Jo Holmes, was from Edinburgh. The connection to Indiana and particularly to Edinburgh was not quite strong enough to gain entrance, but my daughter-in-law's father had been the first person to lease land to Marriott in Colorado, and, with his input on top of the Edinburgh connection, I had access to Willard Marriott through Durbin.

Marriott was reluctant to commit to the extent the Pritzkers did. Perhaps they felt constrained by being a publicly owned company. In the end, by the time Forum Group came to public hearing, a deal was in the works with Marriott for whatever retirement centers had not gone to the Pritzkers.

Chapter 23

CHANGING CHALLENGES

FRED," I SIGHED, "I just don't want to build a Sugar Refining Company." Fred, Paul Shively, and I were sitting in the office in Indianapolis, contemplating the grim realities of Forum's impending demise. We had figured out the Life Care with Equity financing mechanism with the facility we built in Naples and then sold to the Huizengas. Cupertino we had figured out along the same lines. It was simple to raise the necessary cash for the retirement center at Cupertino, California, because we had our financing worked out in advance. If we had only to worry about those two locations, the future looming over us would not have been quite so cheerless.

"Oz, what are you talking about?" Paul asked, turning his head slowly sideways to stare at me blankly.

"He means," explained Fred, "he doesn't want to leave a skeleton to mar the Dallas skyline, like that old bag of bones they just finished downtown in Indy." Fred thought me funny. "Just because it happened to them doesn't mean it has to happen to us, you know, Oz."

THE PHANTOMS OF FAILURE

I did not share either Fred's amusement or his optimism. For as long as I could remember, the ghost of the Sugar Refining Company's building on West Street had haunted my trips to downtown Indianapolis. A relic from the days when they poured walls instead of using steel, the frame of the building sat and sat and sat, a memorial to a business venture gone awry. Every time I drove past it, year after year, I'd think, "I wish they'd just finish that old building!"

The building had finally been completed only a few years prior. Its half-baked shell had housed various dilapidated business concerns for twenty-five to thirty-odd years, and then Indiana University-Purdue University Indianapolis moved into the area with its thirty thousand plus students.

At this particular moment, the shadow of its tortured torso fell over Dallas, Texas, where, in my mind's eye, I saw the construction site of Forum Group's last retirement center—a barren plot with gray girders protruding forlornly out of the ground. Forum's chief financial officer had just finished yet another long diatribe in favor of halting construction and letting the project die a quick death in bankruptcy.

All I could see was the driving vision of my life's work skewered by cold steel and left to rot, unburied beneath the Texas sun.

The present was hard to face and the future difficult to anticipate. In fact, there didn't appear to be much of a future left for us.

But the three of us, sitting there in our office that day, agreed that the Lord would take care of us. We were people of the Book. Fred and I had lacked humility. When everything you touch turns to gold, you may grow overconfident and optimistic about your future. But when all that collapsed, we found at the bottom we were still people of faith.

We'd succeeded at so many things businessmen were not supposed to be able to do. Someone was always coming to talk to us, asking, "How would you do this? How would you do that?"

The Dallas property had always been an oddity. Zoning laws were peculiarly restrictive. Our plans had originally called for a midsized building, but Dallas laws restricted building height to two stories. We had to redesign from one building nineteen stories high to multiple buildings two stories high. The change altered our use of allotted land space, and we had to bury our parking garages beneath the buildings. The ground itself, because it fronted the Central Freeway, was very expensive at one million dollars per acre, and difficult to procure.

But faith, like salvation, is not of our own doing. It is "…the gift of God, lest anyone should boast." Steadfastly we resisted the CFO's urgings. We continued pressing forward with the Dallas building, and we finished it.

It was fully leased successfully, and just as we finished and sold the retirement center at Cupertino, California, we sold Dallas.

We had agreed that the Lord would take care of us, and He did.

Dallas had been built on the old system of constructing a rental retirement community. There had been nothing unique about the financing at Dallas. It consumed capital, but it was the last one ever to do so.

THE END OF AN ALMOST PERFECT PARTNERSHIP

After the bankruptcy of Forum Group, Fred and I began to go our separate ways. Having Fred as a partner had helped make me successful, and having me as a partner had helped make Fred successful. We had functioned as an almost-perfect partnership. I always wanted to sell early, but Fred always wanted to sell late. His patience balanced my impatience, and my impatience countered his patience. We made an extremely solid and reliable team.

But the disintegration of Forum took its toll on both of us, as individuals and as partners. I had exhausted myself finding buyers for Forum's assets. Fred and I together disposed of our retirement centers to Hyatt and Marriott.

In the midst of the disintegration of Forum Group, we had acquired Indiana Telecom. Sargent & Greenleaf, partly because of the security restrictions placed on ownership by the federal government, had never been a part of Forum. Sargent & Greenleaf remained our principal avenue of growth.

Dictograph had become one of the largest residential alarm service providers in the United States. I had the expectation that John Risk would buy Dictograph from us and run it as part of our consolidated businesses. Instead, we sold Dictograph to Holmes Protective Services, and negotiated for a no-compete agreement so that John could enter into the commercial alarm business. He proceeded to partner with Bill Nelson and start a commercial alarm business.

John Risk was the key figure in acquiring Indiana Telecom. Fred and I weren't interested at the time, but we supplied the money and John chased it and made it work.

Indiana Telecom eventually became the largest privately owned pay telephone business in the United States. Other than being the financier and the challenger of concepts, I didn't do much for that business. I supplied 50 percent of the money to buy it, and our family made quite a bit of money out of it. Indiana Telecom didn't generate a sensational amount of profit, but it made a consistently strong profit. When it was sold in 2000 to the largest public company in the pay telephone business for the princely sum of three thousand five hundred dollars per phone, we set a record. That sale brought us a substantial amount of money: Fred's children benefited, my children benefitted, and to a lesser extent, Fred and I benefited.

The critical role of diversification in the merger and acquisition business could be cited as the last great lesson of my professional career.

I and mine had certainly benefited from the acquisition and development of Indiana Telecom. But Fred and his had likewise benefited from the acquisition and development of entities such as Masterfit and Sargent & Greenleaf that I had pursued.

In 2000, we sold Indiana Telecom to People's Telephone. In 2005, with the sale of our cornerstone company, Sargent & Greenleaf, the Fred Risk/ Oz Mutz partnership was effectively dissolved. Both Fred and I began focusing on our children's interests.

For almost thirty-five years, the most productive years of our professional careers, Fred and I had been partners.

SOWING INTO THE FUTURE

I remember Danny Danielson's call vividly.

"There's a guy I want to bring out, John Erickson, and it won't take over thirty minutes of your time, Oz. Just let me bring him out."

Donald C. "Danny" Danielson served as the vice chairman of City Securities, the investment bankers we used in public offerings of our companies. Even when Forum had become almost a satellite of Drexel Burnham, we maintained strong ties with Danny and his brother-in-law, John Peterson, who managed City Securities. This particular conversation occurred long before any association with Drexel Burnham.

I knew it was not a social call because Danny didn't make social calls. He wanted something from me, it was just a question of what. Chances were, I was going to give him what he wanted because he took care of our financing needs.

Shortly afterwards, Danny brought John Erickson to my office. John was in a blue blazer and tie, Danny wore a suit. John was the official spokesperson for an organization called the Fellowship of Christian Athletes (FCA), and Danny was obviously its unofficial head. They solicited me for a contribution, and I was as gracious as possible under the circumstances.

"Well, I'll give you something, and I'll try to make it reasonably generous," I agreed, "but this wasn't part of my plan for the year."

When Danny called me again not too long afterwards and wanted to meet for lunch, I was a bit chagrined. Either I had given too little or too much. I wasn't sure. But soliciting more support was not on Danny's mind.

"Oz," he asked, "would you consider joining the board of directors of the FCA?"

"Danny, I don't have the qualifications," I objected. "I'm not a great football player or basketball player."

In the back of my mind, I was pretty sure I knew what had happened. Danny had married into a family I knew through Peerless connections. Frank and Harold Mutz had bought and sold small amounts of stocks and bonds with localized investment bankers in the Indianapolis community. I had known the Peterson siblings since high school.

Patty Peterson's sister, Sally, had married Bob Ravensburg, an All American football end during my days at Indiana. I had helped Bob through three or four classes at Indiana University. He had probably told his brother-in-law that I would be a good addition to the national FCA Board.

Consequently, I became acquainted with such notables in the sports world as Bunker Hunt, Tom Landry, Jim McCormick, Kent Benson,

Danny Lotz (the son-in-law of Billy Graham), and Don Lash (who won the mile event in the 1936 Olympics).

I never played basketball in high school, but I had watched Carl Erskine, a founder of FCA, play basketball. As baseball fans will recall, he became a game-winning pitcher for the Brooklyn/Los Angeles Dodgers. I had certainly supported Sam Wyche, who coached Indiana football for one year. During that year, Sam, Fred, and I, and a couple of others, formed the Twelfth Man Club, a base of supporters who attended football games by standing until the game was over. The tradition was started at military schools to foster solidarity. Sam had come to Christ through the FCA when he played football in college for the University of South Carolina. He briefly coached Indiana University before he moved to the Cincinnati Bengals. It was Sam Wyche who developed the no-huddle offense that made Peyton Manning famous.

Don Lash donated land in Indiana for an FCA camp. Eventually, I served as the board member with stewardship over the camp. In the late seventies, I managed to have the place air-conditioned, and Carl and I negotiated the pavement of the roads. Carl was president of a small bank at the time and made a deal that paid for most of the project.

Situated on over six hundred acres, it was the only camp of its kind that FCA owned.

The Responsible Stewardship of Land

We accumulate wealth for the good we can do with it, never for the sake of the wealth itself. This means we are its stewards and never its owners, and because we are its stewards, our wealth can never own us.

Fred Risk and I accumulated wealth by consolidating fragmented businesses. Consolidation involves buying, building, and selling. This meant we had to keep alert to changes in the industries affecting the businesses being consolidated, and to new legislation that would significantly impact them. It also meant we would have to know how to buy, build, and sell.

The two of us had made a verbal pact, of which all of our subordinates were aware, that neither of us would settle on a land purchase that the other didn't like. If I didn't like it, we didn't buy it. If Fred didn't like it, we didn't buy it.

Rarely did we disagree on land. Over the course of our thirty-five-year partnership, there were only two instances in which we invested significant money, in land, that time eventually showed was money misspent. Three principles guided our purchase of land:

1. Any investment in land must be made very judiciously.

2. Three alternative locations should always be identified.

3. More land should be bought than is thought needed, and the buyer should not be afraid of selling off parcels (the Irwin Miller admonition).

By following these principles, we found ourselves typically well served by the land we purchased even when it cost us one million dollars an acre.

However, one cat on the back of anyone involved in buying, building, or selling of land is the Environmental Protection Agency. When we sold the Horton Company at Jacksonville, Florida, after owning it for several years, we supplied the buyer with a Phase One inspection. They turned us down when it wouldn't pass because cleaning fluid had once been ingested into the land.

The source of our problem was the dry cleaner a half block away. Their cleaning fluid had leached into the land and affected our property. Our only option was to do a Phase Two inspection, which involved drilling wells eight inches in diameter and running water through them to sample for contamination. Samples were checked every quarter, which amounted to at least a year-long process. Had the samples been contaminated, we would have flunked Phase Two.

Fortunately, we were given the all clear with Phase Two, but EPA regulations can be the biggest headache for anyone who owns, sells, or develops real estate. We became a little gun-shy whenever a potential buyer would tell us, "We will buy this, subject to Phase One approval." What they meant was that if we didn't pass Phase One, we didn't get a check.

We had passed both a Phase One and a Phase Two inspection on our Sargent & Greenleaf property and had a letter from the Kentucky state EPA to verify it. Fifteen years later, in the wake of amended legislation and new concerns, we were asked to repeat the Phase One inspection. We failed it and were forced to remediate our land.

Zoning laws are another area of concern in the process of consolidating fragmented businesses. When we began to plan the Life Care with Equity facility at Naples, the ideal location was obvious. Fred and I had second homes in Naples, and we understood the community. Our multistory condos were not going to be over five stories tall and were centered around a wide area of shared open space. In spite of our consideration, we lost our zoning petition. The people in the surrounding buildings (people we thought would be clients) protested against a retirement center where a bunch of ambulances would be running around at night.

We brought in residents of our units from a variety of other locations to testify that the drivers always turned their sirens off, but to no avail. Ironically, locals who opposed the construction of our center near their homes in Naples were signing up for shares in our co-ops in other locations.

In any kind of building development, floor plans and specs must combine homogeneity and flexibility. After it has been determined what people want, a floor plan must be developed that gives them these features and still can be overlaid into a number of first-floor footprints. The plans must be adaptable to being transplanted to locations under a wide variety of zoning variances. While our nineteen story high-rise worked well in Houston, we had to translate it into multiple units two stories high in Dallas because of the city's zoning regulations.

We built five retirement communities in Texas, including sites in Austin, Dallas, Fort Worth, Houston, and San Antonio. Our first nineteen story high-rise retirement community in Houston failed us near term but proved very successful long term. The center was located on North Post Oak Road in Houston, just down the street from President George H. W. Bush's retirement condo. Mrs. Bush, after being on our property to vote in an election, decided ours was the ideal place to get her hair done. Our beauty shop was open to the public, but we kept our prices high enough to encourage a limited clientele.

One day, as Barbara Bush left, one of our operators said to another, "You will never guess who I had for a client today!"

"No, I couldn't," her coworker replied. "Who?"

The first operator had trouble containing her excitement. "It was the governor's mother!"

Actually, at the time, Mrs. Bush was the president's mother! When Mrs. Bush heard the story later, she had a big laugh out of it.

The land next to our retirement community butted up against ground owned by the First Baptist Church. We built a multistory parking garage for our retirees that also serviced the congregation of the church. Consequently, the church supported our petition for a zoning variance so we could build our high-rise.

MANAGING THE PROCESSES OF CONSOLIDATION

With any industry, consolidators must stay on top of negotiations with labor unions and any mandated approvals from state and local governing bodies. In the wake of sudden, sharp market turns, a manufacturer may impose new requirements on dealers. Is it worth paying the premium to acquire something that already has the necessary approvals or meets current dealership requirements? Or, is it better to take the chance and spend less on something that will need to procure these approvals to meet these requirements in the future? Part of the answer to that question will depend on the length and complexity of the approval process and the governing entities involved.

Even when the official paperwork is in place, things can be very different from what they seem. When we purchased American Medical Centers from Dr. Ronald Dozoretz, he signed the typical affidavit, stating that he did not know of any deficiency in the structures of the real estate we were purchasing that would cause them to fail any commercial standard. We had owned our new acquisitions for about a month, and I was on my way to inspect them. I started with the hospital at Portsmouth, Virginia, where Dozoretz had opened his first psychiatric hospital in a small building.

I was sitting with him in his main office with a glass wall facing the hall beyond. Suddenly the sky opened up and the rain that followed was a deluge. I couldn't believe what I saw from my perch in Dr. Dozoretz's office: everywhere people came "out of the woodwork" with this, that, and the other wastebasket. Everyone had an assigned place to which they ran whenever there was a thunderstorm.

I knew that he had sold that roof under a warranty.

"Dr. Dozoretz," I said, "I believe we have a little problem here."

"Problem?" he asked, "What problem?"

"You have signed an affidavit that this roof is in good condition and I can plainly see that it is not."

His lawyer, who had put together the corporate papers for America Medical Centers, was intimately acquainted with the details of Dozoretz's mode of operating business. He thought that by refusing to negotiate and forcing us into a lawsuit, we would back off and increase the purchase price.

My dad had grown up in the hardware business and had a sharp eye for good construction. I sent him around to examine all Dozoretz's hospitals and tell us what we needed to do. We fixed gutters, roofs, and drainage ditches, the kinds of things no good building owner would ever allow on properties he intended on selling for a profit.

These improvements paid a handsome return a few years later when Hospital Corporation of America bought our consolidation of hospitals for over two hundred twelve million dollars.

TAKE AWAYS

- If you don't have the capital before you start a building project, no matter how financially successful the entities may become later, you are unlikely to catch up.

- When everything you touch turns to gold, you grow overconfident and begin to presume on your future. When all that collapsed, we found at the bottom we were still people of faith. We had succeeded at many things businesspeople were not supposed to be able to do; there was still a "future and a hope."

- Diversification plays the critical role in the merger and acquisition business.

- We accumulate wealth for the good we can do with it, never for the sake of the wealth itself. This means we are its stewards and never its owners, and because we are its stewards, our wealth can never own us.

- Keep alert to changes in the industries affecting the businesses being consolidated and to new legislation that would significantly impact them. Know how to buy, build, and sell.

- **Three principles to guide the purchase of land:**

  - Any investment in land must be made very judiciously

  - Three alternative locations should always be identified

  - More land should be purchased than thought needed, and the buyer should not be afraid of selling off parcels o Is it worth paying the premium to acquire something that already has the necessary approvals and meets current requirements, or is it better to take the chance and spend less on something that will need to procure these approvals to meet requirements in the future? The answer depends on the length and complexity of the approval process and the governing entities involved.

PART FIVE

HOME AGAIN

Chapter 24

"A GOODLY INHERITANCE"

YOU'RE MR. MUTZ."

The man's keen eyes pinned me against the classroom wall behind us like a moth to a mounting board. Then they flitted over to Jean and inspected her face.

"And you're Mrs. Mutz," he continued dryly. "And you are here to get Mr. Mutz through this class."

Tom Bossort didn't wait for a reply. He returned his attention to his other students and a brief explanation of the course syllabus and left us alone for the rest of that first class. But he had sized us up and sized us up accurately. The premier management professor at Indiana University understood people. For the next two or three weeks of class, he made Jean's life miserable. Obviously, he didn't think she should be there.

We were in our last semester of college. I was simultaneously in my first year of law school, using those credits to satisfy the remaining elective hours of my undergraduate degree, but I still needed two business courses to finish my bachelor's degree. I knew by then I didn't want to stay in law school, but I just didn't have a choice that last semester. I had to take those classes, which meant I would be spending every free moment of my day with a legal text.

Jean has an excellent memory. She could look at a sheet of music once and play the piece without consulting the music again. I had talked her into taking my last two business classes with me so I wouldn't have to read the textbooks.

Tom Bossort had understood the situation perfectly—well, almost perfectly. As the semester progressed and he came to know us better, his attitude began changing. He discovered I wasn't lazy or incompetent, just desperate. Perhaps he appreciated the wisdom of my management of that last semester of my senior year.

Class after class he drilled me, testing to see if "Mrs. Mutz" had done her job. In the end, we became good friends. For the rest of our lifetimes, whenever I needed a fresh angle on a business dilemma or the lead to a good employee, I went straight to Tom Bossort.

But it was Jean who coached me through the tests for Tom's course. A family can provide unique assets of time, talent, and resources that ensure the greatest success in life, but when ignored or underutilized, their absence will rob success of its purpose and sweetness.

A Good Name

The writer of Proverbs counsels that "A good name is rather to be chosen than great riches, and loving favour rather than silver and gold" (22:1, KJV). In his *Biographical Sketches of the Members of the Forty-first General Assembly of the State of Indiana*, James Sutherland emphasizes how Jacob Mutz's stewardship of his resources, time, and people set him apart from the "thousands" of his peers. Ethical and profitable stewardship, in Sutherland's mind at least, could not be separated from that "degree of industry not practiced by many," but whose fruits benefited all.[1]

Jacob Mutz found a place in the annals of Indiana history not just because he was, as Sutherland put it, a "thrifty, judicious cultivator of Western staples," but because those commitments that characterized his personal and family life carried over into the performance of "the duties committed to his care" as a legislator and community leader. His stewardship of these local and state resources, conducted according to Sutherland "in a manner that redounded to the interests of the township," earned him "the approbation of his constituents and secured him much popularity among his neighbors."[2]

While Jacob passed on a certain degree of material wealth to his children, that wealth could easily have worked to the demise of his descendants had he not also bequeathed to them his "good name" and a legacy of industrious and principled stewardship. Jacob's tenure in the Indiana Legislature during the critical Civil War years of 1861 to 1865 reflected his commitment to the conservancy of the Union. He approached every aspect of his life as father, husband, self-taught doctor and lawyer, legislator, and agribusinessman from this same position of conservatorship. He understood it as a Christian imperative to "look after the orphan and widow" and made a home for Dick Francis (among others) when the young Francis lost both parents.

Oscar Ulysses Mutz, my grandfather and Jacob's youngest son, stewarded the good name his father had passed on to him through the next generation. O. U. Mutz financed Dick Francis's pharmaceutical education at Purdue from the profitable investment of agriculturally generated wealth into mercantile concerns. The growth of his hardware business, in addition to the ongoing enlargement of the family's agricultural acquisitions, set the stage for my father and uncle's lucrative venture into manufacturing even in the throes of the Great Depression. In this sense, the Mutz family history is a tapestry of the history of the state of Indiana itself.

But something different simultaneously operated in our family. The work ethic driving the generation and acquisition of wealth throughout twentieth century America was tempered by that insistence on a good name inherited from Jacob Mutz and communicated faithfully from generation to generation by O. U. Mutz and his sons, Frank and Harold.

A CHRISTIAN IDENTITY

Having grown up in the church, gone to catechism, and tried to do the things my parents thought I should do, I prayed as a young person that I would get a "call" to become a minister. Ed McCance served as the young people's leader at Irvington Presbyterian Church in the east-side suburbs of Indianapolis. He was recognized as an awardee at the Banquet of Champions in New York for his running accomplishments, and I was a young running hopeful who looked up to him. He had a profound influence on my life.

The call did come to David Cull, a good friend of mine in high school who wound up going to McCormick Seminary in Chicago. David was ordained as a Presbyterian minister; his first pastorate was at a Presbyterian church in Rochester, New York.

But I didn't get the call. In college I began skipping church on Sunday as often as I could. By the time I began dating Jean, if someone had asked me, "Oz, are you a Christian?," I'd have replied, "Yeah, I imagine."

There was never any "imagining" about Jean's commitment to Christ. Our marriage began on that basis. Our first home was within a block of our church. She volunteered as the secretary, and before I quite knew what had happened, I had volunteered as a youth director with a bunch of kids under my supervision. We both loved music and we sang in the church choir together for thirty to forty years. We attended Bible studies together, although my attendance was not as consistent as hers for the rather obvious reason that I was so often at work.

Marcy and Bill regularly attended Sunday school and church. I served on the Board of Deacons and ultimately on the Board of Elders. Jean held the children to a rigorous Christian ethical code and instilled the foundations of faith into their lives. For many years she was the guiding force that kept us all accountable to God. Her love for Jesus Christ was evident as she joyfully became a Bible student and teacher.

But God was working on me.

Shortly after Marcy was born in 1951, in addition to our church activities, Jean and I began playing cards on Saturday nights with two other couples from our neighborhood, including Jack C. Brown, the US District Attorney for central Indiana. Jack was a good poker player and had a brilliant mind. He drank a fair amount, but we didn't drink at all.

Jack arrived at a point where he was drinking too much, and one night he spread himself out on a highway in a bad wreck. The wreck was bad enough, but there were extenuating circumstances that made things worse. At the time he was the law partner of William E. Jenner, the junior senator from Indiana in the US Congress.

From Jenner's point of view, it was not a good time for Jack to have his accident, but for Jack it turned out to be a very opportune time. Friends who had been trying to get him involved in walking a Christian walk suddenly found their way to the "win" side of that equation. As a result of their influence, Jack became active on a national basis in the Christian Business Men's Committee (CBMC).

We continued to play our weekend card games. Jack would bring his New Testament to the table and sit and read and underline it while the other five of us were trying to play penny ante. I became exasperated with him. I knew historically Jean and I had grown up in a far more Christian environment than either Jack or his wife.

"Make up your mind whether you are going to read the New Testament or play cards, Jack!" I finally snapped one evening.

Our penny ante nights ended right then.

We remained friends and sometimes still met together socially. The Browns moved to a more affluent neighborhood a little while before Jean and I relocated to Virginia. During the next two years, Jack and his wife moved around several times in Indianapolis. By the time we were back in Indiana, at Court Manor West in Columbus, he had become a national officer of CBMC. He would invite me to lunches they sponsored and other things of that kind. Then one February night in 1977, Jean asked me if I wanted to attend a CBMC meeting at someone's home in Columbus.

Since Columbus was the headquarters for Cummins, Cosco, and Arvin, it was not difficult to gather an unusual group of people together in a residential setting, and often a meeting in someone's home was preferable to one in a church or fellowship hall. Invitations were less frequent and fewer in number, but would generally result in a strong attendance by people who might enjoy affiliation with CBMC.

"You know Jack is going to speak here tonight?" Jean asked me, once we had finished the customary greetings and acknowledgments and found a place to sit.

"Jack who?" I asked.

"Jack Brown!" she replied, a bit put out at my density. Then she proceeded to tell me the details.

In the end, Jack had a fairly large audience. He presented his Christian witness and the credentials that authenticated it and concluded with a call to conversion. I responded.

There was no "imagining" about my Christian identity after that. I had committed myself and my life's purposes to Christ. But business was still my life's calling.

A BRUISED REED

Among the privileges of being a Christian businessman are the unique opportunities to partner with other Christians in the work of the kingdom. Relationships that flow out of these kinds of partnerships are deeper and more enduring than the friendships that typically characterize other business endeavors.

I first met Chuck Colson through fund-raising work for his ministry. He became my brother in Christ in the truest sense of the term.

Diverse in his thinking and the eternal goals he so passionately pursued, Chuck's life was fully invested in advancing political thought, historical understanding, and a Christian worldview. Mixed in with this multicolored palette of interests was his hobbyist's enthusiasm for automobiles and competitive team sports, a combination that made him a delightful companion on any kind of trip. His sense of humor was robust and genuine. Chuck and Patty were a great couple with whom to spend time.

An insatiable student of history, Chuck was convinced that the period through which our nation is now passing will result in an ultimate turnaround if politicians listen to their constituents and opt for smaller, rather than larger, government. I shared his conservative views and wholeheartedly supported his work to advance and promote political stability. Jean and I also shared an interest with Chuck and Patty in developmentally disabled grandchildren. Chuck's grandson, Max, was older than our granddaughter, Emma Jean (a Down syndrome child). We decided it was time Max learned how to navigate the deep blue sea. I fully shared Chuck's joy, watching his grandson at the helm of our boat. Contrary to professional expectations, Max's navigational skills carried forward. He remembered how to pilot the boat even after a lapse of months between excursions. Such "little" triumphs make life sweet, and the memories of those days with Chuck and Patty, and their daughter Emily and grandson Max, remain fresh and dear.

But the most significant moment of Chuck Colson's life had happened before I met him. As a result of the White House political scandal in the 1970s (known as Watergate), Chuck had been incarcerated. During this period of his life, Chuck had embraced Jesus Christ as his personal Savior. A man completely transformed by being *Born Again*, he identified with prisoners and committed his life to serving them and their families. This commitment launched his life's ultimate work, Prison Fellowship Ministries. Chuck believed the obligation to serve the least and lost was inseparable from biblical faith. He worked tirelessly and passionately to promote prisoner rehabilitation and reform in the US prison system. He helped create faith-based prison programs for inmates who wished to participate in them.

Chuck challenged the church to break its downward spiral of silence by facing its responsibilities to speak out. Today, Prison Fellowship Ministries operates in over one hundred countries through the work of over one hundred thousand volunteers. One of the largest Christian evangelical movements in the history of the world, Prison Fellowship Ministries established the foundation of the Colson Center, an educational training and networking center for spiritual growth.

Chuck's personal devotion to the Colson Center, the most unique of all his multifaceted evangelical endeavors, makes it a significant resource center for those continuing his work today. Assuming consistent support from the private sector, the Colson Center can provide increasing clarity and direction for our future. Our many discussions about this ambitious undertaking during its early development provided long hours of pleasure and fellowship. His growth objectives and social concerns were always informed by the foresight of a thinker ahead of his time.

The practice of any profession as a Christian brings one into the orbit of men and women of stature in the faith. God had richly gifted Chuck Colson in natural abilities and spiritual vision. The author of over thirty books, he, however, cared most about "little things" and ordinary people. He understood failure and redemption and leaves a legacy of unwavering dedication to transforming the culture with God's truth, encouraging us all as we continue to face the challenge of change:

> A bruised reed he will not break, and a smoldering wick he will not snuff out. In faithfulness he will bring forth justice.
> —ISAIAH 42:3, NIV

THE NECESSITY OF PRINCIPLE

Harold Mutz took me to the Indianapolis Motor Speedway for the first time in 1938 when I was ten years old. I always suspected my mother had insisted I go, along with a case of twenty-four bottles of Coca Cola, because my father's purpose for these trips was never entertainment. He took customers there whenever they were in town for a sales pitch.

Dad had a reserved parking space against the infield fence. I was so close to the race cars, I could see the drivers' faces. The winner of the prior year's race was killed, and usually one driver would be killed; more typically two or three. Pasted against the fence, I think I drank every Coke in the case.

America's top World War I flying ace, Eddie Rickenbacker, owned the Indianapolis Motor Speedway at that time. He had purchased it in 1927, and after closing it to support the war effort in the early forties, he sold it to Tony Hulman, whose family owned Clabber Girl baking powder. I never met Rickenbacker, but I did have contact with him through a mutual associate, Graydon Hall. Rickenbacker's most cherished business venture was Eastern Air Lines. He had sent Graydon to be the district sales manager of Eastern's Indianapolis office in 1952.

Graydon and I met when appointed to the same project team for the Indianapolis Chamber of Commerce. He carried the burden of responsibility for the work and was the key ingredient in its success. I was so impressed, I wrote a letter of commendation to Rickenbacker, thanking him for sending us Graydon. "He's by far the outstanding person among all the airline personnel stationed in Indianapolis," I said.

To my surprise, Eddie Rickenbacker wrote back to me:

> Dear Mr. Mutz,
>
> Your letter of [such-and-such a date] warmed the cockles of this old man's heart.
>
> Sincerely,
> Eddie Rickenbacker

When Graydon was later appointed vice president of Eastern, I received a second note from Eddie, letting me know that my letter had been instrumental in Graydon's promotion. That underscored the developing importance I was placing on hiring decisions. Most of the upper echelons of management never see how their vice president in Chicago or their vice president in Nashville is performing. They depend instead on their résumés. Their distance makes them vulnerable to being misled by their subordinates. Eddie Rickenbacker and Graydon Hall were the real thing.

If you were not the real thing, it would be dangerous to try to snow an Eddie Rickenbacker. He had it all in place.

Stewardship is not synonymous with "successful" management; it is the exercise of principled management that wants to maximize the returns on human performance and time in every area of investment. Subliminally, a constant feed runs through my mind that keeps considerations of time and people as well as resources interrelated and focused in my subconscious. At any given moment I am anticipating the challenges and decisions that are confronting our subordinates. I can't forget the managers. Optimizing their performance is a matter of principled business judgment, not an act of kindness or empty rhetoric.

Stewardship is reinforced by proximity. Fred and I usually traveled in tandem. We shared the same space when traveling because we accomplished more together than apart. We made a point of walking every factory floor with which we were associated. We knew there was no other way to find out what we didn't know about people, processes, and products.

Eddie Rickenbacker had developed habits that kept him connected to the front lines of Eastern Air Lines. He would come to work as normal, but by two o'clock his secretary would notice that he was gone. No one ever asked where he went, but they did know what he was doing.

Eddie would go to an airport, stand in the ticket line for a competitor like TWA or Delta, and buy a ticket for cash to some out-of-the-way city that Eastern did not service. He would fly to that city, maintaining a crib sheet of the airline's services—how the staff treated passengers, whether the plane made it on time, whether or not public announcements were made appropriately, and other performance-related issues. His notes would be the nucleus of a talk to his own people and target areas for increasing Eastern's competitiveness.

On a trip to Eastern's Indianapolis office, Eddie came through the door just in time to witness a secretary throwing a piece of paper with a paper clip on it into the wastebasket. Graydon and his team, who normally lunched together, showed up ten minutes late. Eddie Rickenbacker was sitting on the secretary's desk, waiting for them.

He was not known for being a difficult or hard-headed boss, even though he could be demanding. He had been running Eastern Air Lines at a profit every year since it had started. Gathering the whole office force together, he admonished those who had been late returning from lunch, pointing out that they made money as a team and the company could not afford to pay a team not to work. Then he took them to task for throwing a paper clip away. Eastern bought a fixed amount of paper clips every year at a fixed price. If they saved what they threw away, they wouldn't have to buy any new clips at all.

"If you have to leave early," he told them, "make it up!"

As a young person, it is always tempting to file away such anecdotes in the folder of "old men's tales" along with stories of walking to school through six miles of snow each way every day. The wisdom of the principles and practices of the past, however, is a dangerous thing to forget. Rickenbacker, whose life straddled the invention and explosive development of the automobile, the airplane, and the computer, noted the following:

> If a thing is old, it is a sign that it was fit to live. Old families, old customs, old styles survive because they are fit to survive. The guarantee of continuity is quality. Submerge the good in a flood of the new, and good will come back to join the good which the new brings with it. Old-fashioned hospitality, old-fashioned politeness, old-fashioned honor in business had qualities of survival. These will come back.[3]

A FAMILY LEGACY

"It's too bad Dad doesn't really like me a whole lot," I suggested to my mother, "because there's a whole lot of things I could learn from him, and I think he could learn some things from me too."

It was my sixteenth birthday, and I felt entitled to being sorry for myself. Mother sat beside me on the long blue davenport in our living room. Reflecting on the tragedy of it all, I began choking up; but she was having none of it.

My dad was gone from home for tremendous amounts of time. The country was in the middle of a war, and as she took care to remind me, nobody was working harder or smarter than Harold Mutz to make the most of his opportunities to provide for his family.

She didn't have to recount these details too much, as I was aware of them. What bothered me most were his rare appearances at my high school athletic events. You don't have to be good at a sport to want your father in the stands. Mother led the discussion into a practical exploration of what I could do to get closer to him and what he could do to get closer to me. She obviously related our talk to Harold, and he just as obviously took it to heart. Suddenly, I found myself being invited into his life.

With the purchase of Bex Rex, I had become the proprietor of a particularly good saddle and bridle. Somewhere between my sixteenth and eighteenth birthdays, I sold that saddle for thirty-five dollars (a rather generous sum in those days), and under my father's guidance, I purchased my first tailor-made suit from the Leon Tailoring Company in Indianapolis. The occasion marked the beginning of my career as an employee of Peerless Corporation. Each day that I worked beside my father, I grew to respect him more. I saw what he did and how he did it. He wouldn't have me waiting on him, available just outside his office door. He set me to work down the hall, in another department of the business, responsible for my own job and to a different supervisor.

But I was always there when he paged me. He would query me about some aspect of the business and I would say, "I don't know about that, Dad."

"Well, you loaded the truck, didn't you?" he would insist.

The father/son relationship was transforming into a deep and abiding friendship.

In the business climate of the seventies and eighties, I wouldn't have thought of taking my son with me to business negotiations for fear I'd blow the deal by appearing too unprofessional. Harold Mutz insisted I be a part of the Round Oak–Kaiser Frazer negotiations.

He honored me by trusting me with their relocation, and I honored him by keeping that trust.

When Jean and I began making our wedding plans, I could not think of anyone better qualified to be my best man. For Jean, the idea of her new father-in-law being her groom's best man was a bit too outside-the-box for serious consideration.

"Why don't you think it over, Oz," she suggested.

I did, but I continued to come to the same conclusion.

"He's the one I love the most and would fight for the most," I argued. "Jean, he's really my best friend!"

She wrestled with the unorthodoxy of the arrangement a bit longer but eventually recognized its significance. Harold Mutz was the best man at our wedding, and my best male friend to the day that he died.

When my son, Bill, and his beautiful bride-to-be, Pam, were making plans to marry, I hoped he would ask me to be his best man. But I didn't count on it. Bill, like his grandfather Harold, is popular with everyone, and he was always surrounded by close male friends.

Bill was around fourteen when we moved back to Indiana from Virginia and began building our new home, Court Manor West. We had purchased a field outside Columbus where I had just begun my new job with Cosco. My Uncle Bill, the one whose blood transfusion saved my mother's life, represented the firm hired to construct the house and barns and to lay out the fields. The three of us—father, son, and uncle—witnessed the setting of the first fence post.

For the next four years, my son Bill and I would sit at the table after dinner and talk farm. He grew into adulthood on farms in Virginia (Court

Manor) and Indiana (Court Manor West) where he was responsible for farm management related to two annual crops: grass and American Saddle Horses. Bill would update me on how our horses were doing, how their training was progressing, and provide any other detail I might think I needed to know to manage my farm well.

What I didn't realize was that I wasn't managing the farm at all. He was. Those evening discussions around the table did not just "catch me up" on what was going on around Court Manor West. They were brainstorming sessions with my farm manager. Bill was using the time to strategize, evaluate, and plan for the farm's future. When he left for college at eighteen, I suddenly found my farm interests floundering.

HOME

Everyone runs from home sometime in life. I found my solace in heading to my Grandpa Mutz's when I was four. Under the threat of Laura Mutz's switch, broken from the apple tree outside our back door, I hid in the shrubbery outside the Amoses' house.

When each of my children hit the road, they used their bicycles. Marcy jumped on hers and rode madly for a half mile. She knew I could still see her. Her anger spent, she dismounted, turned around, and waved an arm at me. I knew then it was time to go fetch her home.

Bill's flight was more nerve-wracking. He had a ten-speed, and when he left, he disappeared from sight too quickly. I hunted him for two hours in ever-increasing concentric circles. My agitation grew as all the things that could have happened to him began parading through my head. I took myself to task with bitter recriminations: perhaps I had caused this, or I had been insensitive; if my son were hurt, it was my fault.

I should have gone directly to the barn. Had I stopped to think, I would have known Bill would go there to lick his wounds, among the horses he and I both loved. When I finally gathered my wits enough to consider the situation objectively, I found him waiting for me, sitting on a tack box in the aisle between the stalls.

"Where in the world have you been?" I demanded, bristling self-righteously. "What are you doing here?"

Bill looked at me uncertainly. "I didn't figure there was any reason to go too far away." His voice wavered a bit. "I knew you'd come after me."

He had begun to worry that I wasn't going to come for him, and I had been worried that I wasn't going to find him. The tension between us instantaneously dissolved. We found ourselves laughing and crying at the same time.

Years later, when Bill honored me by asking me to be the best man at his wedding, I felt with fresh force the relief of that moment in the barn.

I accepted his offer hurriedly before he could change his mind.

And no solo in a lifetime of singing gave me more pleasure than singing "The Lord's Prayer" at his wedding.

In 2002, all singing ended with the loss of a lung. One lung still houses within me; the other was removed by Dr. Dan Miller in his first pneumonectomy at Emory University after relocating from Mayo Clinic. I have lived thirteen years on one lung, and I am grateful for being given those thirteen years.

I know I won't live forever, but I know now there is an eternal, heavenly inheritance ahead of me. The family inheritance I leave behind in the care of the Mutz generations who follow my admonition is in Isaiah 51:1b: "Look to the rock from which you were cut and to the quarry from which you were hewn" (NIV).

They, too, are at a Crossroads of America.

"When I called him," the Lord says of Abraham through the prophet Isaiah, "he was only one; I blessed him and made him many" (see Isaiah 51:2).

May the many continue to be blessed through the principled stewardship of the resources, times, and people handed down to them in Jacob Mutz's gift of a good name.

TAKE AWAYS

- A family can provide unique assets of time, talent, and resources that ensure the greatest success in life, but when ignored or underutilized, their absence will rob success of its purpose and sweetness.

- Most of the upper echelons of management never see how their managers in other locations are performing; they depend instead on their résumés. This distance makes them vulnerable to being misled by their subordinates.

o Stewardship is not synonymous with "successful" management; it is the exercise of principled management that wants to maximize the returns on human performance and time in every area of investment.

o Subliminally, a constant feed runs through my mind that keeps considerations of time and people as well as resources interrelated and focused in my subconscious; at any given moment, I am anticipating the challenges and decisions that are confronting my subordinates. I can't forget the managers. Optimizing their performance is a matter of principled business judgment, not an act of kindness or empty rhetoric.

o Stewardship is reinforced by proximity.

o The wisdom of the principles and practices of the past is a dangerous thing to forget. "If a thing is old, it is a sign that it was fit to live. Old families, old customs, old styles survive because they are fit to survive. The guarantee of continuity is quality. Submerge the good in a flood of the new, and good will come back to join the good which the new brings with it. Old-fashioned hospitality, old-fashioned politeness, old-fashioned honor in business had qualities of survival. These will come back."—Eddie Rickenbacker[4]

EPILOGUE

REFLECTING OVER EIGHTY-FIVE years of "conscious living," I agree with my parents: I would have chosen no other time to be alive. The birth of heavier-than-air flight spawned by the Wright brothers, Captain Charles E. "Chuck" Yeager's flight faster than the speed of sound, the live landing on the moon by Neil Armstrong, the development of atomic energy, and the host of technological marvels that have marked my life, coupled with the advancement of Christian doctrine, combine to make me grateful for the time in which I live.

The joy of two wonderful children, fifteen grandchildren, and twenty-two great-grandchildren have all contributed to the happiness of sixty-seven years of fulfilling marriage shared with my beloved wife, Jean. We are grateful for the blessing of this time together and thankful for the contributions of modern medicine, air-conditioning, and skilled health care professionals to the lengthening of our life expectancy.

The challenge of change is ever with us, coupled with the wisdom born through experience; this book documents what can happen in one's life when that challenge is embraced and made a foundation for what follows. It is our hope that it may grow in scope and positive results.

The Wizdom of Oz

NOTES

Chapter 1: "Look to the Rock from Which You Were Cut"

1.   George Sluter, et al., *History of Shelby County, Indiana, from 1822 to 1876* (Shelbyville, IN: Self-published, 1876),15.

2.   Ibid.

3.   Ibid.

4.   Ibid., 25.

5.   Ibid., 14.

6.   James Sutherland, *Biographical Sketches of the Members of the Forty-First General Assembly of the State of Indiana* (Indianapolis, IN: Indianapolis Journal Company, 1861), 143.

7.   Ibid.

8.   Ibid.

9.   Sluter, et al., *History of Shelby County, Indiana*, 23.

Chapter 2: To Everything Its Season

1.   "A Woman of Ninety-three Who Gave Three Sons to the Ministry," *Indianapolis News*, April 25, 1902.

2.   Ibid.

3.   Rev. John G. (Gilbert) Sawin, "Hoosier Listening Post," *Indianapolis Star*, n.d., n.p.

Chapter 24: "A Goodly Inheritance"

1.   James Sutherland, *Biographical Sketches of the Members of the Forty-First General Assembly of the State of Indiana* (Washington, DC: Library of Congress, 1861), 143.

2.   Ibid.

3.   Eddie Rickenbacker as quoted on Forbes.com, accessed February 17, 2014, http://www.forbes.com/quotes/author/edward-rickenbacker/.

4.   Ibid.

BIBLIOGRAPHY

"A Woman of Ninety-Three Who Gave Three Sons to the Ministry." *Indianapolis News*, April 24, 1902.

Rickenbacker, Eddie. "Forbes Quotes: Thoughts on the Business of Life." Forbes.com. http://www.forbes.com/quotes/author/edward-rickenbacker/ (accessed February 17, 2014).

Sawin, John Gilbert. "Hoosier Listening Post." *Indianapolis Star* (no date).

Sluter, George, et al. *History of Shelby County, Indiana, from 1822 to 1876.* Shelbyville, IN: Self-published, 1876.

Sutherland, James. *Biographical Sketches of the Members of the Forty-first General Assembly of the State of Indiana.* Indianapolis, IN: Indianapolis Journal Company, 1861.

ABOUT THE AUTHOR

I T's 1928. THE United States has three national radio networks. Switzerland is hosting the winter Olympics. New York City announces plans to build its first municipal airport, Floyd Bennett Field. President Herbert Hoover is elected. Alexander Fleming discovers penicillin, which changes the world of modern medicines by introducing the age of antibiotics. Mickey Mouse appears in "Steamboat Willie," an animated short film produced by Walt Disney. Alligator Oxfords sell for $5.95 and three cans of Van Camp's pork and beans sell for twenty-three cents.

FEBRUARY 12, 1928, OSCAR ULYSSES MUTZ IS BORN. O. U. "OZ" MUTZ

Born and raised in Edinburgh, Indiana, Oz learned the challenges of navigating life following the Great Depression and World War I. He earned a BS from Indiana University. With knowledge gleaned from his father and uncle, and a college education strongly supported by his mother, Oz marries Jean Greiling August 22, 1948. The two of them set their sights on the future.

A manufacturing executive, merchant banker, chairman, partner, owner, and officer of significant companies, Oz and his family move to Columbus and Indianapolis, Indiana; Harrisonburg, Virginia; and Naples, Florida. Oz retires and ultimately settles in Lakeland, Florida, in 2003.

Two children—Marcy Mutz-Wickenkamp (David) and H. William Mutz (Pam) join the family and it grows to fifteen grandchildren and twenty-two great-grandchildren.

Oz writes his memoirs to leave a legacy to his children and grandchildren, and to share business knowledge and experiences with the reader.

CONTACT THE AUTHOR

Oz Mutz

5119 Lake in the Woods Boulevard

Lakeland, Florida 33813

Telephone: (863) 644-4485

E-mail: ozmutz@aol.com